GEOFF WHITE is an investigative journalist who has covered technology for numerous outlets including the BBC and Channel 4 News. He is the writer and narrator of the BBC podcast *The Lazarus Heist* and creator of the Audible Original series *The Dark Web*.

Further praise for *Crime Dot Com*:

'Beginning with a tour of hacks from the 1980s through to the 2016 election (and a thrilling account of the 2015 Bangladesh Central Bank heist), this is a fascinating primer on the dangers of the cyber underworld.' – *Globe and Mail*

'Anyone who wants a casual read on how cybercrime affects our contemporary world should take the time to read this . . . Recommended.' – *Choice*

'Geoff White writes with insight and flair about a subject that concerns everyone – or should do. Criminals, hooligans, hostile state actors and terrorists attack our computers and networks every minute of every day. Our money, security and freedom are at risk . . . *Crime Dot Com* joins the dots, painting a well-informed, easy-to-understand and up-to-date picture.' – EDWARD LUCAS, author of *Deception: Spies, Lies and How Russia Dupes the West*

CRIMEDOTCOM

FROM VIRUSES
TO VOTE RIGGING,
HOW HACKING
WENT GLOBAL

GEOFF WHITE

REAKTION BOOKS

For my wife, my mum and my dad
– may he rest in peace.

Published by
Reaktion Books Ltd
Unit 32, Waterside
44–48 Wharf Road
London N1 7UX, UK
www.reaktionbooks.co.uk

First published 2020
Reprinted 2020 (twice)
First published in paperback 2021
Copyright © Geoff White 2020

Printed and bound in Great Britain
by CPI Group (UK) Ltd, Croydon CRO 4YY

A catalogue record for this book is available from the British Library

ISBN 978 1 78914 443 7

CONTENTS

Author's Note

All quotes in this book that are not referenced are taken from interviews conducted by the author, either face-to-face or online. I am indebted to the many people who have spared their time to help me.

INTRODUCTION

There is a reason cybercrime has surged up the news agenda. It's not just because of society's growing dependence on vulnerable technology. And it's not just because journalists, politicians and powerful institutions are increasingly targeted by hackers. Cybercrime has boomed thanks to a little-noticed confluence of the world's most powerful hacker groups. In the years since the turn of the millennium, a cross-pollination of tools and tactics between these shadowy operators has shaped the technological threat we see today, elevating cybercrime to an omnipresent hazard. As our society has moved online, they have begun striking at the critical services on which we all rely: our hospitals, power stations, news media and political processes.

There are three forces driving this new wave of attacks: organized cybercrime gangs, 'hacktivist' movements and nation-state hackers.

Organized crime has been present from almost the earliest days of computer hacking and has now become firmly entrenched, as its members have realized how much safer it is to rob people and institutions virtually, rather than in person. Their tactics run on a high-volume, low-margin model: if they can steal £5 from a million people the victims might not even notice, but the hackers are still £5 million richer. This has spawned a sophisticated industry that runs its lucrative criminal enterprises like Silicon Valley start-ups. But as the gangs' indiscriminate attack tools have leaked out, the losses have been far more than simply financial.

Hacktivist groups may have started out as digital protest movements, but their tactics were quickly adopted by cybercriminals and are now being heavily exploited by others with more cynical and sinister motives. Their ability to create publicity and co-opt journalism to their cause has had ruinous effects on their victims, who've seen their corporate reputations trashed, and in some cases their companies destroyed entirely.

Perhaps most worrying of all, nation states are increasingly getting in on the act, adding hacking teams to the arsenal of weapons available to their military and intelligence establishments. These are not illicit, backroom operations, but rather highly skilled, professional and well-funded outfits. In the past, their work was often stealthy and tightly focused on selected targets. But as you'll see in this book, that is not how it's remained.

In recent decades these three groups have emerged and grown in influence as humanity has become increasingly connected and reliant on technology. Now, the worlds they inhabit are starting to merge. Organized crime has adopted the powerful techniques of nation-state hackers. Hacktivists have descended into attacks indistinguishable from those of organized crime. Nation states have harnessed the public shaming tactics of the hacktivists and the devastating, often indiscriminate tools of the online crooks.

The term 'cybercrime' might once have been associated mainly with credit card fraud and online bank theft. But thanks to the bleed-across between these three different groups, it's increasingly difficult to draw clear lines of separation. As this book shows, cybercrime is no longer just about money – what's being hacked is, in some cases, the very fabric of society.

This book goes inside the murky world of these disparate hacker movements, exploring the fascinating and sometimes little-known stories of how their crimes are carried out and how they came to collide with each other. It starts with the hippie hackers of the 1970s and traces the path all the way through to the present day – and to our possible futures.

To be clear: it is a male-dominated world. Right now you will find few women, not only among the criminal hacker community but in the legitimate cybersecurity industry. There is evidence that the gender balance is changing, but only gradually.

Writing a book on cybercrime that is simultaneously comprehensive, compelling and concise presents challenges. Hacking attacks that others might consider pivotal have been left out entirely; timelines have been collapsed to speed the story along; and perhaps most heinous of all, much technical detail has been omitted in order to keep this book accessible.

If you are a techie, please bear in mind that this book is aimed at a general audience. Hopefully you will forgive its deficiencies, in the knowledge that less tech-savvy readers might gain from it an insight into and respect for the world you understand so well.

For the non-technical reader: if (as I hope) this fires your enthusiasm for the endlessly fascinating and increasingly important world of cybersecurity, there is a short Further Reading list to be found at the end of the book.

As will become apparent, the cybercrime threat is now so large and so pervasive that our governments, employers and the tech companies themselves stand little chance of protecting us from every attack. If we're not careful, as technology takes a greater place in the running of our world it is the criminal hackers – those who understand, control and manipulate technology – who will dictate its future. It's up to us to defend ourselves, and knowledge is the first step.

ONE

MEET THE HACKERS

I t's 30 degrees in the shade and I'm standing, sweating, at the entrance to a sprawling street market in the Quiapo district of Manila, capital of the Philippines.

On a piece of paper I've written the name of the person I'm searching for: a Filipino man named Onel de Guzman. I've heard he might have worked among the mass of stalls spread out before me . . . maybe . . . several years ago.

I start showing the piece of paper to people at random. It seems an impossible task. The wildest of goose chases.

I don't know what de Guzman looks like now, because the only photo I have of him is almost twenty years old. Even worse: in the grainy shot, taken at a chaotic press conference, de Guzman is wearing sunglasses and covering his face with a handkerchief.

The young student had good reason to hide. He'd been accused of unleashing the Love Bug, a high-profile and extremely successful virus that had infected an estimated 45 million computers worldwide and caused billions of dollars' worth of damage.[1]

The virus was groundbreaking. Not because of its technical complexity or the disruption it caused, but because it showed how to utilize something far more powerful than code. It perfectly exploited a weakness not in computers, but in the humans who use them – a tactic that has been used in countless cybercrimes since. But de Guzman had never admitted to anything. He'd mumbled his way through the press conference, given a couple of non-committal interviews to the media and escaped without prosecution. Then he'd gone to ground and hadn't surfaced in two decades. No social media, no online profile. A ghost in the digital world he'd once been accused of terrorizing.

It had taken me a year to get any kind of lead as to his where-abouts. There were rumours he was in Germany, that he worked for the UN in Austria, that he'd moved to the United States or even that he'd been hired by Microsoft. And now I was stumbling through a market in Manila, showing his name in the hope someone would recognize it.

If I could find him, maybe I could ask him about the virus and whether he understood its impact. And perhaps I could get him to tell me, after twenty years, whether he was really the one behind it.

But as I brandished his name, all I got were blank looks and suspicious questions. Then one of the market stallholders grinned at me.

'The virus guy? Yeah, I know him.'

Before continuing with Onel de Guzman's story, it's important to understand a little about the technological and, more importantly, social tectonic plates that shifted in the years before the Love Bug hit the headlines in 2000.

Such viruses are a relatively recent phenomenon, but they are not without a history. The modern hacker has been decades in the making, and represents a synthesis of several distinct groups. To really understand cybercrime you have to understand how those groups emerged, and to do that, you have to go back to the beginning.

In late 1969, a few months after humans first set foot on the moon, scientists in the U.S. made a breakthrough that would arguably have a greater impact on civilization than NASA's moonshot.

The Department of Defense had been looking for a reliable way of sending messages between its disparate network of computers. Experts hit upon the idea of breaking the messages up into equal-sized chunks and sending them from one computer to another in a series of hops, using the telephone system. The idea of linking up computers along phone lines wasn't new: the issue had always been how to do it on a large scale, and with a system that could easily expand to include new entrants. With this new approach, any computer that signed up to a common system could join the group, and thus send and receive chunks of data. This paved the way for smooth and speedy growth as it spread beyond the military. It would create an interconnected network of computers, or 'Internet', and the system for relaying the messages from one to the other was known as 'Internet Protocol' (IP). Each machine that signed up would have a unique address (an IP address), and to send a chunk from one computer to another would simply involve attaching the right address, so that all the other computers in the chain knew where to send it.[2]

The Internet and the World Wide Web are often conflated. In fact, the latter only came along much later, in 1989. Prior to this, a document could be shared via the Internet, but it might look radically different on different computers. The World Wide Web is, at its heart, a way of publishing using the Internet, standardizing how things look when they're shared between machines.[3]

Combined with the Internet, the Web would propel the two technologies to global domination from the early 1990s. But for almost two decades prior, the Internet chugged along quite happily without the Web. It was in this era that the first computer hackers emerged, and their development was largely fostered by what was effectively a vintage version of Facebook.

The idea that all hackers are unsociable loners is, as you'll see throughout this book, usually wrong. Their behaviour might sometimes be antisocial, but most of them have as much drive as any of us to find kindred spirits. For many early computer users, the route to companionship lay in the Bulletin Board Systems, or BBS, now a largely forgotten technology that ran in parallel to the Internet for around twenty years. The bulletin boards were very simple, public message services where users could hang out and chat. They could read each other's posts and then respond – a process that could sometimes stretch over days.

As one BBS user put it: 'It was like having a conversation. But very, very slowly.'[4]

For non-techies who observed this process, it often seemed less like a technological revolution and more like a pointless waste of time. But when you talk to early users of bulletin boards, the appeal they had is obvious. At a time when very few people understood computers, their love of tech made them outsiders. Suddenly, this arcane system linked them up with people who shared their interest.

From a cultural point of view, these bulletin boards were vital for tech's evolution. The early Internet was largely controlled by boffins in well-funded labs. But the ethos of this new, networked world, its lore and mores, was increasingly thrashed out on BBS. Inevitably, it was here that the first hackers came together. Out in the emerging cyberspace, among the free-flowing bulletin board chats, several forces were combining to create hacker culture. The first of them came about thanks to a bunch of psychedelic refugees fleeing the collapse of the hippie movement.

At the tail end of the 'flower power' era, as the sunrise of Woodstock became the grim twilight of the Altamont Free Concert riots, a magazine called the *Whole Earth Catalog* emerged from the U.S. It promoted self-sufficiency and living outside the mainstream.

Creating a computerized version of the catalogue was a natural evolution. It needed constant updating, which was easier to achieve electronically. In addition, some of the people overseeing it had been part of American communal living experiments in the 1970s, and their aim was to create the same vibe in the catalogue's digital forums. The online version, called the *Whole Earth 'Lectronic Link* (or WELL), was launched in 1985 and it quickly became the bulletin board of choice for the West Coast counter-culture community.[5]

Its hippie credentials were given a massive boost by the arrival in 1986 of a man whose spirit would seep deep into hacker culture: John Perry Barlow, lyricist for legendary rock band the Grateful Dead.

Barlow's fascination with the Internet and bulletin board life seems to have been motivated less by tech knowledge and more by anthropological curiosity. He observed the comings and goings of this emerging community with a lyricist's eye; a down-home, Mark Twain-esque voice in a strange, new, high-tech space: 'In this silent world, all conversation is typed. To enter it, one forsakes both body and place and becomes a thing of words alone.'[6] Soon, the WELL bulletin board was a draw for tech-savvy 'Deadheads', as the band's followers were called.

'There were principally two communities that formed the basis of the WELL in the early years,' recalls one user. 'One was Deadheads, who used it to stay in touch with each other in this nomadic kind of way, and the other were . . . tech experimenters. And so it was a very interesting mix of the technical and the counter culture.'

It's not clear whether Barlow followed the Deadheads onto the WELL, or the other way round, but his presence cemented the board's reputation as the post-hippie hangout par excellence. It also put him on the front line of an opening skirmish in what would become an ongoing battle between law enforcement and those at the fringes of computer culture.

Just as cops might surround the Grateful Dead's gigs in the not unreasonable belief that crimes would be committed, so law enforcement began to circle these early online spaces. When word got out that a confidential file from the newly formed Apple had been leaked, the police swooped. One of the addresses they hit was, perhaps inevitably, John Perry Barlow's.

With his lyricist's wit, Barlow described a bizarre visit in summer 1990 from an FBI agent investigating the crime. It was an iconic moment in old-world law enforcement meeting new-world technology. Barlow wrote that at times he had to walk the agent through how email worked, and what software code looked like:

> He took to rubbing his face with both hands, peering up over his finger tips [sic] and saying, 'It sure is something, isn't it?' Or, 'Whooo-ee.'

You know things have rather jumped the groove when the potential suspects must explain to law enforcers the nature of their alleged perpetrations.[7]

Barlow's report caught the attention of Mitch Kapor, an early tech entrepreneur who'd made a fortune founding the Lotus Development Corporation, a company that went on to develop a wildly popular spreadsheet programme in the era prior to Microsoft's Excel. Kapor, it turned out, had received a very similar visit from the FBI in connection with the same Apple case.

'The most striking part of the experience was that it was clear to me how ignorant they were of everything having to to do with this matter,' said Kapor. 'They didn't understand code, diskettes, intellectual property, anything, and it was disturbing to me – because these were the guys with guns.'

Kapor wanted to meet, and handily he realized his private jet was scheduled to pass nearby Barlow's house, so he stopped off to visit the musician at his ranch.

It turned out they'd both been caught up in an ill-conceived law enforcement attempt to round up 'hackers' who had committed a crime, although the FBI seemingly struggled to work out what that crime was, let alone how to prosecute it. They weren't the only ones: computer users across the U.S. were being swept up in a series of raids, some of which were heavy-handed and on very thin legal pretexts.

But beyond the bewildered FBI officers and occasionally hamfisted prosecutions, Barlow saw something deeper going on: he sensed old, entrenched institutions muscling in on the emerging post-hippie community of places like the WELL.

Along with John Gilmore, another early Internet entrepreneur who'd worked for Sun Microsystems, Barlow and Kapor set up the Electronic Frontier Foundation: an organization focused on preserving civil liberties online.[8] The EFF has been a thorn in the side of governments ever since (and was also pivotal in the creation of the 'dark web', as we will discover later). As society tried to get a handle on what this new term 'hacker' meant – both legally and culturally – the EFF was a leading force in mapping the territory. Barlow (who died in February 2018) was instrumental in this, embodying and vocalizing the early computer community's streak of counter-cultural anti-authoritarianism.

In 1996, Barlow wrote the 'Declaration of the Independence of Cyberspace', which begins:

> Governments of the Industrial World, you weary giants of flesh and steel, I come from Cyberspace, the new home of the Mind. On behalf of the future, I ask you of the past to leave us alone. You are not welcome among us. You have no sovereignty where we gather.[9]

From today's perspective, when the world's four most valuable companies are Apple, Alphabet (Google's parent company), Amazon and Microsoft, Barlow's words may seem in need of revision. But his anti-authoritarian polemic – a middle finger to those organizations who misunderstand the online world and try to lock it down – remains lodged deep in the hacker mindset.

The sense that the online space lies beyond the purview of traditional authority; that it is a world conjured by the dreams and nightmares of its users; a play-space where people can reimagine themselves free from fusty, old-world orders: these sentiments settled hard into the hearts of those on the cutting edge of early digital society. But it takes more than just iconoclasm. Feeding into the rise of hacker culture were two other zones of influence that emerged in the U.S. as the tech boom began.

Boston, Massachusetts, may not have the global reputation of California's Silicon Valley, but during the 1990s it had another thing going for it: really great dustbins.

As John Perry Barlow was manning the virtual barricades in defence of cyberspace, some of Boston's techies were feasting on the spoils of the city's growing high-tech industry. Would-be hackers were dumpster-diving through the industrial waste of computer companies, scavenging discarded kit, then repurposing and reanimating it to equip their ad hoc labs.

'You could get all kinds of things, old computers, hard drives, floppy disks, whatever you could get your hands on,' recalls Christien Rioux.

Rioux had arrived on the tech-savvy Boston scene in 1994. He'd moved from Maine – a computing backwater for a kid who'd started programming Apple II computers aged five. His solution, of course, had been to use BBS chats to find like-minded folks. Now he was a computer science student at Massachusetts Institute of Technology (MIT), placing him in one of the heartlands of emerging tech. At that time, he says, the university's computer systems had millions of IP addresses – a big chunk of all the links to the Internet, which made the university a hub for the developing online space.

Once he arrived, Rioux discovered another reason why MIT was such a force in early hacker culture: a university penchant for a type of urban trespassing called 'building hacking'.

Rioux says:

It was the idea of getting onto roofs and finding your way down into weird steam tunnels under the buildings and so on.

That sort of behaviour was exploratory and opened people's minds that there were things you could do and places you could go that people didn't expect, but were highly fulfilling if you did.

[It was about] finding yourself in a place that's off-limits. You're up on a roof at dawn and it's gorgeous, and you're the only people that have been there for a year because you figured out how to get out of this one weird window and pick this one lock that only maintenance people use.

Learning about that stuff gave people access to a con-cept of hacking long before computer hacking was a thing. That's really where the culture started.[10]

This trend for building hacking was greatly assisted by the fact that lock picking was a highly popular extracurricular pastime for MIT's tech students, according to Rioux: 'Everyone who goes to MIT, the first year you learn to pick locks, it was just a thing you do.'

As computers became widespread, they simply presented a new trespassing challenge: digital locks, as opposed to physical ones. Rioux was soon hooked on the then fringe world of computer security, and took up the hacker name 'DilDog' – a twist on the name of the pet in the Dilbert cartoons. (Many such 'handles' are like juvenile tattoos; as their owners age, their youthful decisions can seem less and less wise.) He cut his teeth exposing weaknesses in Microsoft's Windows operating system, 'pulling down their pants', as he puts it. At one stage he says he found his hacks being referenced in a course he took as a student, his teacher unaware that the hacker behind the headlines was actually sitting in their classroom.

Rioux felt his activities had tacit, if not explicit, approval from the institution: 'The tolerance that the administration had for it, and almost encouragement to some extent, does help. It's not taboo at all. There were lots of stories about famous MIT hackers, and they're celebrated.'

Rioux joined a hacker collective called L0pht Heavy Industries, so named because they set up shop in a loft once used as a hat-making factory.[11] The group became famous when they appeared in front of a U.S. Senate hearing on government computer security in May 1998. It was a surreal moment of counter-culture meeting the mainstream. A photo of the hearing shows a familiar wood-panelled room, with L0pht's members seated behind a long table giving evidence. It all looks fairly standard until you notice the nameplates. The group didn't want to use their real identities, so the committee organizers used their hacker handles instead. The Senators found themselves taking evidence from 'Space Rogue', 'Brian Oblivion' and 'Kingpin' among others.

Their names may have looked weird, their hair may have been long, but their message was deadly serious: the Internet was vulnerable. L0pht warned the Senate that the system was being pushed way beyond its limits, taking on increasing amounts of responsibility but without the security to back it up – arguments still going on today. They claimed that, between the seven of them, they could render the Internet unusable for the entire U.S. in less than thirty minutes.[12]

This became L0pht's tactic: they would hack, find weaknesses, then go public to embarrass their victims into fixing the problem. Rioux took the same approach: he told Microsoft about the flaws he'd found, only going public after he'd given the company time to fix them.

Rioux didn't earn any money from this, and at this stage there was little financial incentive for L0pht, either. Their motivations were, at least in the early days, non-commercial. They hacked for fun, as an academic exercise, and to see how far into digital property they could trespass. For people like Rioux and L0pht's members, accessing a forbidden space was its own reward. Such targets were an irresistible draw, and the fun of working out the weaknesses in security was an endlessly absorbing task. As one tech expert who's worked with young hackers put it: 'Show these guys a locked door, and even if you only gave them a spoon to use, they'd spend the next week working until they got through.'

As hackers rose to prominence, this laser-focused drive to break through – somehow, anyhow – became baked into their psyche. It aligned neatly alongside the anti-authoritarianism of hippie hackers such as John Perry Barlow: after all, the locked door was an even more tempting target if someone in power told you it was impenetrable.

But to drive hackers to global prominence a third ingredient was required: a mischievous, mocking streak that would ensure they were never far from the headlines. Every deck of cards needs a joker, and in the world of hacker history, one group has by far the strongest claim to the title: the Cult of the Dead Cow.

The year L0pht's members testified in front of the Senate, 1998, the Cult of the Dead Cow launched their latest piece of hacking software. Its name alone gives an insight into the group's mentality: in a twist on Microsoft's BackOffice Server product, they'd called theirs 'Back Orifice'.

The Cult of the Dead Cow's origins are now part of hacker folklore and sound like something from a novel by crime writer Stieg Larsson. The group was formed, the story goes, in 1984 when three hackers named Sid Vicious, Swamp Ratte and Franken Gibe got together, choosing for their headquarters a disused slaughterhouse in Lubbock, Texas. The rumours got even crazier: they'd attacked the Church of Scientology claiming its founder was Heinrich Himmler; they claimed to have given Ronald Reagan Alzheimer's disease; they'd been part of an international war crimes tribunal.

So much for the legends. Could any of it be true?

Although the group still exists, it is now a good two decades past its heyday, and its core members proved predictably tricky to get hold of. I finally got a response from a man calling himself their Minister of Propaganda, who went by the name 'Deth Veggie' (another youthful hacker handle destined not to age well). He now works in the UK, and we arranged to meet in a north London pub. 'Just look for the comic book villain-sized guy with a beard,' he wrote. It was a pretty good description.

Deth Veggie's story turned out to be remarkably similar to Rioux's: a sense of growing up in a backwater, a dad who was into tech, early experimentation with computers (albeit a Sinclair zx80 rather than an Apple II), then the sudden rush of discovering modems and the BBS chat scene. After being hauled over the coals by his parents for running up a $600 bill on long-distance calls, Deth Veggie figured out how to hack into the local phone lines of companies with international connections, allowing him to dial into Bulletin Board Systems across the world at local rates.

It didn't take him long to come across the Cult of the Dead Cow, or CDC, to use its abbreviated form.

They were like the rock stars of the computer underground, that's what it seemed to me as a kid.

What attracted me to them then, and still now, was that so many hacker groups took themselves way too seriously. I don't like people in general who take themselves too seriously, and CDC never did.

Eventually he got an invite to join the group.
'You could never ask to join. You had to be asked.'
Was there an initiation?
'I can't talk about that.'
The slaughterhouse? True, he says.

They used to hang out in an abandoned slaughterhouse, listen to heavy metal music and dream about taking over the world. I made a pilgrimage to Lubbock, Texas, in 1997, and the house was still there. It was this huge abandoned complex, dark and stinky.

The international war crimes tribunal? That turns out to be true as well. During the preamble questioning at his United Nations Criminal Tribunal, Slobodan Milošević cross-examined an American statistician whose expert testimony didn't reflect well on the former Serbian leader. 'Are you in the management board of that group which is known as the "Dead Cow Cult"?', asked Milošević, seemingly out of the blue. The statistician had, in fact, assisted CDC, but the issue petered out into one of the late Milošević's many defensive dead ends.[13]

Where Barlow and the EFF pursued hacking's ideological grounds, and MIT honed its technical development, CDC showed just how much fun hacking could be, mocking themselves and other hackers as much as their targets.

'A CDC slogan early on was "We're only into hacking for the girlies and the money,"' says Deth Veggie. 'The joke being, those were two things you were *never* going to get.'

It wasn't only online that the Cult of the Dead Cow injected anarchy into the system. Its members created the first big hacker conference, HoHoCon, so named because it took place around Christmas, giving its members a chance to escape their families. It also gave an opportunity for the then tiny hacker scene to get together, further disproving the stereotype of geeks as unsociable loners.

Tales of crazy behaviour at such conferences abound. They were held in hotels, and one attendee claims to have seen hackers unscrewing wall panels to hijack phone lines from neighbouring rooms so they could blame the hacking (and land the phone bill) on someone else. Pretty soon Las Vegas's proprietors got wise, says Deth Veggie. 'All the HoHoCons had to be registered under false pretences. It would be called a "computer enthusiasts' convention". That's why they could only be held in one place, once, because then they would get kicked out.'

Over time, CDC's aspirations became more serious: they began to focus on human rights and anti-censorship tools, claiming to help dissidents in China fight against the country's repressive Internet policies. But in its early days, CDC's aim was clear: 'We were the court jesters of the computer underground, to some degree,' says Deth Veggie. As such, they provided an anarchic counterpoint to the freewheeling libertarianism of John Perry Barlow and the EFF, and the technocratic trespassers of MIT.

Combine these three strands together – the libertarian, the technocrat and the anarchist – and you have the DNA of a computer hacker. Some veer towards individual aspects of this trinity; but question them hard, and they'll usually display evidence of all three.

What these characteristics have in common is a deep-seated drive to push at society's traditional boundaries. Push hard enough, as Barlow and Kapor discovered, and those boundaries can easily become criminal tripwires. The FBI's officers may not have known exactly what law was broken when they questioned their suspects over the stolen Apple documents, but they had a strong sense that someone, somewhere had crossed the line. Barlow may have escaped prosecution in that case, but he wasn't naive. He saw that the budding computer scene was attracting wilder elements, losing its innocence, and in his typically poetic way, he described seeing these characters pop up on the bulletin board system: 'These kids were fractious, vulgar, immature, amoral, insulting, and too damned good at their work.'[14]

When one of them, Phiber Optik, hacked Barlow's credit history, the ageing rocker was stunned: 'I've been in redneck bars wearing shoulder-length curls, police custody while on acid, and Harlem after midnight, but no one has ever put the spook in me quite as Phiber Optik did at that moment.'[15]

In the end, Barlow met and made friends with the young outlaw. But he wasn't the only one seeing signs that crooks were starting to get interested in the emerging digital space. Deth Veggie, too, even as he revelled in the gleeful anarchy of CDC, noticed crime circling the fringes of computer hacking as far back as the mid-1990s. His group was able to reprogram mobile phones, meaning they could effectively take over someone's number and make calls on their account.

> There was this guy in Boston who wasn't involved in the hacker scene but was on the outskirts of the social scene. He said 'Can you do that at larger scale? If we bring you phones can you program them?'

The group declined. It was a wise move. 'Turned out later he was involved with the Boston Irish mob.'

So far, I've used the phrase 'hacker' loosely, without defining it. In fact, its definition has changed over time. In the days of Deth Veggie, John Perry Barlow and Christien Rioux, it mostly meant someone who tinkered with technology. Back then, many people had a different term for those who used their skills for out-and-out criminal purposes: 'cracker'. It's a distinction that's been lost over the years, but for the moment, I'm going to revive it because in this book it's these 'crackers' I'm going to focus on.

There are plenty of hackers using their powers for good. An army, in fact, of above-the-board tech security researchers who find and expose flaws in order to make us all safer. They work across government, the military, intelligence agencies, law enforcement and private industry to play a positive role as tech becomes increasingly vital in our society. This book is not about them. It is about those who use their skills for crime, and how their activities have impacted on the rest of society.

In the early era of Barlow, L0pht and the Cult of the Dead Cow, these criminal elements were limited in number, largely because there were limited ways to make big money from hacking. Yes, you could use computerized methods to assist with other crimes (like reprogramming phones for crime gangs). You could get hold of free games and software. You could even steal some credit card data. But the ability to commit a profitable crime at scale using only a computer was a pipe dream.

Within a couple of decades, that would change dramatically, fuelling a crime wave that would make billions for the crooks and unleash hacker tactics on the rest of society. Cybercrime was about to go global, and at the turn of the millennium, one man would show just how vulnerable the world's computers – and those who used them – were to attack.

The Love Bug virus was unleashed on 4 May 2000. It was simple, but devastatingly effective and highly contagious. Once infected, many of the user's files would be overwritten with copies of the virus, so that whenever the victim tried to open the files, they'd reinfect their system. The virus also tried to steal people's passwords. But the true genius lay in how it spread. Once infected, the victim's computer would send an email to everyone in their Microsoft Outlook contacts book. The emails read: 'kindly check the attached LOVELETTER coming from me', and attached was a copy of the virus, disguised as a text file with the title LOVE-LETTER-FOR-YOU.[16]

Faced with such a tempting message, many, many people took the bait, opened the attachment and got infected. It didn't take long for the virus to spread around the world. When you think about the maths, its success becomes easy to understand, and quite fright-ening: if each victim had sent it to fifty people, and each of them infected fifty people, and so on, it would only take six jumps for the virus to infect everyone in the world (presuming they all had com-puters). Panic ensued: systems in banks and factories were infected. In the UK, Parliament shut down its email network for several hours to prevent infection. Even the Pentagon was reportedly affected.[17]

Just a few months previously, the world had been fretting about the risk of a so-called Y2K bug – the fear that computers would fail to cope with the switch from dates in the 1900s to the 2000s. The damage predictions had been massively exaggerated, and the vast majority of systems were unaffected. But just as the tech industry breathed a sigh of relief, the Love Bug virus showed the true scale of devastation that could be caused in an increasingly connected world. Estimates of the damage ran into the tens of billions of dollars – much of it spent on fixing infected computers and pre-venting reinfection. Once it was released, the virus code could be downloaded and tweaked by anyone: within days, researchers were seeing dozens of copycat versions being unleashed.

As the news coverage became ever more shrill, investigators got to work, trying to trace the source of the bug. The passwords stolen by the virus were being sent to an email address registered in the Philippines. Local police traced the email account to an apartment in Manila. The net was closing in.

After some initial questioning, they identified one Onel de Guzman, a 23-year-old computer science student at AMA Computer College, studying at the Makati campus, a grim, grey concrete building in the centre of the city. The virus had mentioned the phrase 'GRAMMERsoft', which investigators quickly established was an underground hacking cell made up of AMA students, some of whom had started experimenting with viruses. De Guzman was a leading member.

As journalists poured into town, de Guzman's lawyer hastily arranged a press conference so the world's media could put their questions to the man increasingly assumed to be at the heart of a global virus outbreak. De Guzman appeared, seemingly terrified, hiding behind dark glasses and holding a handkerchief over his face, covering his prominent acne scars. He hung onto his sister, Irene, who lived in the flat that the police had originally raided. Flashguns popped and news cameras zoomed in as de Guzman took his seat. But anyone expecting clarification was soon disappointed. De Guzman's lawyer fielded many of the questions with vague non-answers.

De Guzman himself seemingly didn't speak much English. Finally, one of the assembled media managed to ask a key question: did de Guzman, perhaps, release the virus accidentally?

'It is possible,' mumbled de Guzman.[18]

And that was it. There were no more questions. The press conference ended, and de Guzman's solitary non-answer was the closest anyone got to an explanation of a virus that infected 45 million machines worldwide.

De Guzman was never prosecuted, because at that time the Philippines had no law against computer hacking. Soon, the cameras packed up, the news crews left and the story slipped off the agenda.

With the true author unconfirmed, suspicion fell on de Guzman's schoolfriend Michael Buen, whose name had appeared on a previous virus, called 'Mykl-B'. Buen denied having anything to do with the Love Bug outbreak, but his pleas were largely ignored. Most online sources still list de Guzman and Buen as the creators of the virus, either jointly or separately, and that's how it's been for twenty years. Until now.

The Minor Basilica of the Black Nazarene is one of Manila's most revered Catholic shrines, and in its shadow lies the labyrinthine expanse of Quiapo market, home to everything from Hello Kitty backpacks to LED-lit Virgin Mary statuettes. It was here, acting on a tip-off, that I came to look for Onel de Guzman.

Eventually, the friendly stallholder who remembered him directed me across town to a different shopping district. I went down another rabbit warren of market stalls, flashing the piece of paper with de Guzman's name written on it, looking like a tourist dad who'd lost his kids. After many, many blank looks and suspicious questions, a bored-looking trader pointed me in the direction of a nearby commercial unit. It was empty, but after ten hours waiting for him to turn up to work, I finally came face to face with Onel de Guzman.

Now 43, his juvenile acne scars have all but disappeared, and his diamond-shaped face has filled out into comfortable middle age. Still as shy as he was at the press conference all those years ago, he hides his gaze under a mop of jet-black hair, his face occasionally breaking into a smile displaying a distinctive set of uniform teeth.

He'd changed so much, I began to doubt I was actually speaking to the real de Guzman, so I started making a furtive sketch in my notepad of the position of the moles on his face, to compare later on with the photo of him from twenty years ago. Back then, in the chaotic press conference, he'd swerved the question of whether he had written the virus, giving the half-answer that's remained hanging in the air ever since. According to de Guzman, it wasn't his idea to be so evasive.

'That's what my lawyer told me to do,' he says, in halting English.

I'd expected to have to extract truth from de Guzman by forensic interview, and I'd lined up my evidence like an amateur barrister. Remarkably, he wasted no time in confessing to a wrongdoing he'd ducked ever since the turn of the millennium.

'It wasn't a virus, it was a Trojan,' he says, correcting my terminology to point out that his malicious software worked by sneaking onto a victim's computer disguised as something benign. 'I didn't expect it would get to the U.S. and Europe. I was surprised.'

The story he went on to tell is strikingly straightforward. De Guzman was poor, and Internet access was expensive. He felt that getting online was almost akin to a human right (a view that was ahead of its time). Getting access required a password, so his solution was to steal the passwords from those who'd paid for them. Not that de Guzman regarded this as stealing: he argued that the password holder would get no less access as a result of having their password unknowingly 'shared' (of course, his logic conveniently ignored the fact that the Internet access provider would have to serve two people for the price of one.)

De Guzman came up with a solution: a password-stealing program. In hindsight, perhaps his guilt should have been obvious, because this was almost exactly the scheme he'd mapped out in a thesis proposal that had been rejected by his college the previous year.

At the time, he says, designing such software wasn't difficult. 'There was a bug in Windows 95,' he says. 'If someone clicks the attachment, [the program] will run through their machine.'

But there's the rub: how to get people to click on the attachment? De Guzman says he would hang out in Internet chatrooms where Manila Internet users gathered, and strike up conversations. He would then send his victims an infected file, pretending it was his picture. It worked. 'I chatted only to people that had no knowledge of computers, to experiment on them,' he says.

De Guzman had good reason to confine his hacking to Manila residents. At this time, Internet access relied on 'dial-up': as some younger readers may be astonished to discover, prior to the advent of broadband, getting online relied on plugging a box called a 'modem' straight into the phone line, which the modem would then use to dial an Internet access number (much to the annoyance of housemates, parents or whoever else picked up the phone). Manila's dial-up passwords would only work on Filipino phones, and since de Guzman was stealing passwords to use on his home phone line, he had no need to target victims outside the city. If he'd kept it that way, his life might have been very different. But, like many hackers, de Guzman was curious, and wanted to push his virus forward.

In May 2000 he tweaked his original code so that it would not simply be restricted to Manila residents. He also made two other changes that would ensure his place in hacker history. First, he programmed the virus so that, once it had infected a computer, it would send a copy of itself to each person in the victim's email address book. By doing so, he created a so-called 'worm' virus, a self-spreading monster with no off switch. Once released, de Guzman would have no control.

His second change was the work of true, if perhaps unconscious, genius. Once the virus spread beyond de Guzman's hands, he needed a way of tempting recipients into opening the attachment that contained the code. His old trick of pretending it was a photo wouldn't work. So he came up with a new tactic: he gave the virus a title that had universal and near-irresistible appeal.

'I figured out that many people want a boyfriend, they want each other, they want love, so I called it that,' he says.

The Love Bug was born.

Like many hackers, de Guzman is a night owl. He finds the dark hours quieter, making it easier to concentrate. It was 1 a.m. when de Guzman found his 'patient zero', the person whose initial infection would go on to spread the virus. He was chatting online to a fellow Filipino who was living in Singapore. De Guzman can't remember who the man was, but he remembers sending him a copy of his new, improved virus.

Unaware of the worldwide chaos he'd just unleashed, de Guzman says he then went out and got drunk with a friend. Within a day, though, his virus had spread like wildfire and investigators were closing in on their suspect.

His mother got in contact. She'd received word the police were hunting a hacker in Manila, and she knew of her son's illicit hobby. She hid his computer but crucially left the disks, one of which had the Mykl-B virus on it, pulling Michael Buen and several dozen other AMA students onto the police's radar.

For twenty years, de Guzman's silence left a cloud hanging over his classmate, Buen, who is commonly listed as the joint author of the virus. Yet according to de Guzman, he had nothing to do with it. The pair had written viruses before, he says, but the Love Bug was written by de Guzman alone.

De Guzman says he had to take a year off after the incident to let the heat die down, during which he didn't touch a computer. He never went back to AMA, never graduated and later became a mobile-phone technician. He says he regrets writing the virus, but he now faces the fate of all wrongdoers in the Internet age: infamy that will never decay.

'Sometimes I get my picture on the Internet,' he says. 'My friends said, "It's you, it's you!" They find my name. I'm a shy person, I don't want this.'

His children are aged seven and fourteen. He knows one day soon they will find out about his role in one of the world's most infamous viruses. He's not sure how he'll deal with that.

At the end of our interview, de Guzman goes back to his job, disappearing into the mall's mass of tiny tech repair stalls, where he sits surrounded by soldering irons, multimeters and disassembled mobile phones. He says he loves his work and that he's content, but as I make my way out of the *Blade Runner*-esque fluorescent-lit maze of cramped computer shops, I'm pretty sure this isn't where he'd imagined his life would end up.

The Love Bug wasn't the smartest computer virus, nor the most disruptive, and it certainly wasn't the most profitable. I've chosen it as a starting point for two reasons: first, the Love Bug was where I had my first (failed) stab at tech security journalism. As the infection became a global news story I sent a mediocre article to *The Guardian* newspaper in the hope they would publish it. They declined, and pointed out that sending them an email titled 'I Love You' during the middle of a virus outbreak with the same name probably wasn't the smartest way to pitch a piece.

But there's a second, much more compelling reason for choosing the Love Bug as an entry point. It's the perfect illustration of a basic truth about much of the computer crime wave currently plaguing our society: it's not about the tech, it's about the people. Many of the stories contained in this book aren't, at heart, about code, software, hardware and so on. Instead, time after time the hacker's way in is through exploiting human frailty. Their first step is to fool people into doing things they shouldn't. The trick is how to convince their victims to perform such actions, and that relies on psychological acumen every bit as much as technical skill. A good hacker needs an instinctive grasp of human behaviour, and a deep understanding of our desires and fears.

De Guzman was absolutely not the first person to realize this, but in naming his virus he had, almost inadvertently, come up with the greatest lure of all time. His attack succeeded and became a global menace because he hit upon the one thing sought by everyone on the planet: love.

The tactic of 'hacking humans' would be used in countless cybercrimes in the next two decades. Unlike de Guzman, many of his successors would make billions of dollars in profits. Much of the groundwork for this was laid, at least according to police and security researchers, by the work of one man, a genius hacker who emerged from the rubble of the collapsing Soviet Union to create a cybercrime machine of breathtaking scale.

TWO

FALL OF THE
BERLIN FIREWALL

Anapa is a well-turned-out seaside resort on the Black Sea coast in southwestern Russia. Among the tidy tower blocks at the southern end of town is 120 Ulitsa Lermontova, a popular, sandy-coloured summer retreat where wealthy out-of-towners from Moscow and Siberia go for some sea air.

The block's residents probably didn't take much notice as the man on the fourteenth floor hurriedly packed and left one Friday in May 2014. If they knew anything at all about Evgeniy Bogachev it was that he worked in computers, and they almost certainly had only the vaguest understanding of what that meant. As the 31-year-old and his wife put their daughter into the car and drove off, there was nothing to hint at the reasons for their sudden departure, no police sirens, no squealing tyres, no camera crews. The secret life of their neighbour would only be revealed to them over the next few days, as allegations emerged placing Bogachev at the heart of a multimillion-dollar global cybercrime operation.

From his flat in Anapa, the FBI claimed, Bogachev had wrangled a network of computers infected with his virus that were used to steal from some of the world's biggest banks, in a digital fraud campaign that stretched back for over seven years. But this was not just another hacker on the make. According to those who had tracked Bogachev's alleged career through the online underworld, his effect on the emerging cybercrime community was immense. They watched him take the fledgling virus industry and revolutionize it, copying Silicon Valley tactics and applying them to cybercrime, gaining the same level of success in the underground as the likes of Apple and Microsoft have achieved in the world of legitimate commerce. His work laid the ground for hacking to become a global force.

In Anapa all that was left was a deserted home which Bogachev's chauffeur would occasionally visit to tie up the loose ends.

Bogachev's speedy exit was the last in a series of narrow escapes. Investigators claim that, through a combination of persistent paranoia, guile and outright manipulation, Bogachev had managed to build the world's largest cybercrime network, palm it off to a man who was then arrested for it, build up another network, escape the dragnet that shut it off, then build up a third empire and once again flee just as it all came crumbling down: the online world's equivalent of Keyser Soze, the enigmatic mastermind in Bryan Singer's 1995 film *The Usual Suspects.*

These days, Bogachev stares out from the FBI Cyber's Most Wanted list: shaven-headed and slightly tubby, with a genial smile on his face. The fact that he looks a dead ringer for a Bond villain has not escaped the attention of the media who've covered the case. Adding to his larger-than-life persona is a photo in which he's pictured in a leopard-skin all-in-one cuddling a similarly patterned cat. But those who would see Bogachev as just another idiosyncratic suspect from the bizarre world of hackers are wrong. According to the criminal charges against him, the work he did and the chain of events he set in motion had repercussions that would last for years.

The Love Bug virus had shown how vulnerable the world population's increasing reliance on networked technology could make us. Bogachev didn't just take that ball and run with it – according to the prosecutors who continue to pursue him, he turned it into an Olympic event.

The seeds of Bogachev's alleged rise to prominence were planted in the economic rubble of the fall of the USSR. On 26 December 1991, the Republics of the Soviet Union were granted independence, bringing to an end almost seven decades of centrally managed political control.

The ensuing economic and social fallout has been well documented. Russia's gross domestic product flatlined. News footage of tanks rolling through Moscow gave way to bleak scenes of empty shop shelves and destitute, bewildered citizens. On TV, it always seemed to be winter in Russia. Unemployment rose from just over 5 per cent in 1993 to 13 per cent by the end of the decade – particularly disorienting for a country where most people had spent their entire lives under a command economy that filled jobs, albeit often at the whim of the state.[1]

Another statistic from this era, although harder to find, is far more important for understanding the emergence of cybercrime. Previously unreleased figures from the Institute of Education reveal that, throughout the 1980s and early 1990s, around 600,000 students were entering Russia's prestigious universities each year, and that consistently almost half of them studied technology and engineering. By contrast, medicine hovered around 5 per cent. Even as humanities subjects and economics caught up during the late 1990s, tech and engineering were still far outstripping all other subjects, producing 30 per cent of all graduates.[2] In short, with its economy stagnating, Russia was churning out hundreds of thousands of tech and engineering graduates into a job market that had ever fewer places to accommodate them.

Many of the country's brightest minds were being schooled in exactly the kind of technical skills that were becoming so valuable in the rest of the world as it accelerated towards the dotcom boom, when the share prices of tech companies ballooned in the exuberant closing years of the millennium. But Russia's ailing economy struggled to connect the talent with the trade. For some, the solution was emigration, leading to a so-called 'brain drain'. In the first few years of the 1990s, around two million people left the country, according to Russian government figures.[3] Among those who stayed, a small minority found a different outlet for their new-found technical skills: crime.

Among them was Igor Klopov.

Online, Klopov's communication is staccato, monosyllabic and terse. I knew he'd got into cybercrime in the 1990s in Russia. I knew he'd been lured to the U.S., arrested in a sting operation, and had served several years in prison.[4] I was keen to fill in the biographical details, but Klopov's dour responses were getting me nowhere. Then one day he sent me the story of his life, typed out over 54 pages. It detailed how a talented student had got on the wrong side of the tracks, ending up in New York's Rikers Island prison. I was sceptical of its veracity and of Klopov's motivation for writing it, especially given his past career as a fraudster. But his tale didn't read like an attempt to downplay his offences. Instead, it provided a remarkable insight into one man's descent into hacking, and a perfect illustration of how credit card fraud became the driving force behind a wave of cybercrime in 1990s Russia.

Klopov wrote that he got his start at school in 1997 dealing in 'warez', a slang term for software that had been hacked into and tweaked to remove its anti-piracy protection, enabling it to be distributed free to other users. He mainly dealt in ripping off software used to build websites.

Pretty soon, Klopov faced a problem: the most sought-after software could not be obtained without a credit card payment. Once he had the software, Klopov could remove the anti-piracy locks that stopped it being distributed beyond the original buyer's computer. But to get the software in the first place, he would need to pay. That's when he discovered something remarkable. He claims that during this era, software sellers would accept any valid credit card number, releasing the goods immediately without first checking whether the card number was good for the payment or not.

Klopov created a program to generate valid credit card numbers and used them to buy expensive software, which he then pirated. It was his first entry into credit card fraud.

When the software companies started to close down the hole that Klopov had exploited, he started working with a schoolfriend who would hack into online retailers to steal legitimate users' card details. Klopov used the stolen cards to make online payments for software he would then pirate.

His ambitions escalated. Klopov recruited a network of middlemen in the U.S. to participate in shipment scams: they would receive fraudulently obtained goods and send them on to addresses in the former Eastern Bloc, not realizing that when the fraud was uncovered, they'd be held liable for the goods. Klopov used stolen personal information to set up fake U.S. identity documents, then used the documents to generate fake cheques, which he cashed through his middleman network. This led to his downfall. In 2007 he bought gold bars in the U.S. with a $7 million fake cheque (it would be his last criminal job, he promised his then-girlfriend, before they settled down together).[5] Unfortunately for Klopov, the chequebook he faked belonged to one Charles Wyly Jr, who was worth around $1 billion and was a major donor to the Republican party. The transaction was flagged as suspicious, and unknown to Klopov, his scam was exposed.

The U.S. Secret Service began working on a sting operation: to seal his gold bullion deal, Klopov was told he would have to come to the U.S. personally. The Russian touched down on American soil and climbed into the limo waiting for him at the airport, expecting to go to California to pick up his ill-gotten gains. Instead, as he stopped to take a souvenir photo on Brooklyn Bridge, he was tackled and handcuffed. He spent the next two and a half years in custody after pleading guilty in February 2009 to fraud and identity theft charges. Now in his mid-thirties, he lives in New York and is working, like so many former hackers, in IT security.

Successful as Klopov was prior to his arrest, he wasn't a pioneer of cybercrime and he didn't have God-like computer coding skills. What he did have was a nose for opportunity, a moral compass wonky enough to ignore the illegality, and sufficient computing acumen to make the scheme work. And it all started with credit cards.

He wasn't alone. Card fraud became the engine that drove a new criminal industry during the 1990s. It would make many millions for the few who mastered it. But the community didn't remain at the scale of Klopov's schemes; pretty soon it would organize, creating the groundwork for a truly global crime wave.

Usefully, the history of credit card fraud during this era has been summarized by someone with first-hand experience – a man who became legendary among the 'carders', as they were known. In July 2003, a fraudster by the name of Script wrote a brief time-line of the emergence of such crime in Russia. It was typed out in broken English and posted on an online carder forum, seemingly as a precis to educate new arrivals on the scene:

'Beginning from year 1990, first carder activity conspicuity [*sic*] in countries of former Soviet Union, at the time when even CD orders went with using of generated card numbers.' The reference is to the loophole found by Klopov, where criminals could simply enter any valid card number and make a purchase.

He goes on, 'When shops send anything to all parts of former Soviet Union, that's exactly when a tremendous up growth of carding began.' Again, this is a reference to Klopov's technique of getting goods shipped from the USA. The next of Klopov's moves was to acquire stolen card details: 'In year 1994–5 teams of hackers shared the credit card numbers they got from hacked servers.'

It was then that the clampdown began in earnest, Script explains. 'In those years America began to understand the money flow-out and started to ban former Soviet Union countries.'[6]

Shortly, you'll see how the Russian gangs managed to get round that ban. You'll also learn more about Script, the author of the above text. But first it's important to understand the online commercial factors that were driving the massive expansion of credit card use, ultimately putting millions of those cards into the hands of people like Script and Klopov.

In 1989, Tim Berners-Lee developed the World Wide Web, spark-ing the creation of a network of websites that could be stored on, and navigated around, using the Internet technology honed during the previous decade or so.

The e-commerce industry, as it was then called, was relatively quick to spot the opportunity. Amazon launched in 1994 and eBay in 1995. It's no coincidence that the two behemoths of online retail were born so close together. In order to make e-commerce work, the Web needed a payment method, and the obvious (though not inevitable) contender was credit cards. In 1994, the Web browser Netscape, precursor to the likes of Microsoft's Internet Explorer and Google's Chrome, introduced a system that enabled card details to be sent securely over the Internet. Of course, sending the details securely to the website didn't necessarily mean that the recipient site would keep them secure thereafter, as Klopov's story shows. Nonetheless, digital trade boomed. Online retail sales totalled just over $5 billion for the final three months of 1999 alone, and were growing at twenty times the rate of all other commerce.[7]

Simultaneously, credit card fraud went through the roof. It is true that there were more cards being issued than ever before, but the growth in fraud wasn't uniformly spread across all types of crime. Losses and thefts of the physical cards themselves actually declined, for example. The increase was dominated by one trend: 'cardholder not present', or CNP, fraud, meaning stolen details being used to make purchases that the real cardholder (who was still in possession of the card) hadn't authorized.

As online retailing took off during the late 1990s, CNP fraud grew at an astonishing rate. In the UK it doubled from 1998 to 1999, then doubled again the following year. By 2008 it accounted for more than half of all card fraud losses.[8] As Script described, Russia's gangs were already proficient in defrauding credit cards, and as their use rapidly expanded online, the thieves simply followed the money.

There's also evidence that some Russians saw this type of crime as a patriotic duty. Around the turn of the century a slew of carder websites were created. They offered for sale not only stolen credit card information, but fraud advice and tools (such as machines to encode blank, fresh cards with stolen data). One such site was badb.biz, set up by a hacker who used the handle BadB. It put a nationalistic spin on the pursuit of cybercrime.

Visitors were welcomed by an animated video which showed hackers being presented with a medal by a cartoon version of Russian president Vladimir Putin. Text running underneath the video emphasized how many credit cards had been stolen from u.s. citizens, and exhorted: 'We are awaiting you to fight the imperialism of the usa. That way we invest u.s. funds in Russian economy and make it grow bigger.'⁹

It's unclear exactly how heartfelt this patriotism was, however, because there was another good reason for hackers to claim to be stealing cards for the love of their country. It's likely that almost all the carder groups were on the radar of Russian intelligence and law enforcement. The hackers probably believed that as long as they stayed away from targeting Russian cardholders and focused on the u.s. instead, their country's law enforcement would leave them alone.

But whether one believes BadB and his accomplices were driven by patriotism or not, it's clear many hackers were working to a more prosaic logic. Several Russian former carders I have interviewed said their motivations were less about hegemony and more about profit. They say they targeted u.s. and Western European victims simply because that's where the biggest growth in online credit card use was taking place.

Ironically, if history had played out differently, that boom might have happened in Russia itself. During the 1960s, as Americans were laying the groundwork for the Internet, Russia was cooking up a plan for its own massive interconnected network. Computer scientist Viktor Glushkov had proposed a countrywide system of machines that could help manage the Soviet Union's immensely complex nationalized industrial structure, an early incarnation of today's 'cloud'-based computing. The scheme never took off. As the media historian Benjamin Peters writes, General Secretary

Brezhnev eschewed a key meeting, and the project faltered amid Soviet infighting.[10] The episode is now wittily summed up as the 'inter-nyet'. Instead, the U.S. and Europe made the running in creating both the Internet and the Web. Perhaps, subconsciously, the Russian carders saw their crimes as a chance for revenge for an opportunity missed.

Whatever the carders' motivations, the stage was set for an explosion in online payment fraud, and at the turn of the millennium, as Internet purchasing boomed and credit cards flooded the Web, the ad hoc, underground industry of carders represented by the likes of Klopov and BadB was about to make the leap into organized crime.

In May 2001, a now-legendary meeting was held in Odessa, bringing together several dozen of the world's leading Russian-speaking carders, including BadB. As a result of the meeting, these individuals and small-scale carder groups soon began to coalesce around a single website, called CarderPlanet, where deals could be made and information and expertise could be pooled.[11] Script created the site and it was phenomenally successful, with thousands of members flocking to it for advice on how to cash in on the credit card boom. But it hit a snag, as hinted at in Script's account.

By the end of the 1990s, the fraud problem had become so bad that the (mainly American) financial companies were cracking down, heavily scrutinizing the use of their cards in transactions linked to the former Eastern Bloc. Fraudsters there faced a frustrating problem: thanks largely to the hackers, they had an abundance of card details stolen from companies' computer servers, but it had become increasingly difficult to get anyone to accept payments using these cards. The solution to their woes came partly in the form of a resourceful American career crook called Brett Johnson.

Johnson has the good-humoured charm of a Brooklyn bartender and looks as if he spends his spare time overhauling Harley-Davidson motorbikes. But despite his easy-going demeanour and good-ol' boy likeability (or perhaps because of it), he was at one point a pivotal member of a criminal network that spanned the world, under his hacker alias GOllumfun.

By his own admission, Johnson got into fraud early, learning to hustle from family members. His scams moved online. His first one, he claims, involved a Beanie Baby soft toy. Blue ones were more valuable, so Johnson took a beige one, dyed it blue and sold it online for a tidy profit. Initially, like Klopov, Johnson stayed at the grey end of the market, getting involved with a website called the Counterfeit Library, where users could pick up advice on making fake IDs and perhaps even find someone to create fraudulent documents for them.

It was borderline legal, but as the site attracted more and more fraudsters, Johnson was soon neck-deep in the emerging world of cybercrime, running a forum with 3,000 members and vetting any wares they wished to sell on the site (which, conveniently, gave Johnson first look at any interesting new fraud tips and products coming along). Script was one of the site's users and the only Ukrainian, according to Johnson. With his frauds being increasingly blocked by the credit card companies, Script went to Johnson for a solution. The American was sceptical: some users of Counterfeit Library believed Script was actually a law enforcement official, because his offer of stolen credit cards looked too good to be true.

As a test, Johnson tried out one of Script's stolen credit cards. He bought a top-of-the-range Dell desktop PC for $5,000, fully expecting the transaction to be declined. Instead, the purchase went through without a hitch, and the computer was duly posted out.

Johnson was hooked.

'Overnight, we changed from an identity theft site into a credit card theft site,' he recalled. Carding was now an international operation.

In 2002, Johnson created a new business to supersede Counterfeit Library, called ShadowCrew. Once again, it would be a gathering place for crooks, but this time firmly focused on carding. A fruitful collaboration emerged: the mainly Russian-language site CarderPlanet pulled in the Russian fraudsters with their stashes of stolen credit card data, ShadowCrew's mainly English-speaking members would turn it into cash. It was Glasnost for the cybercrime era. Johnson claims the network's members were at one point withdrawing $40,000 a day from ATMs, after they discovered a flaw in the security embedded within credit cards.

But there was a problem. Among the senior members of ShadowCrew was a figure called CumbaJohnny, in real life a chiselled computer-obsessive in his early twenties called Albert Gonzalez. Unbeknown to Johnson, the police had arrested Gonzalez in 2003 as they were investigating the Russian site CarderPlanet (according to Johnson, Gonzalez was picked up after a pair of cops watched him stuffing $20 bills into his backpack at an ATM). Gonzalez turned informant for the Secret Service. He managed to become an administrator on the Russians' site too and fed information to the U.S. authorities from his key positions at both CarderPlanet and ShadowCrew. Clearly, the days were numbered for both criminal operations. In October 2004, the hammer fell, and dozens of people across the world were arrested in Operation Firewall.[12]

Brett Johnson managed to escape, but was picked up later on separate charges and served six years and three months in prison. He now works as a cybercrime consultant. Script wasn't rounded up in Operation Firewall. He had shut down CarderPlanet some months before ShadowCrew was taken down. But that didn't mean he was off the hook.

In 2005, Ukrainian police raided a well-protected flat in Odessa. As described in Misha Glenny's book *DarkMarket*, when they got inside they found that the occupant's computer equipment had been wiped.[13] They claimed the man inside was Script, real name: Dmitry Golubov. He denied the claims, and after a brief prison spell he was released, later being cleared by a court in Kiev. Despite the failure to convict Script, Operation Firewall was a hugely successful sting for the FBI. But there was a problem waiting in the wings, and once again it came back to Gonzalez, and more generally to the U.S. law enforcement tactic of trying to use criminals to ensnare other criminals.

It turned out that Gonzalez, even though he'd turned inform-ant, never really stopped his cybercrime work. Far from it, in fact. Even as he watched his former accomplices rounded up in Operation Firewall, Gonzalez himself was about to perpetrate a giant fraud. Using his years of hacking experience, he worked with a gang that targeted U.S. shops and businesses with a tactic called 'wardriving'.

Today, we're used to the idea of a WiFi box sitting in the corner of a room, beaming out signals, but in the early twenty-first century it was still relatively new technology, and often not well secured. Gonzalez and his crew capitalized on this. They drove along the South Dixie Highway in Miami, using a laptop and radio receiver to hoover up signals leaking out of big retailers like Barnes & Noble. The signals gave them clues about how they could hack into the companies' networks. Perhaps if they could transmit the right code on the right frequency, the company's computer net-work would respond, allowing the hackers a backdoor into the business.

It worked, and on a massive scale. Gonzalez's wardriving en-abled him and his accomplices to break into companies including TJX, owner of the TJ Maxx retail empire (known as TK Maxx in the UK). They stole forty million credit cards: at the time of his convic-tion in 2010, the largest cybercrime ever perpetrated.[14]

When the 28-year-old Gonzalez was sentenced to twenty years in prison, his links with the Secret Service and Operation Firewall emerged.[15] The fact that their star informant had subsequently embarked on a massive, eighteen-month hacking spree didn't look good for the U.S. authorities. The next time they wanted to take down a card fraud gang, the police wouldn't rely on a mole; they would go undercover themselves, and it didn't take long for the opportunity to present itself.

In 2005, police in the UK and U.S. got word of a new site, DarkMarket, an English-language forum where British card fraudsters, among others, were cooperating with Russian gangs. It was the successor to ShadowCrew and CarderPlanet, but this time law enforcement used a new tactic to bring down the criminal network.

An FBI agent called J. Keith Mularski infiltrated the website and gathered evidence from inside. Mularski had already created an underground alter ego on previous carding sites, under the handle Master Splyntr (a reference to a character from the *Teenage Mutant Hero Turtles* cartoon). Splyntr worked his way up through the forums' ranks and ended up running the server on which the DarkMarket website was stored. From this superb surveillance position Mularski (and therefore the FBI) could see all communication between the carders, and, more importantly, the Internet addresses they were accessing from, potentially revealing their real-world locations.

In summer 2007, law enforcement pounced on DarkMarket, and sixty people were arrested worldwide. But the site lived on for more than a year, and the backgrounds of those who ended up running it showed just how far cybercrime had evolved. As Misha Glenny revealed in his book, DarkMarket had effectively been taken over by crime gangs. The site had started as the bedroom project of a group of criminally minded geeks, but as its success grew it became the possession of highly organized criminal groups with links to operations that stretched far wider than online credit card fraud. These traditional crime groups had started to subsume the hackers' new criminal tactics.

It was to become a repeating pattern, and one that permeates this book.

When DarkMarket finally shut down in 2008, it looked like the end of an era. Card fraud was becoming an ever harder target for the crooks. Card companies were increasingly aggressive in tackling dodgy transactions, and law enforcement had shown they could successfully infiltrate carder websites. And even when infiltrations weren't successful, the suspicion that they might have been was poisonous to the trust relationships the sites struggled to foster among already paranoid thieves. (BadB, incidentally, was identified as Vladislav Horohorin. He pleaded guilty to fraud charges in October 2012.[16] His online profile says he's now free and working in Israel as a cybersecurity consultant.)

The credit-card-shaped hole through which Klopov, Script, Johnson, Gonzalez and others had grabbed their cash was getting a little smaller, but a global community of fraudsters had been awakened to the possibilities of online scams and they weren't going to give up. They were searching for a new cash cow. Thanks, allegedly, to a man called Evgeniy Bogachev, they were about to get it. And once again, online financial innovation created the opportunity: this time, the boom in Internet banking.

The banks hopped aboard the online revolution with gusto as the new century arrived, spurred by the growth in e-commerce (and perhaps with an eye to the cost-cutting potential of having fewer staff and premises). Estimates show that around eight million households worldwide took up the new services in 1995. By 2003 it was 130 million.[17] Take-up of Internet banking in the u.s. doubled from 2000 to 2002, reaching 30 per cent of account holders; it then climbed steadily to almost 60 per cent by the end of the decade.[18] Consumers in the u.s. and Europe flocked to access their accounts online. As the credit card fraud window narrowed, the carder community spotted a new opportunity. But making it work would require a step change in tactics – one that would open up a new vector for hacking.

The types of fraud developed in the 1990s and described earlier in this chapter were, in a way, not so much cybercrime as 'cyber-enabled' crime. Yes, the hackers were exploiting technology to grab credit card details, as Albert Gonzalez did with his wardriving attacks. But once the card details were stolen, it was often traditional criminal methods that were used to convert them into cash (buying goods and selling them on, for example).

Relying on such tactics had a number of drawbacks: for a start, it involved more people, which meant more to share the profits with, and more potential informants. And as Script and his accomplices found out, reliance on the purchase of physical goods was vulnerable to card companies clamping down on postage to particular countries and addresses.

What came next was a move towards a purer form of cyber-crime, a trajectory that has continued ever since. The constant drive of cybercriminals is to kick freer and freer of the physical world where they are more vulnerable to being caught. They want to get ever closer to the source of money, and as money becomes increasingly virtualized and digital, the cybercriminals' job has become more and more lucrative.

The emergence of online banking was a key step on this journey. It meant the thieves could target their victims' money directly, rather than having to go through the steps of turning stolen credit cards into goods and thence into cash.

Previously, financial institutions had been hard targets. U.S. bank robber Willie Sutton is famously quoted as saying he attacked banks 'because that's where the money is' (an utterance he later denied). But the logic works both ways: bank security tended to be tighter because, well, that's where the money is. Or was. As the twenty-first century dawned, suddenly the money wasn't just in the banks' safes; it was on the customers' computer screens, it was in the stream of ones and zeros that flowed from the banks' networks to the account holders' laptops and back: a stream that proved fatally vulnerable to hackers.

Now, instead of only one door to the bank vault, there were as many potential doors as there were customers. And as we dis-covered in the previous chapter, humans are susceptible to being tricked. The hackers turned their attention from the companies to the people who used them. The question was how to get into a victim's machine. Spreading viruses from computer to computer wasn't a new concept, as we saw from the Love Bug incident. But after a slew of such Internet 'worm' viruses, computer networks and companies had fought back, closing off the holes that allowed viruses such as the Love Bug to propagate.

Email, though, had achieved near-ubiquity and provided the best chance of unilaterally reaching victims. Even now, email is invariably the number one vector for cybercrime – the germ-laden sneeze in the elevator. It's also what drives the mega-hacks on businesses, in which hundreds of millions of customer records are stolen. One of the first uses for such information is to extract the email addresses and start targeting them. Sending millions of spam emails is not only relatively cheap to do, but you need only a fraction of recipients to fall for the scam to give you tens of thousands of potential victims. (Brett Johnson reckoned that for every two million spam emails sent, the spammers would receive around 20,000 positive responses.)

So, let's imagine you have a stack of email addresses, each one representing a potential target for your scam. You know that a good percentage of them will be using online banking, and you want to send them a virus that gives you access to their accounts. But where do you get such a thing? If you can't write the virus yourself, how on earth can you acquire it? If only there were a piece of software you could buy off the shelf, something that worked intuitively, like Microsoft's Word or Apple's iTunes. Enter Evgeniy Bogachev.

Bogachev was barely out of his teens when he first appeared on the carder forums, according to the FBI. During his time on the forums, he would have witnessed the rise and demise of a succession of card fraud sites: CarderPlanet had given way to ShadowCrew had given way to DarkMarket (plus the many others I haven't detailed above: mazafaka.ru, carder.org, carder.ru, CardersWorld, CardersMarket, and on and on). Most of them had been brought down by infighting, betrayal, law enforcement infiltration or some combination of the three.

In Bogachev's vision of the future, now mapped out in the various criminal charges against him, this would come to an end. Instead of vulnerable websites run by vulnerable teams, there would be one virus to rule them all, masterminded by one man. Appropriately enough, it was christened after the king of the gods in the ancient Greek pantheon: Zeus.

Released in 2007, Zeus was a Swiss army knife of a virus: once installed on a victim's computer, it could be used for multiple different tasks. It could record anything that the victim typed into the keyboard, it could steal passwords, it could install more programs, and it could secretly send out emails containing copies of itself to snare more people. Once on a victim's machine, it effectively gave the hacker remote control. But to smuggle such a program onto a target's computer is an art form in itself.

First there's the challenge of how to send it. Try sending a virus from your Gmail or Outlook account to a thousand people and see how long it takes for your account to be shut down. Anti-spam services are constantly on the lookout for the email addresses (and computers' IP addresses) that send dodgy emails, so the spammers must constantly switch addresses, as well as the computer servers they're sending from. That's why an essential function of the Zeus virus was to get the victim's computer to send out more spam itself, to infect yet more victims with Zeus. Anti-spam services can spot a hacker's infrastructure, but it's not so easy if the victims themselves start infecting people.

But Zeus's real genius was what it did to website pages once it had been installed. Zeus could change what users saw on the screen in real time. When a victim connected to their bank online, Zeus could show them a screen that appeared to show that everything was fine, meanwhile manipulating what was going on behind the scenes, secretly siphoning money away. And since Zeus stole banking passwords, hackers could log in at a later date and continue with the theft, with the victims none the wiser until they next logged in themselves and saw the true picture.

Most importantly, with Zeus installed, all of this took place within the victim's own computer. This meant that the banks didn't see a suspicious login from an unknown machine, which could immediately have raised the alarm. And when the police turned up to investigate, it initially looked as though the victims had made the transactions themselves.

At the time, many banks required customers to log in by entering their whole password, making them susceptible to password stealers like Zeus (something that's now been corrected: most banks ask for, say, three random letters from the password). In addition, during the Zeus era many banks allowed customers to set up new payees and transfer money directly from the bank's website, whereas now they often require customers to use a separate keypad or a code sent to their mobile phone in order to set up new payees (so-called 'two-factor authentication').

These security improvements might have stopped Zeus in its tracks, but they came too late to protect the many, many people who fell victim to the virus. Among them was an industrial plastics manufacturing company called AEV, headquartered near Liverpool, UK. If you've ever taken the casing off your TV, or other gadget, and looked at the tangled array of electronics inside, all carefully wrapped in brightly coloured plastic, then you've seen the kind of stuff AEV makes. Much of the manufacturing happens on an industrial estate in Birkenhead, where vats of noxious-smelling gloop sit ready to be turned into useful bits and bobs.

Such was the capriciousness of the Zeus virus: AEV is not a massively wealthy business or a big brand name. It's just a normal company, with normal employees, who of course use email. And one day in September 2013, one of those employees received a message with Zeus hidden in an attachment. The spammers got lucky. The employee was in the finance department, and had access to AEV's corporate accounts.

The email appeared to show that AEV was overdue in its tax payments, so the employee dutifully opened the attachment, unknowingly installing the Zeus virus. Next time she logged into the company's bank account, she entered her password, and within minutes two transactions had gone out: €100,000 to

Cyprus, $30,000 to Ukraine. Because of Zeus's ability to hide its tracks, the employee had no idea what had happened until she logged into the bank again and saw the missing money.

The Managing Director of AEV is Jonathan Kemp. He's down to earth and so is his trade. He's not shunting abstract financial products around a computer screen, nor coding a mobile app that's worth billions for reasons no one can understand. He's got a factory that makes actual stuff that people actually want, and he employs people to make it.

It wasn't a pleasant experience for Kemp admitting to his employees what had happened, telling them about the virus and about the £100,000 hole that had suddenly appeared in the company's finances. Fear spread. It was a sizeable part of the firm's profit, and if it couldn't be sorted, they worried redundancies might have to be made. Christmas was round the corner.

Kemp decided to go public. That was a very unusual move, because most businesses hit by cyberattacks want to keep it as quiet as possible.

'People were embarrassed, they didn't want the publicity. I think there was definitely a sense of shame and stigma,' said Kemp.

He believes the banks played on this. He claims that when he initially contacted his bank for help they implied the hack was a rare event. But the more Kemp talked publicly about it, the more fellow victims he found. Dozens came forward, with losses in the millions of pounds. Zeus had infected innumerable computers around the world. From his small office in Birkenhead, Kemp was uncovering the tip of a very large iceberg.

He was also unimpressed with the response from the police. He says his local force were mystified by the incident. He was told to report it to Action Fraud, the national police system, but says he never received a reply. Such responses added to his nagging, gnawing sense of loss. 'It was the most bizarre sensation,' he told me. 'It would have been easier if I'd had my wallet stolen and £100,000 taken, because physically I could have felt

I'd been robbed. With the cyberattack, I just couldn't get it out of my head.'

Kemp was criticized by some for not installing better protection at the company before the attack. That's all changed now; he spends what he considers a significant portion of the company's money on cybersecurity. He pays 'ethical hackers' (officially called penetration testers) to try to break in and advise him on any holes they find. They do tests every month. 'I know it's over the top,' he says. 'Once or twice a year would probably be fine. But this way, I sleep easier.'

The bank eventually refunded the money. Good news for Kemp and AEV. But an outcome that, when you think about it, simply shifts the problem rather than solving it. In many cases, victims of cybercrime get their money back from the bank or financial organization, leaving the impression that no one loses out. There are several counter-arguments. First and most strikingly, this 'victimless crime' perception is precisely the logic the criminals themselves often use to justify their actions. Credit card fraudster Script summed it up in an interview with the Russian magazine *Xakep* when he said that this kind of crime was 'guilt free'.

Card fraud, he said, 'isn't as heinous an occupation as it might seem. It's a lot less shameful than robbery. We don't cause card owners any problems; they'll get back everything from the banks, right down to the last penny if they ask for it.'[19]

If you believe cybercrime doesn't matter because banks give refunds, you're playing right into the criminals' hands.

Second, the repayment to AEV from the bank was discretionary. It's by no means guaranteed that the bank will refund the money. Kemp was in touch with around eighty other corporate Zeus victims. Those with a turnover under £1 million and fewer than ten employees were refunded under a special banking scheme. But of the larger companies, many did not get their money back.

Third, it's wrong to believe no one pays just because individual victims are refunded. In fact, we all pay in lots of ways. In the AEV case, for example, the bank had to recoup the missing £100,000 somehow, and it probably did so through fees and charges. Every time you pay an overdraft charge, every time you get a poor rate on a financial product, every time you spend twenty minutes on hold because the bank's call centre is understaffed, you're effectively making a tiny payment to the hackers. Cybercrime is increasingly a tax on online life, and if you resent being overtaxed, you should resent this.

Meanwhile, whoever stole AEV's money was never caught. Ultimately, it became just another dollop of cash in the coffers of the growing gang of people utilizing Zeus: all they had to do was buy the software, learn to use the controls, email it out and wait for suckers.

Zeus was massively popular. Within two years of first being spotted in 2007, it was on more than three million computers in the U.S. alone.[20] Key to its success was its creator's unceasing drive to refine his product. Through underground online forums like cardingworld, he liaised closely with his customers, listening to their needs and providing for them by releasing continually updated versions of the virus.[21]

We know this, because one of his potential 'customers' was Don Jackson. At the time that Zeus was spreading like wildfire, Jackson was working as a cybersecurity researcher at a U.S. company called Secureworks. It has a low profile among the public, but it deals with governments, police forces and giant companies around the world. Its clients were starting to notice Zeus infections, and so Jackson decided to make contact with the people behind the virus.

Using fake identities, he and his team managed to talk their way into the Zeus creator's online chat sessions (at that time, they only knew his hacker handle, Slavik). Jackson and his colleagues sounded convincingly like cybercriminals: they asked all the right questions and knew all the right hacks. It was no surprise they talked the cybercrime talk – after all, they had watched the hacker community from the other side as they tried to prevent companies being attacked.

What they found in Slavik was a software developer running the kind of tight customer service operation offered by eager tech start-ups. Potential Zeus buyers would suggest improvements, Slavik would provide them. He carefully labelled each new software release, the same way companies like Microsoft do. When Jackson blogged about his findings, for example, Zeus was at version 1.3.4. New for this release: the ability to hack the Firefox web browser, in addition to Internet Explorer.[22] Prices started at $3,000 for the basic Zeus package, but extra add-ons could also be purchased. For example, for $2,000 you could buy the ability to hack the newly released Windows 7 operating system (without it, you'd be limited to victims using the older, xp version of Windows).

Jackson found Slavik to be professional, responsive and diligent, with code that was well written and easy to use. He knew the value of his product, and was fiercely protective of it. Slavik used what Jackson called a hardware-based licensing system: in plain English, once you downloaded Zeus you could only use it on your own computer. For a group that had, like Klopov, partially started life by ripping off others' software, things had finally come full circle: Slavik was protecting his investment like a legitimate software company.

Jackson published his findings in March 2010, and it was clear that he wasn't the only one getting close to Zeus's inner circle. Law enforcement and other tech security companies were on the trail too.

Slavik had been phenomenally careful not to give away hints that might reveal his identity. Not one of the hackers I interviewed for this book claims to have known who he really was. Nonetheless, as the net closed in, the cybercrook showed wisdom way beyond his years. Unlike Klopov, for Slavik there would be no doomed, Hollywood-cliché 'one last big job'. He had a better plan: he would fake his own virtual death.

Aleksandr Panin wants more life. Not just for himself, but for everyone. Many, many more years of life, way beyond our current quota. But unlike many with the same aspiration, Panin is doing something about it. He's studying molecular biology with the aim of tackling cancer and has written detailed texts about possible solutions.[23]

Unlike many students, however, Panin is publishing his work from Yazoo City Low Security Correctional Facility in Southern Mississippi (coincidentally, the same prison where Albert Gonzalez, the TJ Maxx hacker, is serving out his time).

As he explained to me in a series of emails from a prison computer, Panin has been in the U.S. custodial system since July 2013, shortly after he arrived in the Dominican Republic on holiday. Up until then, life was going well. Up until Panin got involved with Slavik, Zeus's creator.

Panin had always had an interest in life extension, and while studying for a place at Moscow State University he started researching mind uploading, which offers the prospect of taking the contents of a human brain and transferring it to a computer. Panin quickly hit a snag: funding this kind of research is pricey, the experts told him. Panin claims this, along with family pressures, drove him to explore cybercrime.

Around the turn of the millennium, Panin was working for a student website and was tasked with boosting visitor numbers. His solution was to create a 'bot', a piece of software that would visit the site, pretending to be a real user, upping the number of hits. He realized the bot could also be used to click on website adverts. Since advertisers got paid by the number of clicks, the bot could be used to generate money and Panin would get a cut. This is what's called 'click fraud'. Someone got in touch and suggested the same software could be used to launder stolen credit card information, by automatically entering it into websites' payment systems en masse.

From here it was a short hop for Panin, now under the hacker alias 'Gribodemon', to one of the many fraud forums running at the time; and from there, he learned of the legendary Zeus virus. But as a hard-up student, Panin says he couldn't afford the $2,000 that was being charged for Zeus at that time. So he set out to create his own version.

SpyEye was a cut-price equivalent of Zeus, and by Panin's own admission, it was not the professionally crafted work of software engineering that Zeus was. But that didn't matter, because Panin originally didn't think anyone else would end up using it but him. Panin says the fact that he never intended to sell SpyEye to others meant that, unlike Slavik, he didn't do much to protect his own identity while he was developing it; a decision he would later regret.

Panin claims he ended up selling the software out of desperation when he got $500 behind with the rent on his apartment. Short of cash, he decided to hawk his hacking tool to the growing cybercrime community using Zeus. But before he could sell SpyEye in the crime forums, it had to be approved by a moderator. In Panin's case, he claims the moderator was none other than Slavik, Zeus's creator. He approved SpyEye. The reasons why would become clear as the next few months unfolded.

Launched in January 2010, SpyEye was wildly popular. The u.s. Department of Justice (DOJ) claimed in 2016 that the software had been used to infect a staggering fifty million computers worldwide. It was also lucrative; the DOJ claims Panin sold it for between $1,000 and $8,500, to at least 150 customers.[24] But it couldn't match the grace of Zeus, and Panin was constantly having to patch holes and weaknesses in his software. Then, in November 2010 (a few months after Don Jackson went public about his Zeus findings), Panin got a miraculous offer: Slavik contacted him and offered him the source code for the Zeus virus.

Source code is different to the software that customers download. It's the original code that the developers use to build the program, which is then turned into the customer version, which can't be turned back into source code. You might have a copy of

Microsoft Word, for example, but the source code belongs to Bill Gates and Co., which is why he's richer than you.

With the source code, Panin controlled Zeus: he could tweak it, improve it and sell new versions. He could also use it to improve SpyEye, and according to the DOJ, he was planning to release SpyEye version 2 when he was arrested.

Why had Slavik handed over his Crown Jewels to an up-and-coming cybercriminal? Here's what Panin told me:

> I asked Slavik why he is doing it. Well, he said that he was tired of constantly supporting Zeus and decided to quit – he pointed out that his kids are giving him strange looks when he is on the computer almost all of the time, so he decided to quit and start a legal business and move to Cuba.

That turned out to be very far from the truth.

Panin is a contrary individual: he is deeply committed to his study of molecular biology, but oddly detached when it comes to SpyEye. He seems almost happy to be in prison, and resigned to the fact he was going to get caught. He doesn't regret building and running banking viruses, other than the fact that he feels the coding work was below par. He seems uninquisitive and disconnected. As we saw in the case of the Love Bug virus, the best hackers have a keen sense of human psychology. Panin seems to lack this. As he wrote to me about Slavik: 'We didn't communicate at all. I didn't see the point of communication anyways – no one in the field was experiencing desire to become friends in the real world or something like that. It always was just a business.'

Perhaps Panin should have asked more questions.

The younger hacker's earlier lapses in security caught up with him. Unbeknown to Panin, the U.S. authorities had issued a warrant for his arrest via Interpol. In July 2013, as he boarded a plane after holidaying with a friend in the Dominican Republic, police swooped and Panin was soon on a plane to the U.S. (the DOJ claims he was arrested when he flew though Atlanta airport).

Three years later he was sentenced to nine and a half years in jail.[25]

Meanwhile, Zeus's author was far from 'retired', and was almost certainly nowhere near Cuba. In fact, Slavik had simply narrowed his circle of customers and upped his prices.

He was still a career cybercriminal, sailing close to the wind, and the next near miss for him would come as a result of a basic failing in the Zeus business plan: even after spiriting the money out of people's bank accounts, at some stage the hackers had to get their hands on the actual cash. Put simply: if you steal $100,000 using Zeus, transfer it to your own bank account, and then try to withdraw it, you're going to get caught. It's far better to convince ten people to receive $10,000 each, figure out some way to launder the funds, then hand it over to you. But those ten people are going to want a cut of the money.

Ultimately the Zeus hackers faced the same problem as the credit card fraudsters: recruiting so-called 'money mules' meant working with too many people, who were eating away at the profits and creating potential leaks in the operation.

In 2009, three women from Kazakhstan walked into the FBI offices in New York to report an unusual incident. They told officers that they had come to the U.S. to look for work, and had become involved in a strange scheme: a man would drive them to a bank branch and tell them to open an account, telling the bank they were summer students. Then, over the next few days, they would return to the bank and withdraw money from the newly opened accounts, keeping a small cut for themselves.[26]

Over the next year, similar stories began to emerge. The transactions were mostly under $9,000, the level at which more stringent checks kicked in. Some of the mules had been brought to the U.S. specifically to take part in the operation; others were recruited in the country. It must have looked like easy money, especially for someone desperate for cash. According to *Wired* magazine, one woman told investigators that she'd taken the muling gig after her regular job had fallen through, commenting: 'I could strip, or I could do this.'[27] The mules were almost certainly ignorant of the bigger picture.

Investigators tracked the network and linked it to money that had been stolen from bank accounts using the Zeus virus. The authorities were once again on Slavik's trail.

Around the world, dozens of arrests were made. Some were those responsible for recruiting the mules, some were managers of the network and some were mules themselves. The scale of the police bust gave an insight into the size of muling operation required to cash out the millions being stolen using Zeus. There was, inevitably, one key figure missing among those arrested. Despite years of work, investigators didn't even have Slavik's real name, let alone a physical location where he could be put in handcuffs. And it seemed Slavik knew it. After the muling network arrests, far from winding his neck in, he upped the stakes, forming the Business Club, a loose alliance of around fifty cybercriminals.[28]

Together, this club went after larger and larger amounts, targeting ever bigger companies. They also figured out a way to avoid the muling hazards, in the U.S. at least. An emergency restraining order taken out against Slavik by an FBI agent in 2014 stated that the Business Club had 'discovered a mechanism by which to send international payments while avoiding all of the traditional safeguards.'[29] The bank vault was now wide open for cash to flow straight out of the U.S., and the sums were eye-watering.

The same restraining order states that thefts of a million dollars were 'very common'. A single bank lost $8 million in just eleven thefts. The largest single transaction was $6.9 million, in November 2012.[30]

To keep the Business Club stocked up with infected computers, Slavik had created the most powerful version of his virus yet: Zeus 2.0. In all the time Don Jackson had monitored it, the software version number had never shifted from one. Version two was a major departure, as reflected in the new price tag of $10,000.

Slavik had gone back to the drawing board to fix a snag that made the Zeus virus vulnerable to law enforcement tracking. To control the victims' infected computers, Zeus operators needed to send them instructions. These were issued by a so-called 'command and control server', a computer that functions as an online mother ship.

With this one computer controlling all the infected machines, it created a pinch-point in the criminal network: if investigators could trace the instructions, they might be able to get to the hackers – or at the very least get a warrant to disable the command computer, which would liberate all of its slaves. Law enforcement officials had got faster and more effective at doing this, and it was starting to do serious harm to the cybercriminals' operations.

Slavik's new virus, Zeus 2.0, or Game Over Zeus, got round this problem by borrowing from what are called 'peer-to-peer' systems. These had been popularized by a website called Napster back in 2001, which was hugely popular because it figured out a way to offer ripped-off music. Napster's owners realized that if pirated music was held on the site's own computers, the authorities could simply raid the company and shut those machines down, and the music would vanish. Instead, Napster had its users store the pirated songs on their own computers, and Napster would then simply connect a user looking for a song with another user who had it. As a result, Napster proved immensely difficult to shut down, but was eventually closed after rock band Metallica sued, having discovered their entire back catalogue available for free.[31]

Nevertheless, Napster had set a trend, and its lessons were not wasted on Slavik as he set out to build an unassailable version of Zeus. In its new incarnation, infected machines were still controlled by a central command computer. But they also kept a list of the online addresses of other virus-infected computers. Law enforcement could, of course, shut down the command computer, but if the infected machines lost contact with the mother ship, they would now simply contact another infected computer, find a new mother-ship address and keep going. At a stroke, one of law enforcement's most effective takedown tactics was rendered almost useless.

Ever the entrepreneur, Slavik took the opportunity to intro-duce another innovation into Zeus 2.0. As a shrewd businessman, he didn't want to waste any effort. What if his virus infected a computer that didn't do online banking? Slavik came up with an alternative tactic: blackmail the computer owner. He tweaked Zeus to be able to spread 'ransomware': a virus which scrambles files on a computer before charging a fee to unscramble them. Handily, the fee could be paid using Bitcoin, the virtual, 'anonym-ous' currency. Suddenly, the Zeus thieves discovered they could get victims' money sent directly to their Bitcoin accounts. This meant even less reliance on the muling networks which eroded their profits and increased their vulnerability to law enforcement actions.

Slavik didn't invent ransomware, but the scale of his suc-cess showed how profitable it could be. One researcher traced payments and discovered that $27 million had been extorted worldwide in just two months.[32] This was another of Slavik's legacies: he sparked a boom in ransomware – a legacy that would go on to cause harm way beyond the Zeus gang's crime spree.

The Business Club, the group of fraudsters of which Slavik was a member, perfected yet another tactic around this time: a type of digital smoke grenade to allow them a clean getaway. After they'd hit a bank account and stolen the money, they would use their network of virus-infected computers to inundate the bank's websites with junk requests, overwhelming its computer systems and forcing parts of them to shut down.[33] It made it much harder to see what had happened and to investigate the theft. This is what's called a DDOS or Distributed Denial of Service attack. Once again, Slavik didn't invent it, but it's become yet another key weapon in the cybercrime arsenal.

And the Business Club had one more trick up their sleeve: remember the click-fraud that Aleksandr Panin carried out, making his bot software click on ads and then getting the cash from the advertisers? The Zeus 2.0 virus did that too.[34]

In summary, Slavik had helped create an online crime machine the likes of which had never been seen before. It's unclear quite how much he personally made from these years of cybercrime, but if the FBI is right in asserting he was 'at the very top' of the Zeus operation, he would be a multimillionaire, a lifestyle reflected in his champagne-inspired choice of email address: bollinger.evgeniy.[35]

Slavik's success meant that he'd trodden on a lot of toes: law enforcement in multiple countries who had seen victims lose millions; big tech firms like Microsoft who had to deal with his mayhem impacting upon their systems; and security companies who'd had enough of constantly playing whack-a-mole with his viruses hitting their clients.

Quite how the FBI unmasked Slavik is still unclear. Dutch security company Fox-IT says it received a tip-off about an email address that led to a UK server used to run Business Club websites.[36] From there, they discovered Slavik's social media accounts. Even one of the world's greatest cybercriminals, it seems, can't resist the lure of sharing the odd selfie. Finally, law enforcement could claim to put a face and a name to the mysterious Slavik.

A plan was hatched. The big tech companies would be given the Internet addresses of the command computers that controlled Zeus-infected machines, and would disconnect them. Then, as the infected computers sought out a new mother ship, they would be redirected to a 'sinkhole', connecting them to an Internet address from where they would be blocked from ever finding Slavik's network again. The takedown would happen on Friday 30 May 2014. In the meantime, the DOJ had been working on charges against Slavik. They decided they would go public, brandishing his photos and his alleged real name, putting a face to the anonymous cybercriminal who by this time they were blaming for hundreds of millions of dollars of losses.

The press conference would happen on Monday 2 June, following the three days of the technical takedown. Everyone was set. And then there was a slip-up. One of the tech security companies helping the operation made a mistake. On Friday, they mistakenly published a blog post describing the secret operation that was about to unfold.[37] The post was swiftly removed and the technical takedown began. Meanwhile, in Anapa, Bogachev packed the car.

When the story broke, journalists swooped on the Ulitsa Lermontova tower block. They found a surprising set of reactions. When they heard the news of what he was alleged to have done, some of Bogachev's neighbours lauded him as a hero for getting one over on Russia's enemies. One police officer reportedly said he'd like to pin a medal on the cybercriminal, in an eerie echo of the animated Vladimir Putin in BadB's promotional video.[38]

The reality is that even without the early tip-off, it's almost certain Bogachev would not have been arrested. For a start, relations between Barack Obama's White House and Vladimir Putin's Kremlin had been in deep-freeze for years; there was little chance that Russian law enforcement would cooperate with a u.s. investigation. But American investigators had a much more compelling reason to doubt Russia would help, linked to a shocking accusation they'd made as they circled tighter and tighter around the Zeus gang and its leader. Bogachev, it's alleged, had made his virus product available to download for buyers, but he had left a backdoor in the code, seemingly known only to him. Once Zeus was installed, the backdoor could be used to search victims' computers for keywords and documents. As investigators seized more and more Zeus infrastructure, they started to see what was being searched for, and it cast a whole new light on the man behind Zeus.

Researchers at Fox-IT claim they saw Bogachev searching tens of thousands of computers for classified Ukrainian secrets, and email addresses belonging to Georgian intelligence officials and leaders of elite Turkish police units. The company claims Bogachev was the only person who knew that Zeus, which had infected several million computers from 2006 to 2014, could be used as a global surveillance tool. 'Bogachev, it appeared, was a Russian intelligence asset,' the company wrote in its blog.[39]

The Russian government did not respond to requests for an interview for this book.

In 2016, following the hacking attacks targeting the u.s. presidential election, outgoing president Barack Obama issued sanctions against four Russian military officials, as well as branches of the Russian government itself. Tacked onto the list was a notable addition: one Evgeniy Bogachev, blamed for $100 million of thefts.[40] The accusations levelled against him were separate to those of the alleged election hackers, but his inclusion on the same document adds to the suspicion that Bogachev was, effectively, working for the Russian government.

If this were true, it is another reason why Bogachev should be seen as such a pivotal figure in the history of cybercrime. If the allegations are founded, his work represents a key moment when the wide-scale, indiscriminate hacking by organized gangs started to merge with nation-state interests – a trajectory that would have significant consequences in the ensuing decade.

Unsurprisingly, perhaps, I have not managed to find Bogachev during my research for this book. It's assumed he's still in Russia (partly because attempting to visit other countries would leave him perilously exposed to extradition to the u.s.). Investigators who tracked the case are prosaic about his fate, especially given their assumption that he is now working full-time for the Russian state. One ex-policeman who worked on the uk end of the Zeus takedown told me: 'He's very probably in a Russian government building, being constantly watched by Russian law enforcement, and having to use their computers. That's punishment enough.'

This, then, is the modern world of cybercrime policing: you spend years tracking a ghost, and even when you find out their true identity, you stand almost no chance of seeing them face justice.

Rather than arrests, law enforcement bodies increasingly rely on working with private companies to do technical damage to the criminals' networks, just as they did by destroying Zeus's mother ships. It's often effective (today Zeus infections are running at a fraction of their heyday peak), but not as satisfying as seeing someone in handcuffs. It also leaves the criminals free to come up with new schemes, and shows other would-be hackers that jail time is seemingly not something they need to fear. And so the demise of the Zeus empire did little to dent the rise of cybercrime. Instead, Bogachev's alleged tactics of ransomware, hacking for government surveillance and Denial of Service attacks all became part of the growing culture of hacking.

As the second decade of the twenty-first century bedded in, cybercrime had come of age: it was organized, distributed and had established links with government-level hacking operations. But at heart, money was still driving it, and the search for new ways to steal continued unabated. Some of the older methods had got harder: credit cards were more difficult to defraud and online banking had been strengthened against attack. But what about the banks themselves? That's ultimately where the money is, after all. What if hackers could break into the digital bank vault itself? Instead of chiselling money from bank customers day in, day out, they could steal huge lump sums in one go.

At the very moment Bogachev was leaving Anapa, the groundwork was being laid for a crime that would make Zeus's multimillion-dollar spree pale by comparison. In a sign of times to come, the hacking tactics of organized crime gangs were being harnessed by governments and used to pursue their own agendas. What came next was possibly the most audacious heist ever attempted: a bank in chaos, a digital smash-and-grab raid, and a billion dollars spirited away through an Internet traffic jam.

THREE

OCEAN'S 11 DOT COM

I t's summer 2015, and across four countries the groundwork is being laid for a billion-dollar hacking attack.

In Bangladesh, an employee of the country's central bank is reading a courteous email from a job applicant before clicking a link to download his CV.

In Sri Lanka, an aspiring politician is courting charity donations from wealthy Japanese backers, pulling in millions of dollars.

In the Philippines, a bank manager is opening five accounts for people using fake drivers' licences.

And somewhere inside North Korea, a Google user called amazonriver1990 is researching the term 'CVE'. The abbreviation stands for Common Vulnerabilities and Exposures – the kind of software glitches that, if used correctly, can help get you inside the digital doors of an online bank vault.

These people may not have known one another, but within a year they would all be part of a modern-day bank robbery. The crime was high-tech, but the plot unfolded like a classic heist movie: assemble the crew, case the joint, do the break-in and make the getaway. And according to the investigators who picked over the crime scene, the digital fingerprints point to one suspect: the government of North Korea.

It's not easy to get a clear picture inside the swirling geopolitical snowglobe that is one of the world's most secretive states. There is a cohort of North Korea experts who read the tea leaves of occasional official announcements, and glean titbits of information from the few defectors who make it out. These researchers are constantly working with limited information, and the same applies in the online world. On the map of digital connections, the Democratic People's Republic of Korea is a dark expanse compared to its neighbours. Perhaps the most illuminating tech perspective comes from an American who, for several years, taught computer science in the so-called 'Hermit Kingdom'.

Will Scott had just finished his masters at Washington University and was deciding what to do with his future when he spotted that Pyongyang University of Science and Technology was looking for teachers. Within a few months, he was on a plane to the capital, where he taught for three terms over three years at the college, which is North Korea's only privately run university and is funded by foreign sources.[1] The big change during his time, Scott says, was the technology:

In 2013 some of them had phones, some of them had tablets. By 2015 most of them did, and most were starting to have computers and laptops as well. These were the years when tech was booming and getting mass adoption.

Of course, Scott's not talking here about the vast majority of North Koreans, who according to the UN are more worried about malnutrition than mobile reception.[2] The kids Scott was teaching were from the country's minority middle class.

And the smartphones they used were not the kind that most of us know and love. Yes, they had apps, could play music and take photos, but Scott says the vast majority of users could not connect to the World Wide Web. The government controls all communications, and online access for the country's reported five million mobile subscribers is strictly limited.

Scott's students did have Internet access, though, via a series of Windows computers in the university. 'They could use it occasionally, and generally in order to do research for classes or to find things, but were not recreationally using the Internet for anything outside of direct reference for a project,' he says. Concern over surveillance seemed to have quashed their inquisitiveness, or perhaps stymied its growth in the first place.

It was an experience echoed by Sophie Schmidt, daughter of Google's then executive chairman Eric. She visited North Korea with her father in 2013 as part of a diplomatic trip, and later wrote a warts-and-all blog about the experience. On an official tour, she was taken to a university 'e-Library' where students could access the Web. She described it as an 'e-Potemkin Village', a reference to an extravagant charade created to fool the viewer. She saw ranks of North Koreans with the digital world at their fingertips, but when she looked closer she realized the students showed little interest in it. 'A few scrolled or clicked,' she wrote, 'but the rest just stared.'[3]

Yet, according to researchers, North Korea has created one of the most high-profile and dangerous hacking groups in the world. How did a nation with such an apparently awkward relationship with online computing achieve such cyber prowess? The reality is that the folks whom Schmidt and Scott saw timidly skirting around the Web were not the country's future cyberattackers. Those people come up through a totally different system designed to identify the most skilled people, according to Martyn Williams, who runs the website North Korea Tech (an affiliate of 38 North, a North Korea-focused website that is, in turn, backed by a U.S. think-tank).[4]

Right at the primary school level, they'll initially identify kids that have an aptitude for mathematics, and they'll be given additional exposure to computers. At the high school level they now have an annual programming contest. And that's at city, provincial and national level, so you get the best of the best selected that way. Then the best of those will go off to the specialist universities. A certain amount will go to military hacking schools. There's a system to find the best of the best.

North Korea needs such a system because, unlike more developed countries, it can't rely on a culture where hackers are often self-taught, honing their skills on laptops in their bedrooms. 'You can't do that in North Korea because homes don't have computers or Internet access, so it's all done through the school system,' says Williams.

It's a tactic that's been decades in the making. Kim Jong Il, the country's late Great Leader (1941–2011), knew the importance of cyberspace in conflict. 'The victory and defeat of modern warfare depends on how we do electronic warfare,' he's reported as saying in a set of military guidelines from 2005.[5]

Four years later, the North Korean administration created a department called the Reconnaissance General Bureau, pulling together its cyberwarfare units and shifting them up the pecking order of the country's rigidly arranged and well-funded military hierarchy.[6] Within a few years it would create one of the most high-profile and disruptive state hacking teams on the planet, according to security researchers who've tracked its rise. It became known as the Lazarus Group – a reference to its ability to survive and thrive inside its victims' systems even when it seemed it had been eradicated.

Part of the appeal of cyberoperations for countries like North Korea is its low cost: cheaper than tanks, fighter jets and missiles, and certainly cheaper than a nuclear weapons programme – perfect for countries with limited resources looking to take on more powerful opponents.

According to some reports, North Korea has around 6,000 'cyberwarriors'.[7] News coverage of this is often alarmist – it's worth remembering that cyberarmies exist in many countries, including the UK, which since at least 2013 has been developing 'full-spectrum military cyber capability, including a strike capability'.[8] But where many governments' hackers are focused on intelligence gathering or strategic advantage, researchers see a key difference with North Korea's cybersoldiers: they're hacking for cash.

As the Lazarus Group grew in reputation, tech security experts started to discern that its most attention-grabbing attacks were motivated by a need to feed its government's coffers. There are good reasons why this might be true: despite a patchy rapprochement with the u.s. and South Korea, the current North Korean regime has been the target of crippling sanctions, particularly following increased missile testing under Kim Jong Un, Kim Jong Il's son and successor as Respected Supreme Leader.

Among the sanctions, in March 2013 the UN Security Council passed Resolution 2094, blocking North Korea from bulk cash transfers and severely limiting its ties to the international banking system.[9] A country starving for food was now being starved of financial access.

Earlier we saw how Russian cybercrime gangs had milked the growing online banking system for hundreds of millions of dollars. The lesson wasn't lost on North Korea's hackers who, according to testimony given to UN investigators, set out to boost government income as the sanctions bit.[10] And they didn't mess about with credit cards and consumer banking. Instead, according to the FBI, they took it to a new and frightening level, hacking straight into the banks themselves.

Pulling off such an audacious raid would require North Korea to solve a crucial problem: the country has almost cut itself off from the world, digitally as well as diplomatically. This helps control its citizens' exposure to outside influence, but those same limits also mean its hackers are themselves vulnerable to surveillance. The country's Internet access is provided by a North Korean company called Star, which for several years has been run as a joint venture with a Thai company called Loxley Pacific (although the latter reportedly pulled out in early January 2018).[11] Star, in turn, gets its Internet connections from a Chinese company. Between them, these providers offer an extremely limited connection that gives North Korea a narrow doorway to the Internet. Whereas a country like the UK might have millions of IP addresses linking its computers to the outside world, North

Korea has barely more than a thousand. With so few links, it is painfully vulnerable to surveillance. Any attempts to hack from inside North Korea could be quickly spotted by foreign intelligence agencies.

The country's solution, says the FBI, was to rely on its longest-serving ally: China. The Americans claim North Korea runs at least one front company in the country, called Chosun Expo, just over the border in Dalian.[12] It was originally a joint venture between North and South Korea, and it seems it attempted a variety of different activities. Archives of the company's website show a bewildering corporate journey, from selling mushrooms and vases to offering bespoke computer programming services. My attempts to contact the site's current owners proved fruitless.

The firm was once seen as an important bridge-building exercise between the two countries, but at some stage, South Korea pulled out. Now, claims the FBI, Chosun Expo is a cover for North Korean cyberactivities which they link to the Reconnaissance General Bureau, its hacking unit. To back up their claim, the FBI quotes a witness 'who had direct dealings with Chosun Expo' and said some employees 'who were dispatched to China kept only a very small fraction of their salary, remitting the rest to the government of North Korea'.[13] The U.S. also says that Chosun Expo's website was registered using an email address that was later accessed by someone using a North Korean IP address.

Archives of Chosun Expo's website from 2015 state that the company is based in North Korea. But the U.S. insists that it was from within Chosun Expo's China office that North Korea's hackers launched their raids deep into the heart of the Western financial world.

A high-tech heist was about to play out in four acts, but before targeting the banks, the hackers would first hit an icon of American soft power: Hollywood.

THE DRY RUN

Actors Seth Rogen and James Franco do a good line in puerile comedies, and their 2014 Sony movie *The Interview* was no exception. The plot sees two bumbling journalists travel to North Korea for an exclusive interview with Respected Supreme Leader Kim Jong Un that turns into a farcical assassination.

Ahead of the film's release on Christmas Day, trailers were aired from June that were predictably mocking in their portrayal of Kim. The film closes with a graphic computer-generated sequence of his character dying in a burning helicopter. Many saw nothing unusual in the trailers; after all, the Kims and their quirks had been objects of derision for years. But it seems the film quickly raised hackles in the Democratic People's Republic of Korea (DPRK).

On 27 June, North Korea's ambassador to the United Nations sent a letter to the international body claiming the film had sparked 'towering hatred and wrath' in the country. 'Those who defamed our supreme leadership and committed hostile acts against DPRK can never escape the stern punishment to be meted out according to law, wherever they might be in the world,' it said, closing with the threat of 'strong and merciless counter-measure'.[14] According to the FBI, North Korean actions against the film didn't stop at official letters. In early September, two actors who starred in *The Interview* had attention-grabbing comments posted on their Facebook timelines, says the FBI, offering 'Nude photos of many A-list celebrities'.[15] The comments included a link which, if clicked, installed a screensaver containing a few photos of a female model. In fact, it was a smokescreen. Behind the scenes, the screensaver was also attempting to infect the computer with a virus.

According to the FBI, the comments were posted by a Facebook user named David Andoson, who logged in using an email address linked to Chosun Expo, the North Korean front company in China. North Korea, it seemed, was targeting the stars who mocked its Respected Supreme Leader, and trying to hack them using salacious links on their Facebook accounts. If this was indeed the case, it shows a surprisingly shrewd grasp of pop culture for a nation supposedly sealed away from the outside world. Just two weeks earlier, nude photos of A-list celebrities had indeed been leaked onto the Internet. A timely link to a fresh leak of intimate pictures might have been just tempting enough for a Hollywood star to click on.

It's not clear whether Sony knew about these messages and the letter to the UN, but even if it did it seems unlikely the company would have backed down and cancelled the movie. It later emerged that Sony was intensely aware of the political controversy the film might stir up, but proceeded nonetheless. In hindsight, it was an unwise call. (Sony Pictures Entertainment did not respond to requests to comment.) It later emerged that the hackers had been inside Sony's systems since the end of September 2014, when an employee had inadvertently clicked on a phishing email, believing they were downloading some advertising videos. An FBI investigation found that the employee had instead unwittingly downloaded a virus that allowed the hackers to start finding their way around Sony's internal computer systems and eventually to pilfer swathes of deeply sensitive corporate material.

After months of stealthily stealing insider info, Sony's attackers were ready to drag the company's name through the mud. But first they wanted to take it offline.

On 24 November 2014, a Sony employee in the UK logged into their computer to be confronted with a message that looked like a schlock horror movie poster. A red skeleton leered out of the screen, along with the message 'Hacked by #GOP' (later revealed as an abbreviation for Guardians of Peace, an as-yet-unknown hacking group). Just to add to the bizarre, almost comic impression, the message included an audio recording of gunshots, followed by a scream. The message was so full of hacker clichés that it might have looked like a practical joke. The consequences, however, were deadly serious. Guardians of Peace, according to investigators, was the Lazarus Group, North Korea's hacking team. They had unleashed a worm virus inside Sony. One by one, the company's computers were infected and their screens frozen with the same doom-laden 'Hacked by #GOP' message. Like all modern companies, Sony was highly networked, and the virus spread quickly, wiping the memory banks of every machine it infected. Around 8,000 computers had to be disconnected to contain the outbreak.[16] Within days, staff at the company were reportedly forced to rely on paper, pens and fax machines, as one of the world's biggest media conglomerates went into digital shutdown.[17] But things were about to get worse, as the hackers weaponized the reams of confidential information they'd been stealing for months.

The cybercriminals had demanded payment to cease their attacks, but received nothing. On 26 November, at least four senior Sony Pictures Entertainment execs received an email stating: 'We began to release data because Sony Pictures refused our demand . . . You are to collapse surely. Damn to gruel and reckless Sony Pictures!'[18]

Once again, the quaintly archaic language belied serious intent. The hackers made good on their threat: thousands and thousands of highly sensitive, confidential emails from Sony's most senior executives were published online for all to see.

Journalists had a field day poring over the once-private gossip. The media fallout from the attack will be discussed in a later chapter. But before the salacious Sony emails grabbed everyone's attention, some reporters had been trying to work out who was behind the attack. Just a few days after Sony announced it had been hit, there'd been speculation about a link to North Korea and *The Interview*'s mocking treatment of its leader.[19] But the Guardians of Peace group hadn't mentioned the film at all, despite making several public announcements about their hacking of Sony.

That changed on 16 December, three weeks after the hack went public. The hackers posted a message online referencing the film. They also implied that this was no longer about computer crime and data leaks, but that real-world violence could be involved:

> Warning We will clearly show it to you at the very time and places 'The Interview' be shown, including the premiere, how bitter fate those who seek fun in terror should be doomed to . . . Remember the 11th of September 2001. We recommend you to keep yourself distant from the places at that time. (If your house is nearby, you'd better leave.)

Canning the movie was a big decision for Sony. It seemed absurd to turn a slapstick comedy into a freedom-of-speech martyr that might actually result in people being physically harmed. But on the other hand, axing it could be seen as an act of self-censorship, and if North Korea was indeed behind the attacks, Sony would have effectively kowtowed to a nation-state hacking attack – not a good precedent to set.

But under increasing pressure, and with several major cinema chains backing out of screenings, Sony pulled *The Interview* from widespread theatrical release. It was later released online, where it seems the furore did indeed raise its profile – it made $15 million in its first four days (coincidentally the same amount Sony initially set aside for dealing with the aftermath of the hack).[20]

Barack Obama, meanwhile, publicly blamed the attacks on North Korea.[21] It was an unprecedented step – no world leader had ever pointed the finger so explicitly at one state for a hack so soon after it had happened. As such, it was a key development in an issue that had dogged cybercrime investigation as it had risen up the agenda over the years: attribution. Unlike in more traditional crimes, in hacking there are no fingerprints or DNA. IP addresses and email accounts may look like compelling evidence, but they can be manipulated (which is why the FBI's allegations against North Korea remain just that: allegations, and ones unlikely to be tested in any court). Security research firms at the time of the Sony hack were notoriously reticent to pin crimes on any specific country (in public, at least). Instead, each company would come up with its own pseudonymous codenames for the different hacker groups they spotted, such as Lazarus.

But in fact, Obama's decision was a staging post in an ever-increasing drive to dish out blame. In early 2013, a u.s. tech security company called Mandiant worked with the *New York Times* to investigate a hacking attack against the newspaper. As a result, Mandiant eventually attributed dozens of attacks to a specific group, which they claimed had targeted everything from the Coca-Cola company to u.s. power grid firms. This time, Mandiant went way beyond merely attributing the attacks to a hacker group with an obscure codename. Instead, it laid the blame squarely on the Chinese government, not only naming a unit of the People's Liberation Army, but identifying the individual building it alleged the attacks were coming from. The claims were vehemently denied by the Chinese government, which said it 'resolutely opposes hacking actions'.[22] Nevertheless, the *New York Times* decided to go public about the investigation, and it pulled no punches in identifying the alleged perpetrators, even printing a photo of the building where Mandiant claimed the hackers worked.[23] As Mandiant's boss, Kevin Mandia, told me, 'The night before that went public I was talking to the journalist, and he said "This is a big deal," and I said "No it's not, no one's going to pay attention to it."'

Mandia was wrong: the story made waves around the world. For Mandia it was a crucial turning point in bumping cyber-security up the agenda, and attribution of blame was key.

'We felt we were at a juncture,' Mandia told me, 'we'd had this kind of activity happening for seven straight years. If a sovereign nation is pointing fingers at another sovereign nation there might be risks to that, you might not want to do it. So we figured maybe the private sector can do it.'

In the end, the *New York Times* got a great scoop and Mandiant became one of the world's most sought-after security companies

OCEAN'S 11 DOT COM

(it was later bought for a reported $1 billion by another tech security firm, FireEye, which was drafted in to deal with the Sony hack).[24] Since then, the pressure has grown to publicly attribute cyberattacks not just to vague group codenames, but to states and even individuals.

With the Sony attack, Obama had seemingly upped the ante – here was a national leader publicly calling out another country. But despite the president's forthright words, the FBI released almost no specific evidence to back up the accusation, claiming the 'need to protect sensitive sources and methods'.[25] As a result, there was considerable doubt in some quarters as to whether North Korea really was behind the attack. There were suspicious aspects: if the hack was in revenge for *The Interview*, why did the Guardians of Peace only start talking about the film weeks after journalists had mentioned it? Why did they initially demand money from Sony? (North Korea might be desperate for funds, but surely not enough to chisel a movie studio for petty cash?) And why was North Korea suddenly interested in leaking movie moguls' private emails? It seemed an odd set of behaviours, even for such an idiosyncratic country.

In fact, behind the scenes the FBI was accumulating the breadcrumbs of evidence they say lead to Pyongyang: North Korean IP addresses had been used to scan Sony's website in the months leading up to the attack, then the same IP addresses were used to set up the Facebook accounts that sent messages to actors from *The Interview*. Those addresses were also used to access the computer server that held the virus hidden behind the screensaver, and to set up the accounts which sent phishing emails to cinemas promising to show *The Interview*.

The hackers, it seemed, were leaving digital fingerprints all over the place, partly because of North Korea's narrow window on the Internet. But they either didn't know or didn't care – and they were already preparing for their next attack. They were now ready to knock over a bank. And not just any bank, but one guarding the precious billions of a vulnerable and struggling country.

As in any good heist movie, carefully planned surveillance was the next scene on the storyboard.

CASING THE JOINT

In late January 2015, as the furore over *The Interview* was dying down, several members of staff at Bangladesh Bank received a politely worded email from a potential job applicant called Rasel Ahlam. 'I am extremely excited about the idea of becoming a part of your company,' wrote Ahlam, 'and am hoping that you will give me an opportunity to present my case in further detail in a personal interview. Here is my résumé and cover letter. Thank you in advance for your time and consideration.'[26] The email contained a link to a website where Ahlam's CV could be downloaded in a compressed '.zip' file.

The staff members didn't know this, but the message came from an email account that had been used to target Sony Pictures Entertainment. Whoever had hacked the media giant was now sniffing around a new, far richer target.

Bangladesh Bank is the country's national financial institution, its equivalent of the Bank of England. It has around $32 billion of foreign currency reserves. For Bangladesh, a country with a population of 165 million and a gross domestic product of around $250 billion[27] (compared to the UK's 66 million people and $2 trillion GDP), the bank's stability is absolutely vital. The employees who received Ahlam's email were not picked at random. Someone, somewhere had done some careful research about the recipients, along with Bangladesh Bank in general. FBI agents who investigated the Sony hackers found one of the Google accounts connected to that hack was also used to conduct these searches.

The email attack on the bank's employees was unsophisticated, but the trick worked: FBI analysis showed that three computers at Bangladesh Bank had opened the résumé, and at least one was infected with a virus that the hackers would gradually use to open a wider door into the bank's systems.[28] The tools of the hackers' trade have arcane names and this intrusion was no exception: viruses such as Nestegg, Macktruck and SierraCharlie were among those used by these hackers, who by March 2015 had established a permanent, digital backdoor into the bank. Working carefully and quietly, they could now manoeuvre their way through its systems and eventually redirect the flow of money out of the vault. The hackers were potentially looking at billions of dollars in spoils.

But first, they had to prepare a way to spirit the money away once they'd pulled it out of the safe.

The Jupiter Street branch of the Filipino bank RCBC is inside a small, bland building in Manila's well-to-do Makati district. Above it are a dentist's surgery and a handbag repair business. Despite its humble outward appearance, the bank's entrance is guarded by a bored-looking security guard equipped with a frighteningly large pump-action shotgun, the standard-issue weapon to protect Manila's financial institutions and high-value offices.

In 2015, the branch manager was Maia Santos Deguito. In May, a few months after the hackers first gained access to Bangladesh Bank, she was asked to set up five new accounts. The exact circumstances are still under dispute: Deguito says she met all five account holders in person. Other witnesses have claimed she didn't, and that she set up all five accounts through a single intermediary she met in a casino. Either way, what is clear is that the drivers' licences used to set up the accounts were fakes. There were other suspicious signs too: the five applicants all claimed to earn exactly the same salary, with the same job title, but at different employers. Welcome letters sent to the new account holders were returned unopened.[29]

Something was amiss, but perhaps at the time it didn't seem to matter: the accounts sat dormant with their $500 initial deposits untouched as the months went by. But in time, those five accounts would become part of a global money-laundering operation that would leave Deguito faced with spending the rest of her life in prison. Her branch was being lined up as an escape route for the Bangladesh Bank hackers' ill-gotten gains, and she wasn't the only one being targeted. The hackers were scouring the world to find dozen of avenues through which to channel the funds.

Three thousand miles away from the Philippines, Shalika Perera was thinking about cows. More specifically, about a dairy project she hoped to establish in Matale, a mountainous region a few hundred miles inland of the Sri Lankan capital Colombo.

Perera ran a charity in Sri Lanka called the Shalika Foundation, a philanthropic enterprise she hoped might also burnish her credentials as she attempted to move into politics.[30] As the charity's president, Perera worked with another Sri Lankan and a Japanese middleman to source big donations. It seems to have been a lucrative collaboration: the Shalika Foundation website boasts of tens of millions of dollars in contributions, much of it from Japan.

Things were going well and projects from housing schemes to electricity generators were starting to get funding, according to the website. But it turned out Perera's local Sri Lankan charity had been identified by the hackers as another potential conduit for the stolen millions. She, too, would soon be dragged into the spotlight. And she wasn't the only one being primed to receive the stolen money: in all, 36 accounts around the world were lined up. The hackers (or more likely, a network of accomplices) spent months creating this global system of recipients for the hundreds of millions they planned to pilfer from Bangladesh Bank, which was still unaware that criminals were hiding inside its systems.

By the beginning of 2016, the getaway routes were established, and the scene was set for the heist to go down. Like all good bank robbers, the team wanted to give themselves the maximum amount of time for the break-in.

THE HEIST

The Bangladesh working week runs from Sunday to Thursday, meaning Bangladesh Bank would almost certainly be minimally staffed on Friday and Saturday.

The Philippines, where Maia Santos Deguito had set up the five accounts at RCBC, had a national holiday for the Chinese New Year on Monday 8 February 2016. If the hackers timed it right, between the Bangladeshi and the Filipino working hours they would have four clear days to move most of the money.

And as an added bonus, they could play a third time zone to their advantage. This was because of how Bangladesh Bank's money was stored. The bank was headquartered in Dhaka, but that's not where all of its money was actually kept. Instead, Bangladesh Bank held around $1 billion, the majority of its international deposits, in an account at the Federal Reserve Bank in New York (the prestigious 'New York Fed').[31] The hackers aimed to take almost every cent of that money.

When Bangladesh Bank wanted to pay someone from its New York account, it would send instructions to the New York Fed to make the transfer via a network called SWIFT (The Society for Worldwide Interbank Financial Telecommunication). It's a system installed in more than 11,000 banks around the world, and is one of the main tools used to send instructions to move money globally from bank to bank.[32] If the hackers wanted to clean out Bangladesh Bank's dollar reserves, the most effective way to do it was to send SWIFT messages ordering transfers to be made from its account at the New York Fed. Because the transfer requests came from Bangladesh Bank's internal computers, they would look like genuine SWIFT messages.

On 29 January 2016, exactly a year after first breaking into the bank, the thieves started work. So far, they'd compromised the banks' computers, carefully disguising the Internet traffic they were sending in and out so they wouldn't raise suspicion. But the computers they'd hacked were not the ones controlling the money. The hackers needed to get to the terminals running the SWIFT system. So they spent the next few days moving from computer to computer, using stolen logins and other tricks to hop from machine to machine. By Thursday 4 February, they had wormed their way to their prize: the computer that managed the SWIFT messages. It's a piece of software that most people outside the banking industry have never heard of and wouldn't have a clue how to use. The hackers, it seems, had no such problems.

'They already knew once they got in,' says Eric Chien, a senior researcher at tech security firm Symantec who investigated evidence from the bank attack. 'They had an understanding of how SWIFT works, and they had the software ready to go. It was as if they were sitting at that machine and opened up the software, and made the transfer as if they were the bank teller.'

In fact, they'd had the chance to practise before, according to the FBI, on at least two other banks' SWIFT systems. In December 2015, Thien Phong Bank in Vietnam said it foiled an attempt to send $1.1 million to a Slovenian bank via an attack on its SWIFT systems. FBI investigators subsequently found viruses on a Vietnamese bank's systems that were also used to hack Bangladesh Bank. The FBI found other examples of similar malicious software at a bank in the Philippines, whose SWIFT system was under attack from late 2015 to early 2016, though no money was transferred in the end.[33]

And the Bangladesh Bank hackers were by no means the first to target SWIFT. Documents allegedly stolen from the U.S. National Security Agency (NSA) and released in April 2017 appear to show that U.S. agents broke into Middle Eastern and Latin American banks by targeting their SWIFT systems as long ago as 2013. PowerPoint slides bearing the agency's seal boast of access to five Middle Eastern banks.[34] There's no evidence the agency stole any money via SWIFT, though, and the suspicion is that they used their access to monitor terrorism funding. The NSA declined to comment on the leaked documents.

Even prior to 2013, SWIFT was being discussed on cybercrime forums. Research for this book conducted by tech security firm Digital Shadows has thrown up mentions of SWIFT from as far back as 2010, including someone offering to sell their access to the system.

It really shouldn't come as any surprise that spies and crooks were aggressively targeting SWIFT: it's a system that moves billions of dollars around the world. But it's important to note that this doesn't necessarily mean there are inherent problems with it. The company that makes and maintains the software (a cooperative owned by its members) claims that many of these hacks only worked because of weak security surrounding the banks' SWIFT systems, rather than SWIFT itself. A corrupt employee selling their access, for example, is more of a human failing than a technical one. The company also says it has made improvements since the hacks came to light to help prevent further attacks.

None of that helped Bangladesh Bank, though, which was about to face catastrophic consequences.

In the movies, hackers' computer code streams down the screen in a tidal wave of arcane terminology (usually in green text on a black background, typed in by someone wearing a hooded top).

Reality is slightly different.

Inside Bangladesh Bank's SWIFT system, the hackers initially changed just eight characters of code. To the untrained eye, swapping 0x75 and 0x04 for 0x90 and 0x90 looks inconsequential. For the hackers, it forced the SWIFT software to skip over a key authentication check. These two simple tweaks turned a computerized 'no' into a 'yes', and helped swing open the door to a billion-dollar bank vault.[35] It allowed the hackers access to the part of SWIFT that controlled the messages instructing other banks to make transfers.

The hackers began manipulating these messages, lining up a series of transfers out of Bangladesh Bank's New York Fed account that would net them almost a billion dollars. But first, they had to tackle something that threatened to blow the whole operation. In the Bangladesh Bank office was an HP LaserJet 400 series printer. Its job was to print out records of the SWIFT transfers. If this printer started churning out details of the thieves' transactions, any employee who took even a casual look at the papers would instantly spot the crime. The hackers created code that would change the documents being printed, so the printer just spewed out blank pages.[36] It was the digital equivalent of putting a loop of video onto the CCTV cameras to hide their movements. Now the thieves could be left to work in peace.

In the end, they lined up 36 transactions totalling $951 million: almost the entire contents of Bangladesh Bank's account at the Fed. The time-zone differences were working to their advantage: they had first logged into SWIFT in Bangladesh Bank at 8.36 p.m. local time on Thursday 4 February, after the bank closed for Bangladeshi weekend. But that meant it was 9.36 a.m. in New York, meaning that the Federal Reserve Bank had the entire day to action the payments.[37]

As in the best heist movies, there was a moment when the thieves' plans were almost derailed: the hackers' transaction orders had failed to include details of the intermediary banks to which the New York Fed was supposed to send the money. The transfers were initially declined, but the hackers quickly corrected them and the money was on its way.

The digital safe was being cleaned out, but the hackers had one last trick up their sleeve. At 3.59 a.m., Bangladesh time, they logged out of SWIFT, and their viruses began deleting key files that would have helped investigators trace the money.[38]

They'd covered their tracks – now all that remained was to launder the loot.

THE GETAWAY

As the cybercriminals moved in on Bangladesh Bank, Shalika Perera received some great news about her dairy project. Via her Sri Lankan colleague, her Japanese fixer had sent her a letter dated 2 February 2016 (two days before the hackers started pulling money out of Bangladesh Bank). The letter appeared to have come from JICA, the Japanese International Cooperation Agency, a well-established organization that uses Japanese government money to fund overseas causes.[39] 'We are pleased to inform you that we are agreeable to donate funds towards the above mentioned project submitted to us,' said the letter. It seemed Perera's Japanese middleman had come good.

'Nothing can be compared to the wealth from the sale of milk and milk products,' the letter went on to say, apparently quoting Perera's charity's marketing. Twenty million dollars, the letter said, would be on its way. Perera's Sri Lankan colleague, who had brokered the deal, told her he would take $11 million for his own project and leave the rest to Perera's charity. She was promised another $25 million in due course, she later told me in an online interview. In fact, the letter was a fake. JICA says it had no idea its name was being used, and had nothing to do with the transfer.

In hindsight there were obvious red flags in the JICA letter: 'electrification' was spelled incorrectly, and there was a grainy picture of a wad of banknotes tied up in a ribbon, which didn't seem entirely fitting with a $20 million donation from a sovereign wealth fund. But Perera was happy the money was coming. She insists that neither she nor her colleagues did anything wrong. And as it turns out, the idea that JICA might want to send millions of dollars to a philanthropic project via Bangladesh wasn't that outlandish: according to documents on Bangladesh Bank's website, the Japanese agency had been working with them since 2012.

The hackers knew all of this. They knew JICA worked with Bangladesh Bank, they knew Perera's charity was accustomed to receiving Japanese money and they had someone send the letter to the Shalika Foundation to prepare the ground. Somebody was back-channelling information to put the charity in the frame, teeing it up to receive its share of the stolen money. So when the hackers filled out a transaction for $20 million from Bangladesh

Bank, marked as being from JICA and bound for a charity project, it raised no suspicions – at least, apparently, none in New York. But as it travelled to Sri Lanka, the payment went via another bank, Pan Asia, before reaching the Foundation's account, where a diligent employee raised an eyebrow at the size of the transaction. Further suspicions were raised when it turned out the payees had spelled Shalika Foundation as 'Fundation'.

Urgent calls were made to the New York Fed, which not only reversed the Sri Lankan payment, but cancelled the remaining transactions from Bangladesh Bank. The heist was grinding to a halt. But for Bangladesh Bank, there was bad news: before the cancellations had taken effect, four payments had slipped through and were now winging their way to RCBC bank in the Philippines. In total, $81,001,662.16 had been raided from the bank's account at the Fed, and would now enter a system almost tailor-made to ensure the money would disappear without trace.

Eight thousand miles away from New York, in Manila the accounts opened almost a year previously at the RCBC branch in Jupiter Street suddenly sprang into life, and the woman who'd set them up would find herself at the centre of a global heist investigation.

On Friday 5 February, four account holders instantly became multimillionaires: 'Michael Cruz' was suddenly $6,000,029.12 richer. 'Jessie Lagrosas' had $30,000,028.79. 'Alfred Vegara' got $19,999,990.00. And 'Enrico Vasquez' was sitting on $25,001,573.88.[40] Mathematically rigorous readers will notice we've already lost $40.37 from the total amount stolen from Bangladesh Bank. Get used to it: this process leaks like a sieve.

Once again, the hackers had exploited Bangladesh Bank's connection with JICA to create a cover for the massive money movements. The four transfers sent to the Philippines all carried the names of legitimate projects that JICA had funded in the past.

Meanwhile, the stolen money was entering the financial equivalent of a washing machine. Some of the cash was transferred to an account created that day in the name of an existing

RCBC customer. The account was set up, and thirteen minutes later it suddenly received $22 million.[41]

Around $45 million was pulled out of the four fake millionaires' accounts and deposited in other accounts at the bank. That took eighteen minutes. It seems the launderers also tried to withdraw some of the money in cash, but at this point they hit a problem: the branch didn't have enough money in the vault. A bank employee later told an investigation that $380,000 in cash was ordered from another branch. When it arrived at Jupiter Street this money was put in a cardboard box and a little while later, according to the employee, a dark grey Lexus saloon pulled up at the bank, rolled down its window, and the box was loaded into the car.[42] Again, it's not clear whose car it was, and investigations hit a dead end when it emerged that the bank's CCTV cameras had been out of operation since the day before. According to Bangladesh Bank's lawyers, the cameras remained out of action until all the money had left the RCBC branch.[43]

From there, the bulk of the stolen funds ended up in the accounts of a Filipino company that changes dollar currency into local pesos and back. In the meantime, though, Bangladesh Bank had rumbled the theft and was frantically trying to stop the cash leaking out of RCBC. But once again, the time-zone differences would give the thieves a critical few hours' advantage.

The bank sent several stop requests on Monday 8 February, but by that time it was after 5 p.m. in Manila, seemingly too late for a response from RCBC in the Philippines, where in any case it was a national holiday. And by the time the Filipino bank responded, it was later on the following day – a day during which much of the stolen money had been hurriedly rushed out of the door.[44] By now it was a full five days after the heist had started, and Bangladesh Bank stood almost no chance of catching up.

By the time RCBC got round to freezing the four accounts, of the original $81 million, only $68,305 remained – chump change, relatively speaking; like a smattering of banknotes floating in the breeze after the vault doors have been blown open. The sum was duly returned to Bangladesh Bank. Eventually, on 12 February, RCBC filed a suspicious transaction report. Referring to the four overnight millionaires, it summarized the transactions thus: 'Amount involved not commensurate with the business or financial capacity of client.'[45] It was a massive understatement. RCBC did not wish to comment for this book, citing ongoing legal proceedings.

Meanwhile, elsewhere in Manila, Bangladesh Bank's money was being funnelled into the final stage of the laundering process; a secretive universe of fabulous wealth that most of us don't even know exists. Even if we did, we'd stand no chance of getting inside. It's a world of plush seats, chain-smoking, expensive booze and eye-watering sums gambled on the roll of a dice. Welcome to the high-roller rooms of Manila's casino scene.

By gambling the cash and walking away with their winnings in 'clean' money, the thieves hoped to ruin investigators' chances of following the stolen funds. Police might be able to trace it to the casino's accounts, but if the money launderers did their jobs well, it would be impossible to track its journey as it was being bet and recouped across the casino's tables.

The money-changing company that had ended up with most of the cash split it between two Manila casinos: around $29 million was sent to the bank account of Bloomberry Resorts Corporation, which runs a casino called the Solaire. A further $21 million went to a company called Eastern Hawaii Leisure, run by a Filipino called Kim Wong, who had allegedly helped create the fake bank accounts at RCBC all those months before. As for the rest, bundles of cash were handed to a Chinese man called Wei Kang Xu, who has not been heard of since.[46] Ultimately, the vast majority of the money ended up inside two casinos: the Midas and the Solaire.

For anyone who's not visited a high-end casino, it's hard to convey the jaw-dropping opulence of places such as the Solaire. Shopping options include Bulgari, Prada and Bang & Olufsen. There's a theatre showing a full-scale performance of *Phantom of the Opera*. But the thing that really sticks in my mind is that it's the only place in my years of travel where I have ever been offered a special 'handbag stool', just for my bag to sit on.

With millions in stolen money now deposited in accounts both here at Solaire and at the Midas casino, the money launderers could start washing the cash. But they faced a problem. How exactly do you launder tens of millions through a casino without losing it all? You can't just take the whole lot, bet it on number thirteen on the roulette wheel and hope for the best, no matter how lucky you feel. Besides, gambling the money among the general public on the casino floor might have raised suspicions. Instead, in order for the criminals to make sure they got a guaranteed return, the cash would need to be laundered in carefully controlled conditions, away from the public gaze.

The solution was to put it into so-called gambling 'junkets'. These are special events for invitation-only players to indulge their habit in all-expenses-paid private gaming rooms. They have exotic names like Sun City and Gold Moon. The gambling chips used in these junkets can only be played in these rooms, making it an easily controlled environment for the money launderers (the gamblers can't just walk off with their winnings, for example, because they have to exchange all their chips through the junket organizer). Much of the $29 million that went to the Solaire was converted into such chips for three junkets, then sent up in special cages to the junket rooms. There, a group of seventeen Chinese gamblers frittered away the chips playing baccarat.[47] A similar process was happening at Midas.

Like everything else in this story, baccarat was a carefully calculated decision. Unlike the spin of a roulette wheel, baccarat has only two outcomes on which to bet: the players' cards or the dealers'. And on average the casino's profit margin will be between 1 and 11 per cent, according to experts who investigated the case. With such controlled conditions, the money launderers could now start their work, dishing out the money little by little, examining the odds and making bets and counter-bets to recoup 90 per cent of the funds or more.

To run this kind of balanced system takes time. Unlike instant-aneous bank transfers, gambling tens of millions of dollars in this way takes weeks. So, by the beginning of March the Chinese gamblers were still sitting in Solaire and Midas, knocking back the cognac and playing cards, a full month after the truth had emerged about the $81 million raid on Bangladesh Bank.[48]

Why were the Filipino authorities unable to stop the stolen money leaking away? In short it's because in the Philippines, until after the Bangladesh Bank heist, casinos were not covered by money-laundering legislation, meaning very few questions were asked of people bringing in and taking out large sums of money – something the thieves almost certainly knew only too well. Bloomberry, which owns the Solaire, has stated it had no knowledge that the funds were stolen and has worked to dis-close the identities of the gamblers, stating it 'was a victim and not complicit in this case'. Midas did not respond to requests for an interview.

Partly as a result of this loophole in legislation, there are no criminal charges against the casinos. There are also no charges against Kim Wong, the man who allegedly helped create the fake bank accounts, or the higher-ups at RCBC. Attempts to chase down the Chinese gamblers met a dead end at the Chinese embassy, according to Filipino prosecutors. The Philippines Anti Money Laundering Council is still pursuing criminal legal action against the money-changing company, and some executives at RCBC. They're also trying the civil courts to get money back from the casinos.

But as it stands, in the entire $81 million heist there is only one person who's been convicted: Maia Santos Deguito, the branch manager of the RCBC bank in Jupiter Street (and, incidentally, the only woman to be prosecuted), who faces up to 56 years in jail and a fine of $109 million. She is appealing her conviction and declined to be interviewed for this book.

While the criminal justice system may have failed, on the civil prosecution side the banks have lawyered up. At the time of writing, Bangladesh Bank is suing 45 different people and organizations, including RCBC, the casinos, the Chinese money recipients, Deguito and Wong.

Part of the bank's claim against RCBC is the fees the bank allegedly earned from the various transfers of the stolen money and conversions from pesos to dollars, which according to Bangladesh Bank's lawyers and the Filipino Senate add up to more than $100,000. For its part, RCBC says it followed proper banking procedures, and is suing Bangladesh Bank in the Filipino courts for defamation over its claims.[49] The heads of both banks resigned in the wake of the scandal, and RCBC was issued with a record $20 million fine by the country's central bank.[50] The laundering of $81 million raised some serious questions about the robustness of the Philippines' banking and casino system, and the country's government did its best to investigate, holding a Senate Committee hearing that lasted for weeks and interviewed most of the key players. They were frequently stymied in their attempts to get to the bottom of the matter, however, as RCBC repeatedly invoked secrecy laws to avoid handing over details.[51]

Such was the confusion and conflict between the testimony that when they added up all the amounts given by different witnesses, the Senate Committee found a $17 million discrepancy. Kim Wong later managed to find $15 million of that sum, which was handed back to Bangladesh Bank. He denied knowledge of any money-laundering scheme.

In a bizarre postscript, the committee's report into the incident was never made public because it was handed in an hour too late to be ratified by the outgoing Senate.

If the hackers were seeking a jurisdiction with the right combination of compliant financiers, unregulated multimillion-dollar casinos and a weak government, they found it in Manila.

For Bangladesh, there was a taint of national shame at having been so monumentally robbed, losing money that is much needed in a country dealing with more than its fair share of tragedies. Days after the Filipino Senate finished its inquiry, for example,

Bangladesh was ravaged by a storm that forced half a million people to flee their homes. In one area alone Cyclone Roanu reportedly destroyed $38 million worth of crops and homes – the amount gambled on Manila's casino tables in just a few weeks.[52] At the time of writing, Bangladesh is still fighting to recover the stolen money.

So what happened to the cash after it left the casinos in Manila? The assumption is that it made a few more hops, then came into the hands of the team that originally hacked Bangladesh Bank. And the American investigators, for their part, have no doubt who that is.

In addition to the North Korean links behind the emails targeting Bangladesh Bank, the FBI claims it found North Korean IP addresses controlling parts of the virus used to attack the bank. One of the Gmail accounts used to target Sony also had an address book full of Bangladesh Bank employees' email addresses. The trail, the FBI says, leads directly to Pyongyang, and a country under financial sanctions is now potentially $81 million richer.

The FBI was apparently assisted in its investigation by the hackers' decision to use American technology companies for their communications. Despite their leaders' venomous anti-U.S. rhetoric, it seems North Korea's cyberarmy relied on Gmail and Facebook just as much as the rest of us. This left them fatally exposed to surveillance by the American authorities, who can use the U.S. legal process to gather evidence. As the FBI points out in its criminal complaint against one North Korean allegedly involved in the hack, U.S. investigators submitted 'approximately 100 search warrants for approximately 1,000 email and social media accounts accessed internationally by the subjects of the investigation'.[53]

Once again, North Korea's limited exposure to the Internet and lack of local IT services allowed investigators to zero in on their suspects.

The Bangladesh Bank case attracted global publicity, and journalists, particularly from Reuters and Bloomberg, ferreted out masses of information. The cybercriminals' tactics were picked over in minute detail. But even as their workings were made public, the hackers didn't rein in their activities. Quite the opposite, in fact: they continued their spree and even intensified their tactics.

The hacks continued over several years and on different continents, meaning that the true scale has escaped most people's notice. But thanks to the FBI's documents, a United Nations Security Council report and my own research for this book, it's now possible to map much of the Lazarus Group's bank-robbing spree.

In 2015, they targeted Banco del Austro in Ecuador, stealing $10 million,[54] and made failed attempts on two other banks, in Vietnam and the Philippines.

In 2016, as money was leaching out of Bangladesh Bank, the same viruses were used to try to steal $100 million from an African bank, but the heist failed. Later that year, Bank Bumi Arta in Indonesia was hit for an unknown amount. October 2017 saw Far Eastern International Bank in Taiwan lose $60 million, although the bank recovered all but a few hundred thousand dollars.[55]

Up until this point, there were more misses than hits, but in 2018 the hackers' luck changed. They successfully stole $10 million from Banco de Chile.[56] Perhaps their most audacious raid came in August of that year when, according to a UN Security Council panel, they stole $13.5 million from an Indian bank called Cosmos.[57] This time, they didn't just compromise SWIFT, the interbank transfer system. The hackers went considerably further, altering the bank's ATM software and allowing people to withdraw money using fake cards. What followed was a cashing-out operation that is, even by cybercriminal standards, staggering. Over two days, more than 10,000 withdrawals of cash were made in 28 different countries. This was money laundering on a truly global scale. Indian police arrested some of those who made the withdrawals, who they claim also admitted to being part of a $1.5 million raid on another Indian bank.[58]

In total, in under three years at least $122 million has been stolen directly from banks by the Lazarus Group. Once again, as far as UN experts and the FBI are concerned, the blame can be laid at the door of one country alone.

In March 2019, the UN Security Council's panel on North Korean sanctions published a major report covering allegations of North Korean hacking. The authors quote one unnamed UN member state which gives a no-nonsense appraisal of these attacks and what's motivating them: 'These operations aim to acquire funds through a variety of measures in order to circumvent the sanctions.'[59] The accusation is clear: faced with financial punishment from the international community for its missile tests, North Korea simply hacked its way round it and stole the money. The techniques honed by organized crime gangs in the preceding two decades were now being exploited by nation states, according to investigators.

So . . . what does North Korea say?

If the North Koreans were trying to capitalize on their global reputation for idiosyncrasy, they couldn't have done a better job than their UK embassy.

Whereas other countries' diplomats have palatial offices in central London bedecked with their nation's flags, the Embassy of the Democratic People's Republic of Korea is a converted seven-bedroom family house off a noisy suburban dual carriageway in Ealing, west London.

It was here, after several unanswered emails and phonecalls, that I went to ask North Korea's response to the mounting allegations of state-sponsored hacking from UN experts, the FBI and security researchers worldwide. The Americans' allegations against North Korea alone now stretch to 174 pages of dense legal complaint, packed with dozens of email addresses, IP addresses, Twitter accounts and website names, along with dates and times of the alleged attacks. It's a minutely argued case, although one that is painfully hard to interrogate: much of the social media evidence has disappeared, and much of the other evidence lies inside companies such as Sony, Google and Facebook.

The website of North Korea's Ministry of Foreign Affairs seldom backs away from a fight. Its statements frequently include archaically worded potshots at other nations (including the U.S., even while some of its statements welcomed diplomatic approaches from President Trump and his administration). The site contains statements on everything from the crisis in Venezuela to issues in the Golan Heights.[60] Yet on the specific allegations of bank hacking raised by both the FBI and the UN, the ministry's website was silent.

An official made a comment in September 2018 when the U.S. criminal complaint about the Lazarus Group's hacks was released. Speaking via the state's news agency, he denied any North Korean involvement in the hacking incidents at Sony and Bangladesh Bank, calling the U.S. accusations a 'smear campaign'.[61] But with the American investigators having laid so many of their cards on the table, I felt a more substantial response was required. If I'd hoped to get answers at the embassy, I was disappointed.

The gates were closed and locked, there was no answer from ringing the bell, and, on the day I visited, no flag was flying. Perhaps that indicated that the ambassador was out, but if so, he'd apparently left his cars in the driveway: a pair of shiny black Mercedes, one with a personalized number plate.

The embassy bristles with CCTV. The only hint of personality is a basketball hoop in the back garden (Kim Jong Un is a big fan of the sport, after all). The building was the brick-built equivalent of a cold shoulder.

It seems they do answer the door to Royal Mail, though. My recorded-delivery letter asking for an interview was signed for by 'Kim' at 10.27 a.m. on 30 March 2019. At the time of writing I am still waiting for a response.

Even if I'd been able to ask about the bank hacking allegations, it would already have been old news. Investigators claim North Korea's hackers, and others like them, have found a new way to earn megabucks, thanks to a hacking method even more profitable than attacking banks. That's because there's a major problem with the kind of bank hacks covered in this chapter: middlemen.

Consider this: our story began with an audacious plot to steal almost a billion dollars in a high-tech theft worthy of a Hollywood blockbuster. In the end, the closing scene of this real-world heist movie is a bunch of chain-smoking gamblers shunting pesos around casino tables in Manila. Of the original $951 million, how much of it finally ended up in the hands of the bank robbers? How much did they lose to the casinos, to the gamblers, to the financial institutions along the way? Whatever the answers, the amounts that shook out from the bottom of the hopper must have looked like slim pickings compared to the original billion-dollar scheme.

And how much effort went into it? For at least a year, a global criminal network had beavered away, mastering the SWIFT system, crafting the viruses and the fake CVs to hack into Bangladesh Bank, grooming the Sri Lankan charity, lining up accounts and middlemen in Manila. Only to see swathes of the loot ebbing away into a money-laundering maze.

And this applies to their entire bank hacking spree. Over the three years, Lazarus Group tried to steal $1.25 billion. In the end, the amount they actually got, thanks to middlemen, reversed transactions and intercepted money, was $122 million. Not bad, but not what they were aiming for.

If only there were a more direct way to profit from cybercrime. A way to steal money and make sure that the profits were sent directly to the criminal, with no middlemen.

The next chapter will show how the cybercriminals' prayers were answered. Once again, organized crime's cybertools would be harnessed by nation-state hackers; and once again, FBI evidence would accuse North Korea of being front and centre in a new crime wave. And this time, the effects would be felt far beyond banks and developing countries – it would affect the services that are literally a matter of life and death.

FOUR

DIGITAL EXTORTION

H is chest shaved, anaesthetics coursing through his blood-stream, Patrick Ward was finding it hard to concentrate on the trashy crime novel in his hands.

As he lay in bed in London's St Bartholomew's Hospital on a Friday morning in May 2017, he was hours away from the surgery he hoped would transform his life. An ebullient 47-year-old, Ward's hereditary enlarged-heart condition had turned his once-active existence into a succession of curtailed kickabouts, wheezing stair rests and hospital visits alongside pensioners. He'd waited two years for a septal myectomy (an operation to remove a small portion of his heart tissue) at a leading London hospital and was excited at the prospect of getting his fit, sporty life back. His surgeon carried out the operation on only one day each week, and after years in the queue it was finally Ward's turn.

His family had booked into hotels nearby and he'd arranged six weeks off work for recuperation. He'd done his research and was confident this would finally sort him out. And now it was the big day.

But when the surgeon came around, it was with bad news. The operation was cancelled. Something was wrong with the hospital's computer system.

Even speaking two years later, Ward's frustration is palpable as he recalls his reaction: 'I said, "No, don't worry, crack on, come on!" I started swearing a bit. "I'm ready, for fuck's sake. I've been waiting two years for this!"'

A natural optimist, Ward was initially hopeful that the IT problem would soon be fixed. But as the hours passed, it gradually became clear that the glitches weren't going away. He wouldn't go home with his broken heart mended. He'd have to endure his breathless, limited life for some time yet.

Meanwhile, the usually frenetic hospital had been transformed, he recalls:

> I wandered round, chatted to a few people. I went to the nurses' station: blank screens, no noise anywhere. Just really, really odd. Eerie. The nurses didn't know what was going on, nobody really knew what was going on. I got onto my phone. 'Jesus, the NHS has been hacked.'

Three miles away, at a building covered in CCTV cameras behind Vauxhall underground station, officers at the National Crime Agency (NCA) were turning up the volume on the office TV. Something had caught their eye. Sky News was reporting a hack on a hospital in the northwest of England, and it was fast becoming clear it wasn't an isolated incident. Calls quickly started coming into the NCA's National Cyber Crime Unit, with its staff of around 250.

Much like a hospital, the unit runs a triage system to deal with incoming incidents and assign them to the relevant level of expertise. The system was inundated. Police forces across the country were dialling in with reports, and hospitals were among the most common victims.

Staff from the National Crime Agency scrambled to get to the affected NHS locations, keen to exploit the so-called 'Golden Hour' when evidence is fresh. St Bartholomew's was one of the first they reached, shortly after Ward had been discharged. He had stumbled, dazed, onto the street, accompanied by his family, only to be intercepted by the waiting TV news crews who were already following up the story. When he was interviewed by the BBC he still had the bandages on his hands from the cannula that had just been removed.

Still chatty yet clearly bewildered, in his interview Ward summed up the question on everyone's minds: 'Why would anyone want to hack a hospital that's trying to do good?'[1]

But it wasn't just hospitals. In fact, computers worldwide were under attack.

The virus outbreak had started around twelve hours before Ward left the hospital. It first hit in Argentina, according to a source within the NCA, before spreading at an alarming rate.

By mid-morning in Western Europe, it had surfaced in Spain, where it found fertile ground: Spanish telecoms giant Telefónica, with around 120,000 employees worldwide. Some of its Madrid staff watched as their computer monitors displayed a disturbing message. Against a red background, the message began: 'Ooops, your files have been encrypted.'[2] It went on to tell them that to get the scrambled files back they would have to pay a fee of several hundred dollars to the hackers who'd infected them, using the virtual currency Bitcoin. The fee would double after 72 hours, and after seven days the data would be destroyed permanently. A dropdown menu offered instructions for payment in 28 different languages – it seemed the hackers were ready for international success.

Such 'ransomware' attacks are nothing new. As we saw earlier, they had formed a lucrative spin-off from the fearsome Zeus virus during the 2010s, and were in existence long before then (one of the first was distributed via floppy disks sent in the post in 1989).[3]

Over the decades, ransomware had been honed into what was arguably the zenith of cybercrime: a highly evolved form of automated blackmail. A vital element in its success was setting the right ransom amount, which involves an element of psychology. Too low, and it's not worth the cybercriminals' time. Too high, and the victim won't pay. Thus ransomware works on a high-volume, low-margin model: the individual blackmail demands are relatively small, but with millions of infections, the overall profits can be huge. This model kept ransomware out of the headlines for two reasons: on a personal level, many people didn't bother reporting it, regarding it as an annoyance rather than a crime. And on a corporate level, many businesses were afflicted by a type of 'cybershame' that their systems had been caught out in this way. In online help forums for companies' IT staff, the candid advice was often just to pay up, on the basis that shelling out a few hundred dollars was better than spending time sorting it out – or worse, ending up in the headlines.

It's controversial advice, and those giving and receiving it on forums never revealed which companies they worked for. But we do know the eye-watering impact of ransomware on some of the world's biggest companies, because it's now reached such a level they have to report it to their paymasters. U.S. Pharmaceutical giant Merck, for example, told investors in 2017 that it had been hit with a strain of ransomware called NotPetya which meant, in the company's understated corporate-speak, that 'revenue was unfavorably impacted' by $260 million.[4]

Faced with such costs, some businesses have inevitably paid up. But isn't that a risky strategy? After all, if the ransomware comes from crooks, how do you know you're going to get your data back? The hackers have thought of this, and developed a clever trick to incentivize their victims into coughing up. It is a digital version of the 'proof of life' concept in kidnapping whereby, for example, the victim's thumb is sent back to their family. Once a computer is infected, the ransomware often offers the free decryption of a few randomly chosen files, to let the victim know that decryption is possible. This tantalizing glimpse of recovered data could be enough to tempt someone to pony up.

All in all, over the last few years ransomware has become a highly profitable enterprise: multiple crime groups run multiple strains of the virus, tweaking their tactics and splitting their efforts into different campaigns, in the same way that advertisers will run different ads to see which is most effective.

Data from the Cyber Threat Alliance, a non-profit collaboration between tech security companies, showed that in January 2015 the total revenue from just one campaign of one ransomware strain was $325 million.[5] What's more, every last cent of that money would, potentially, flow directly to the cybercriminals themselves without the need to rely on middlemen or money mules, thanks to Bitcoin (about which you'll hear more later in this chapter). For victims who struggled to understand the new currency, some strains of ransomware even included an online support system to talk them through how to make payments with virtual currency.

For the crooks using ransomware, however, their cash cow failed to solve an enduring problem: how to get the virus onto victims' machines in the first place. The standard delivery method was via email. But emailing viruses was a headache – it required a continuous supply of fresh addresses to target, as well as near-constant tweaking to make sure it got through users' regularly updated defences, such as antivirus software. The hackers were seeking a new, easier way of spreading their infection. And in 2017 they got it, thanks to a security weakness in Microsoft computers allegedly discovered by America's spy agency.

Here's how it works: imagine you have a PC in your bedroom with all your music on it, and you want to listen to your tunes on a laptop in the living room. Microsoft computers have a handy feature that lets the two machines share files. The National Security Agency (NSA) allegedly discovered that this handy file-sharing feature could also be used to spread viruses. It seems the NSA didn't rush to tell Microsoft about the flaw so they could fix it, but instead kept it a secret (presumably so America's military and intelligence staff could utilize it). It's also alleged, by Microsoft's president among others, that software for this secret file-share infection trick was later stolen from the NSA by hackers.[6] In April 2017, a hacking group called Shadow Brokers began offering to sell a way of exploiting the flaw. Allegedly short of buyers, they soon made the software available for anyone to download for free.[7] To date, the NSA has not commented publicly on the leaks.

Once again, there was a cross-pollination between the worlds of government hackers and organized cybercrime.

The file-share flaw meant viruses could be spread automatically from computer to computer, and it wasn't long before the ransomware hackers cottoned on. They realized that instead of having to use email, they could simply get the virus onto one machine, and then let it spread itself, potentially generating big profits with minimum effort.

But they faced another problem. Just getting the malicious software onto a computer wasn't enough: it had to be triggered in some way. Previously, the crooks had generally relied on tricking email recipients into clicking on links or attachments to trigger the infection – this was how, for example, Onel de Guzman had spread his Love Bug virus.

For maximum return and minimum effort, what the crooks needed was some kind of trigger to unleash the virus automatically once it had arrived on a new machine. Once again, it's alleged, the NSA inadvertently helped them out. Among the powerful hacking tools leaked by Shadow Brokers was DoublePulsar, the codename for a piece of malicious software that could help detonate the virus once it had spread onto a new computer.[8] The hackers now had in their hands a way of replicating de Guzman's success in spreading a virus and also of ensuring it would go on to infect on a truly massive scale, because it would activate without any action from victims. It was a combination so powerful that, once released, it would take careful coding to stop it spreading out of control. Unsurprisingly, perhaps, this was one aspect the criminals didn't bother with, as they launched their campaign on the world's computer infrastructure.

Microsoft had released a software update in March 2017, the month before the Shadow Brokers leak, which fixed the file-sharing hole. But many users didn't update (or they used an old

version of Windows – xp – that couldn't be updated at that time).
They were sitting ducks.

On Friday 12 May, WannaCry, as the summer ransomware
campaign became known, was unleashed.[9] In less than 24 hours its
automated computer-hopping saw it spread from South America
to Europe and the uk. Pretty soon it ended up inside the nhs,
which is when the real havoc began.

Back in the National Crime Agency, the afternoon of Patrick Ward's
cancelled operation saw the first of a series of cross-department
emergency meetings as the seriousness of the outbreak became
clear, and non-work weekend plans were hurriedly cancelled. The
uk's newly formed National Cyber Security Centre was working
with the nca and other government departments to come up with
a plan to tackle the outbreak.

The virus was having what tech experts call 'kinetic effect',
meaning it had spread way beyond the computerized world and
was affecting physical infrastructure and individual patients like
Ward as they were turned away from long-awaited operations.
The day after the initial outbreak, five accident and emergency
(a&e) departments were forced to divert patients to other hospitals. It wasn't just the health service: businesses of all stripes
were hit, from car manufacturers to logistics firms.

'They were affected, but were for obvious reasons somewhat
less willing to come forward and support law enforcement,' said
one police investigator. 'I guess because they didn't want the
organizational embarrassment of it being known that they have
these really high-tech products, but actually are still running on
[outdated] Windows xp.'

For most people, though, the big focus was the nhs, partly
because it was the issue that was dominating the headlines – a
rare achievement for a cybercrime story. It's hard to overstate
the difficulties faced by tv news when covering cybersecurity: a
subject with such a chronic lack of dramatic footage that it constantly struggles for traction on the news agenda. Finally, with

WannaCry, the camera crews had a cybersecurity story with some decent pictures and a ready stock of case studies. Reporters positioned themselves in front of cameras outside A&E departments as ambulances came and went, picking up interviews with disgruntled patients as they were turned away.

Of England's 236 NHS hospital trusts, 37 ended up infected and 43 others were affected because they were forced to disconnect computers to protect themselves. Six hundred other NHS organizations (such as GP surgeries) were infected. Almost 7,000 appointments had to be cancelled, including more than a hundred urgent cancer cases.[10]

Why was this organization so disproportionately affected? There are multiple answers.

In order to protect against WannaCry, computer owners needed to install the update that Microsoft had released in March 2017. That meant restarting the machine, and that's not always easy in a hospital setting where some of the equipment is keeping patients alive. It also takes time and money, and NHS budgets are squeezed.

Some NHS machines were beyond help, even with the update. One in five computers were using Windows XP, and would have to be upgraded to a newer version of Windows to be protected – again, that takes time and money, and some equipment is so specialized that a software update might have rendered it unusable.[11]

Furthermore, there was very little central government oversight of health service computers. Trusts had been advised to install the update, but were left to get on with it themselves and very often they prioritized other things over IT security. Why not? Most people, including many inside the organization, didn't think the NHS was a target. As Patrick Ward asked: why would anyone attack a hospital?

But with an auto-spreading and self-activating virus such as WannaCry, there is no targeting. The bigger the organization, the greater the risk of getting hit – and as one of the world's largest employers, the NHS was one of the hardest-hit victims of all.[12]

Frustratingly, the NHS Trusts should have known the risk, because they had already been attacked. I'd discovered this when I submitted Freedom of Information requests the year before WannaCry, asking the NHS whether they had encountered ransomware. Of the 152 NHS Trusts I questioned, a quarter admitted to being hit. Some had been forced to cancel operations, others had spent tens of thousands of pounds cleaning up the digital infection. These were the pre-shocks of an impending earthquake, but because of the lack of any central IT oversight, no one was watching the seismographs.

There was one final factor helping WannaCry's spread, something the NHS had that most other organizations lack: a dedicated, high-speed computer network (called N3) connecting all hospitals and many local authorities together. Now being replaced, at the time it was one of Europe's largest virtual private networks (or VPNs), with more than 40,000 connections.[13] The system that allowed patients' scans and diagnoses to be sent quickly to where they're needed was the same system that allowed the virus to proliferate so rapidly.

All of which meant that WannaCry spread like wildfire. But sooner or later it would hit a limit – not just in the NHS, but in any organization in which it landed, it would eventually run out of computers to infect within the organization's network. To be truly nasty, WannaCry needed to be able to hop into new organizations, to find new pools of victims.

The virus writers came up with a neat solution. Periodically, the code would call out to a random computer somewhere on the Internet. If the target computer was running a vulnerable version of Windows, the virus would hop onto it and begin infecting that organization's computer network too. In the end, according to Europol, around 230,000 computers in 150 countries were infected.[14]

WannaCry's creators unleashed something that spread beyond their control. That got some in the tech security world seriously rattled. The inadvertent targeting of hospitals represented a new and disturbing breach of an ad hoc system of ethics that had built up over time in the world of high-level computer hackers. 'It's arbitrarily, meaning indiscriminately, going to have a butterfly effect,' says Kevin Mandia, CEO of U.S. tech security company FireEye. 'Whoever wrote WannaCry . . . they had no idea if it was going to affect 5,000 machines or three hundred million.'

On initial analysis, it seemed that WannaCry had no 'off' switch. In fact, that wasn't true. Buried deep inside the code was a way of bringing the entire outbreak to a halt. It was discovered not by highly paid teams of security researchers, but by a man in his twenties working from a seaside resort in the West of England.

The twelfth of May, the day WannaCry struck, was supposed to be a day off for the security researcher known as MalwareTech. He had gone out for lunch before returning to check the forum he monitored for news of virus outbreaks. His specialism was so-called 'botnets', groups of computers infected with a virus that put them under the control of criminal groups. He'd been working on bank-hacking botnets, but when he saw the mass of reports of NHS infections, his interest was piqued. How, he wondered, was the virus spreading so fast? 'Contrary to popular belief, most NHS employees don't open phishing emails, which suggested to me that something this widespread was something else,' he later wrote.[15]

He managed to get a sample of the WannaCry virus, and on peering into the code he began to understand the automated way in which it was propagated and detonated. But he also spotted something unusual that had apparently escaped others' notice. Before infecting a victim, the virus would try to visit a particular website that had a long, seemingly random address. If the website was up and running, the virus would stop, leaving the victim's files untouched. But if the website didn't respond, the virus would kick in, scrambling the files, demanding a ransom and attempting to infect other machines.

MalwareTech had the bright idea of checking who actually owned the website that the virus was trying to visit. It turned out it hadn't been registered. So he registered it. Sure enough, from then on, whenever the virus landed on a new victim's computer, it would check the website, and on finding it had been registered, the virus would stop. MalwareTech had single-handedly brought the WannaCry outbreak to an end.

It was an incredible outcome; and for the TV news outlets, it was gold dust: not only was it a cybersecurity story they could film, but one with an unlikely hero. MalwareTech was soon unmasked as Marcus Hutchins, a cheery, self-effacing 22-year-old who lived in the sleepy seaside resort of Ilfracombe in north Devon. Newspaper photos showed him smiling in front of his impressive array of computer screens. What most of them cropped out of the pictures was his bed a few feet away. It seems the man who brought down the world's most high-profile virus had cracked the case from his bedroom.

Hutchins's media profile created problems, however. He hadn't willingly revealed his identity, but rather had been outed. Now his name and location were public, and the National Crime Agency feared that whoever designed WannaCry might now go after him.

'From a physical, real-world risk perspective, we're looking at it thinking, "You've spoiled someone's party, and I don't know whose party you spoiled,"' says Mike Hulett, director of operations for the agency's cybercrime unit. 'It could be some other kid in their bedroom somewhere, or it could be some nasty organized crime gang, or a state.' In addition, Hutchins was accumulating some extremely sensitive data. Whenever WannaCry successfully infected a computer, it would call out to the website Hutchins now owned, handing over the victim's IP address. He was getting around half a million such addresses per day, according to a source close to the investigation. The police feared Hutchins was effectively sitting on a giant global database of vulnerable computers, and that also made him a target for other hackers.

Efforts were made to protect Hutchins, according to the NCA. But the agency was simultaneously wary of getting too close to him. They had known of his work prior to WannaCry, and they regarded him as a gifted researcher. But, according to one source in the agency, they also had concerns about whether his techniques were entirely above board, and had declined to enter into a 'formal arrangement' with him.

Subsequently, Hutchins worked with the UK's National Cyber Security Centre, which was also investigating the WannaCry case. When Hutchins discovered the 'off switch' in the virus, the NCSC even went as far as publishing his blog about it on their website, albeit under his alias MalwareTech (his true identity hadn't been revealed at that point).[16]

It was an association that would become awkward for the newly established NCSC in the months after the attack, because as it turned out, the hero who stopped WannaCry had a dark past.

On 2 August 2017, Marcus Hutchins was arrested in Las Vegas, where he'd reportedly been attending Def Con, one of the world's biggest tech security conferences. He was accused of creating a virus called 'Kronos', a tool designed to hack online banking. Hutchins pleaded guilty to the charges in the U.S. courts in April 2019, writing on his blog, 'I regret these actions and accept full responsibility for my mistakes.'[17]

Not only had he created Kronos, he'd done so while using his MalwareTech alias, the same one used to blog for the National Cyber Security Centre. It seemed the NCSC, part of the UK's GCHQ intelligence agency, hadn't spotted Hutchins's criminal history.

The NCSC says it has a background checks procedure in place for vetting the outside sources it works with. Hutchins, they say, wasn't paid for his work, nor was he on a contract with the Centre. And in fairness, Hutchins is certainly not the only gifted tech security researcher with a murky past trying to go straight. As one police cyberinvestigator told me:

There's a kind of accepted truth in this world that a lot of people who are now successful cyber security researchers have probably done something in their past that would

constitute a Computer Misuse Act offence, which is why
they've got their knowledge. Generally they don't get caught
for it.

It was an ignominious end to the story of the man who'd
brought WannaCry to a halt. (Hutchins declined to comment for
this book, citing ongoing legal proceedings.) Nonetheless, thanks
mainly to Hutchins's work, the NHS and other victims got back
to business as usual. Patrick Ward had to wait a month for his
rescheduled operation (Barts NHS Trust staff worked extra even-
ings and weekends to clear the backlog) and is now enjoying
the new lease of life for which he'd waited so long. But for the
investigators, the work had only just begun.

Back at the National Crime Agency, the focus was now firmly on
finding out who was behind WannaCry.

In the past, police investigating cyberextortion cases had
enjoyed success with a tactic used in kidnappings: direct negotia-
tions with the extortionists. In some ransomware instances, police
were able to contact the crooks and trace their communications,
occasionally even managing to pinpoint their exact location and
make an arrest.

They had no such luck with the WannaCry attackers, because
no one was answering their calls. And that's because, as the NCA
and others discovered, whoever had released WannaCry had no
interest in helping their victims pay the ransom and recover their
data. Despite some reports to the contrary, in the vast majority of
cases, even if you paid up, you never got your files back. This was
unusual: most previous ransomware gangs had understood that
failing to unscramble the files would create a lack of trust among
victims, which would be fatal to their profits. The WannaCry
attackers seemingly didn't care. It was among a series of hints that
WannaCry was not the work of a traditional cybercrime group.
After all, if you're going to go to the trouble of creating such a
contagious and effective virus, why not maximize your returns?

The British police had more luck, however, when they took their findings to their American counterparts.

The FBI office in Los Angeles had been working on the hacking of Sony Pictures Entertainment ever since it was attacked in late 2014. As described earlier, they'd amassed a wealth of information about the tools used to break into the media conglomerate. And as the NCA approached them with evidence from the UK attacks on the NHS and other organizations, they started to notice common factors with the attacks not only on Sony, but also on Bangladesh Bank and other victims of the so-called 'Lazarus Group'. IP addresses used to control the WannaCry ransomware had been used to access email accounts which had also been used to hack into Bangladesh Bank.[18] North Korean IP addresses linked to the Sony and Bangladesh Bank hacks had visited a website that published exactly the kind of Windows flaws that the WannaCry virus relied on.[19]

It turns out that the version of WannaCry that hit in May 2017 was just the latest iteration: there had been two previous versions with very similar code, suggesting the same author or team was behind all three campaigns. And buried within the code were pieces of information also seen in viruses used in the hacking of Sony and some of the banks whose SWIFT systems had been targeted by Lazarus.[20] The difference in the May 2017 version was the factor that made it so destructive – the auto-spreading trick that was stolen, allegedly, from the U.S. National Security Agency.

If that was all true, the FBI was now investigating the fall-out from a cyberweapon developed by its own government. As one UK police source put it: 'At the very time when you want the world's intelligence community to come together, there's a certain degree of embarrassment from one of the key members, that this is their ball that got kicked over the fence.'

Nonetheless, the FBI persevered, and in September 2018 they went public, releasing a criminal complaint and naming a North Korean, Park Jin Hyok, as a key member of the Lazarus hacking team that allegedly targeted Sony, Bangladesh Bank and other victims, as well as developing WannaCry.[21] The complaint mapped out the FBI's evidential claims against North Korea, including the information the UK's National Crime Agency had found at the dozens of NHS Trusts affected.

As stated earlier, when the FBI complaint was released, an official from the North Korean Ministry of Foreign Affairs spoke via the state's news agency to deny any North Korean involvement, calling the U.S. accusations a 'smear campaign'. But if, as the Americans believe, North Korea was behind WannaCry, how effective was it?

On a financial level, certainly, it was a washout. Several hundred people paid the ransom, but even at the peak of Bitcoin's value, when the currency surged in December 2017, the total of the ransoms would have been only slightly more than a million dollars. This is peanuts in comparison to even the most moderately successful ransomware campaigns. And the fact that those who paid the ransom rarely got their files back implies the WannaCry hackers were uninterested in creating a profitable business.

Perhaps the idea was never to make money. On a destructive level, WannaCry succeeded in seriously disrupting a key part of UK national infrastructure and causing alarm among politicians and the public. On a PR level, it generated headlines around the world. Besides, according to security researchers and the South Korean government, it seems the North Koreans didn't need to make bumper profits from WannaCry, because they'd already hit upon a new tactic to make megabucks from Bitcoin. Instead of using it for payment from crimes like ransomware, the hackers took to targeting the currency itself. Just as they went after the banks directly via the SWIFT system, the hackers would now start targeting the digital 'banks' that store this new type of money.

It was a crime spree that would make them, by some estimates, more than half a billion dollars. To understand it, you have to understand Bitcoin and the radical ideas that lie behind it. Don't worry: it's not that complicated.

Bitcoin is often described as a 'virtual currency', but in our modern world of online banking and card payments, that's not very helpful: all finance has become increasingly virtual.

In fact, Bitcoin is the end result of a delusional relationship with money that has been going on for hundreds of years, and if you drive out to the Royal Mint in Llantrisant, South Wales, you can see the growth of this financial hallucination close up.

Above the glitzy tourist experience downstairs is the Mint's museum, where row upon row of thin, dusty drawers is filled with a timeline of Britain's coins. Their development is a mirror image of currency inflation: as the centuries pass, they get smaller. Long ago, a pound of value was linked to a pound in weight, a specific pound, at one stage called the 'Tower Pound' because it was kept in the Tower of London where the Royal Mint used to be based. It weighed the same, it was said, as 5,400 fully grown grains of barley. Take a Tower Pound of silver, cut it into 240 coins, and you've got a stack of 'sterlings'.[22]

The problem was that, over time, inflation nibbled away at the pound's value. Research by the UK Parliament found that one pound today buys you only a hundredth of what its equivalent would have bought in 1750.[23] This gradual decline in purchasing power meant that, in an era when a coin's value was directly linked to the weight and metal used to produce it, the coins had to get commensurately smaller. Eventually, they became too small to manage. Beneath the glass in the Mint's museum you begin to see the emergence of tiny slivers of precious metal that were eminently losable, as well as vulnerable to 'clipping': trimming off the edges and melting them down to make a new coin.

In the early 1600s, a decision was made in Britain which helped lay the centuries-long path towards Bitcoin. Perhaps tired of the fiddly coins, James I created a copper farthing that was coated in tin.[24] He wasn't the first to eschew precious metals, not by a long chalk: money made from non-precious material such as paper had existed in other countries for centuries. Over time, across the world, we all accepted the big switcheroo and carried on. After all, if this bit of copper still buys you the same amount of wheat, who cares what it's made of? Currency began to be detached from its inherent physical weight and worth became increasingly 'virtual'.

One of the reasons we accepted the change was that it was backed up by the state and all its power. In the years following James I's new coinage, for example, counterfeiting money in Britain was classed as treason: male offenders were hanged and then dismembered while still alive, and women were burned at the stake (though usually strangled first).[25] Money is an exercise in trust, and it requires the ability to enforce a system. Ultimately, that level of trust has previously resided only in governments, with their police forces, armouries and jails.

One of the ideological streams that fed into Bitcoin's early development was an attempt to evade this need for a centralized money authority backed by the threat of state-sanctioned violence. Interestingly, as the journalist Andrew Smith points out, that's an idea that appeals to both the left and right of the political spectrum: for the left, a currency free of state control offers the chance of a radical redistribution of wealth and power. For the libertarian right, it's the ultimate manifestation of small, hands-off government.[26]

Thus the idea of creating a stateless, virtual currency was born. One of the major stumbling blocks had been the sheer scale of such a global project. It required a world in which everyone had access to a common system for transferring financial information that was cheap and readily available. As computing power increased and the Internet boomed at the turn of the millennium, such a system finally existed. The scene was set for a breakthrough.

There had been other attempts to use computers and the Internet to create an independent currency, but none had survived long. Then, on 31 October 2008, a message appeared on a mailing list for cryptographers discussing the issue. 'I've been working on a new electronic cash system,' it read.[27] The message came from a user with the name 'Satoshi Nakamoto'. It included a link to a highly technical description of how a devolved virtual currency might be created. It was called Bitcoin. The cryptogeeks took the theory apart, prodded it, and decided it just might work.

One of the main issues Bitcoin needed to solve is what's called the double-spend problem. In a truly virtual currency, transfers of money are simply numbers whizzing from one machine to another. In a traditional banking system, banks can keep a track of the numbers, agree who owns what, and appeal to an arbitrator (such as a government agency or the law) if there is a dispute. In a devolved system, there are no banks and governments to supervise, and so a dodgy operator could simply transfer the same money digitally to two people at once: both payees think they've received the funds, but the payer has only spent one virtual 'coin'.

Part of Bitcoin's genius was to find a way to solve this problem using what's called a third-party ledger. In this system, each person's account (or 'wallet' as it's called in Bitcoin) has a unique number, as does each coin. When a transfer is made, the sending and receiving wallet numbers and the coin number are combined into what's called a 'hash'. So if my wallet is called ABC, and yours is XYZ, and I transfer Bitcoin number 123 to you, the hash might be ABC123XYZ. This hash is then published online for all to see, so if someone spots that Bitcoin 123 has suddenly also appeared in wallet DEF, then the alarm bell rings and the transaction is reversed.

This, of course, relies on having people to spot the dodgy transactions, and as the number of transactions increases, that job gets harder. Why would anyone spend their time detecting such double-spend behaviour? Because when they do, they are rewarded every now and again with a freshly minted Bitcoin. This practice of checking transactions is known as 'mining', and it's how new Bitcoins are created.

Every time a transfer occurs, a new hash is added to the public record, which is called the 'blockchain'. Therefore in order to verify each new transaction, a miner will need to go back through the *whole* record to make sure all the transactions line up (so if you were to transfer Bitcoin 123 to someone with wallet number NOP, then the miner would need to match up the hash of the original transaction, ABC123XYZ, with the hash of your new transfer, XYZ123NOP, and so on).

And it's not only Bitcoin transactions that can be hashed in this way. Using computer software you can reduce an entire legal contract to a hash much shorter than the original document, then put it in the public blockchain where it's lodged, immutably, for all to see. If later on someone tries to pull a fast one and tweak the contract, even a subtle change will produce a different hash and you can prove the contract has been altered by comparing it with the original hash. This is the real reason why so many bright minds are excited about Bitcoin – because the underlying blockchain concept is so radical and potentially powerful: it's a permanent, public, irrevocable store of information that can be verified in a flash. Contracts, voting records, company audits . . . many things can be hashed and stored in the blockchain and preserved forever on multiple computer servers spread across the world.

Of course, as more of these hashes are created, the job of mining gets exponentially harder. As more Bitcoin transactions pile up, for example, the miners have to go through more and more transactions to check for any double spends. And since this is all done electronically, it requires an ever-increasing amount of computing power. It used to be possible to mine Bitcoins using a home computer. Now, with more than 300,000 transactions per day,[28] you need hundreds of machines all linked together and industrial-scale cooling facilities to stop the whole rig overheating.

However, no matter how hard mining gets, it's still worth the effort, thanks to another brilliant aspect of Bitcoin: a cap on the total number of Bitcoins that can ever be created of 21 million.[29] As this limit is approached, the worth of each coin increases, balancing out the effort involved in mining them. If you're thinking that this built-in inflation in Bitcoin mirrors those ever-diminishing coins in the Royal Mint museum, you're right. The difference with Bitcoin is that, unlike a physical coin, you can divide a number up almost infinitely without losing it down the back of the sofa.

Anyone with a computer can create a Bitcoin wallet, and can then create new, unique wallet addresses with just a click of the mouse. These function broadly like a bank account number (unlike the examples I gave above, most wallet addresses are around thirty characters long). The wallets are anonymous, and thanks to the coin-mining industry there is a ready supply of new coins with no transaction history. And if you don't want to get into mining, no problem: there is now a plethora of Bitcoin exchanges where you can use 'real-world' currencies like pounds and dollars to buy virtual coins. There are even ATMs where you can deposit cash and top up your wallet.

Back in 2008, though, Satoshi Nakamoto's invention remained, for a few months, the plaything of the cryptocurrency geeks, who tossed it about, carried out mining (which was easy in those early days of few transactions) and racked up Bitcoins that would, unknown to them, one day make them fabulously wealthy.

Amazingly, Satoshi Nakamoto, the inventor of this revolutionary new system (or, perhaps, the pseudonym for a group of inventors), has remained as anonymous as the currency itself. For more than a decade, while Bitcoin has gone from being an obscure techie project to a global success story, no one has come forward to claim the glory. Several have tried, however, and the hunt for Satoshi has taken some journalists on impressively wild goose chases.[30] One thing's for sure: whoever was around at the start and storing up those early, easy-to-mine Bitcoins, if they managed to leave them squirrelled away for the best part of a decade, they are now very, very rich.

Another remarkable thing about Bitcoin has been its resilience. Despite countless predictions of its imminent demise, the currency has survived and thrived. One thing it hasn't been, though, is stable. The value of Bitcoin, although climbing over a long timeline, has experienced wild swings in the short term. Between 2017 and 2018 it went from $1,000 per Bitcoin to $20,000, then back down to $4,000.[31] This leads to questions over whether it can ever work as a currency (what if your coffee suddenly costs twice as much as it did yesterday thanks to a Bitcoin price spike?) or whether it's actually a commodity to be speculated upon like gold, oil or grain. In fact, this dispute is as old as Bitcoin itself. Even in the early days there were signs of a schism between those who believed the dream of Bitcoin as a stateless currency that could radically alter the individual's relationship with government, and those who believed Bitcoin was a speculator's dream ticket to a rollercoaster that promises riches (now known by the acronym 'HODLers', short for Holding On for Dear Life).[32] As its value continues to swing, it's hard to avoid the conclusion that the latter group have it right.

Bitcoin's third-party ledger system didn't just solve the double-spend problem. It also created something invaluable to cybercrime: the potential for anonymity. Banks carry out 'know your customer' checks because the exercise of state power relies on sanctions against those individuals who abuse the financial system (there's little point having a big stick to enforce a system unless you can identify the skulls to crack with it). Bitcoin, by contrast, isn't interested in the names behind the numbers, because it created a system in which the numbers speak for themselves.

As Satoshi Nakamoto's invention blossomed, the criminal underworld finally saw its financial dream come true: a computerized, apparently anonymous currency that enabled worldwide trade with no questions asked.

For most people, Bitcoin came to mainstream attention thanks to crime, and one criminal enterprise in particular: Silk Road. The wild story of this dark web drugs bazaar (and the story of the dark web itself) is covered later. For the moment, suffice to say, Bitcoin drove the creation of such criminal enterprises by allowing, for the first time, a secretive yet secure worldwide payment method for crooks and their customers.

But Bitcoin isn't just a useful payment tool for enabling offences such as drug dealing and fraud. The virtual currency has also been the subject of crime itself – in fact, it was a crime scene almost from the beginning.

Raised on a diet of manga comics in his home country of France, Mark Karpelès had for years dreamed of a life in Japan. But when he got there, in 2009, his life turned into a nightmare. The 24-year-old would find himself at the centre of the biggest heist in Bitcoin's history.

Softly spoken, thoughtful and shy, Karpelès is the polar opposite of the swaggering tech bosses who stride the stage at their glitzy product launches. My first impression was that in the cut-and-thrust world of e-commerce, he'd have been eaten alive. But it seems I was wrong: Karpelès turned out to have impressive stores of resilience.

Karpelès discovered Bitcoin while trying to find a convenient international payment system, and was intrigued by the technology. When the chance came up to run one of the very first Bitcoin exchanges, where people could buy the virtual currency with their dollars or pounds, he took it on as a side project. But there was a problem: very soon after he took over the business, he says he found that thousands of coins had been stolen from its coffers.[33]

Karpelès persevered, believing he could ride out the loss. To understand why he thought this possible, you have to travel back in time and see Bitcoin the way it was perceived in its earliest days when the currency was practically worthless. When the very first coins were created they had, inevitably, a monetary 'real world' exchange value of zero. The new currency needed some time to get going before its worth was proven. It was so experimental, in fact, that there was a website called the Bitcoin Faucet which gave out five free coins to each visitor (unsurprisingly, with each Bitcoin now worth thousands of dollars, the original site is no longer live).

The early view of Bitcoin as an oddball novelty is reflected in the history of the exchange business that Karpelès took over. It was called Mt. Gox, and its roots lay in a computer-and-card game called *Magic: The Gathering*. Players who wanted to swap cards would do so through the website, hence its name: 'Magic: The Gathering Online (e)Xchange', abbreviated to Mt. Gox. When the site started dabbling with Bitcoin, many outsiders would probably have regarded trading this new virtual currency as being on a par with swapping playing cards.

From our current standpoint, it's very hard now to remember this era of Bitcoin, because the currency's subsequent crazy growth skews our impressions like a fun-house mirror. When I first covered Bitcoin in 2011, I simply couldn't understand how a currency could gain traction with no traditional basis of authority. I was wrong, and I wasn't the only one. At the time, each Bitcoin was worth about $5. Had I invested $2,000 at that point and picked the right moment to cash out, I could have bought my London flat outright within two years.

But, like me, back in 2011 Mark Karpelès wasn't to know that his radical sideline was on the verge of exploding in popularity as one of the most disruptive financial innovations in modern history. He believed that, as the business grew, he'd be able to replace the lost coins and no one would be any the wiser. But the price spiralled, trapping Karpelès. When he took over the business, he says $60,000 worth of Bitcoins were missing. Within two years, those same stolen coins were worth $1.8 million. The secret hole at the centre of the company was growing out of control. Meanwhile, Mt. Gox was on a tear: it went from 3,000 users to a million in under three years.[34]

As Karpelès struggled to keep up with the exponential growth in his business, Mt. Gox became the world's dominant Bitcoin exchange. If you wanted to get your hands on this hot, new virtual currency, you likely ended up at Karpelès's virtual door. He himself would probably admit that he wasn't the best person to run such a beast of a business, but Karpelès felt he couldn't hand it to anyone else because he knew the size of the hidden problem he'd been left with. His hands were tied to the Bitcoin balloon. As everyone else enjoyed its meteoric rise, all he could see was the inevitable drop getting bigger and bigger.

Then in 2014, the ground fell away completely, and Karpelès found himself in free fall.

Having a Bitcoin wallet on your computer is convenient because you can use it to send and receive money to and from other web users. It's easy to create wallets – there are websites that will guide you through the process in just a few clicks and store your login information too. But it's risky: if your computer or the website gets hacked, you can lose all your funds.

One way round this is what's called a 'cold wallet'. You set up a wallet on a laptop in the usual way, top it up with Bitcoin, then disconnect it from the Internet and keep it somewhere safe.

Later on, when Bitcoin has (hopefully) gone up in value, you can switch on the laptop, reconnect it to the Internet, open that virtual wallet and start using your stored coins. You can even top up your cold wallet while it's in the safe because, when you finally reconnect it to the Internet, the blockchain system, which has been actively updating and storing your transactions with every new payment, will automatically fill it with all the money it's due. But while your cold wallet is disconnected, transfers can't be made *out* of it, meaning that it's theoretically safe from hackers. In fact, you don't even need the laptop: you can simply store your wallet details on a piece of paper in the safe. Later on, you retrieve the details, log into your wallet online, and the blockchain system will quickly update your wallet, showing your original balance and crediting it with any new Bitcoin that's been paid in while you were logged out.

Because of the large amounts of money now handled by Bitcoin currency exchanges, most of them use a variation of the cold wallet system. They use hot (Internet-connected) wallets for day-to-day transactions, and cold (disconnected) wallets for long-term, high-value deposits. It's like a bank issuing a limited amount of cash to its front-counter clerks, while keeping its major reserves in the vault.

Mark Karpelès followed this strategy. He kept the written details of his cold wallets on hundreds of pieces of paper locked in bank safes dotted around Tokyo.[35] It may seem surprisingly low-tech, but at the time, Karpelès believed this was the safest option. He would transfer money into the cold wallets for safe keeping, happy that these wallets were stowed offline, away from hackers. He tried to check the cold wallets' balances occasionally to make sure the amounts in the wallets were correct and tallied with the amount he'd squirrelled away into them.

Then one day, the amounts didn't match.

As Karpelès frantically checked the offline cold wallets, he found discrepancies. Someone had been raiding his exchange, stealing money, then changing the Mt. Gox corporate records to cover their tracks. The more cold wallets he checked, the more money Karpelès discovered missing. By the end, the losses added up to 850,000 Bitcoins. Thanks to Bitcoin's meteoric rise, Karpelès was staring at a $480 million hole.

'I don't have a word for this, except . . . it's like when you see the floor very close . . .' says Karpelès, in halting English.

'Like when you're falling off a building?' I suggest.

'Yes.'[36]

The business filed for bankruptcy on 28 February 2014, leaving Mt. Gox's many customers locked out of their accounts. It was the beginning of a lengthy and labyrinthine series of legal proceedings, both civil and criminal. Karpelès himself was arrested on 1 August 2015 and spent eleven months in jail.[37] He pleaded not guilty and received a suspended sentence in 2019 for tampering with electronic records, but was cleared of embezzlement.[38]

After the business went under, Karpelès had found around 200,000 of the missing Bitcoins, which by this stage had rocketed so much in value that they were worth more than the dollar-value of the original amount lost. It sounded like great news for the people who had their money in Mt. Gox. Perhaps they could get a share of the recovered coins. But the process was fiendishly complex: would they get their money back in Bitcoin (now worth massively more than when they'd invested)? Or in dollars? Or Japanese yen? And if it was in a 'real-world' currency, what exchange rate would be used? Would it be the rate Bitcoin was worth when they initially invested? Or its value when the site collapsed? Or its present-day value? The fun-house mirror warped the figures so much that it didn't seem fun any more.

The legal proceedings continue, and currently it feels as though the only people getting rich out of this particular Bitcoin story are the army of lawyers fighting the various sides' cases.

Meanwhile, though, you might be wondering what happened to the original 850,000 coins stolen from Mt. Gox (now worth a whopping $4.2 billion). The answer, according to the U.S. Department of Justice, was to be found sunbathing on a Greek beach overlooking the Aegean Sea in July 2017.

Alexander Vinnik was relaxing at a remote resort in Halkidiki when he was suddenly surrounded by about twenty men. They were dressed in shorts and sunglasses, but they weren't fellow holidaymakers.[39] They turned out to be plain-clothes police, and within hours the Russian was in custody in a Greek prison, accused of being at the centre of a global money-laundering enterprise. Vinnik had, according to the U.S. Department of Justice, run a cryptocurrency exchange called BTC-e, which they claimed had 'helped to launder criminal proceeds from syndicates around the world', including handling $4 billion worth of Bitcoin transactions on a no-questions-asked basis.[40]

Investigators say that, of the 850,000 Bitcoins stolen from Mt. Gox, almost two-thirds ended up in accounts run by Alexander Vinnik. They also claim that under his leadership BTC-e was pivotal in laundering the profits from ransomware attacks, including Cryptowall, the virus strain mentioned earlier that had made $325 million in just one of its campaigns.[41] Their allegations against BTC-e are echoed by data from three Google employees, who in August 2017 presented some fascinating research on ransomware – they had attempted to trace the path of the ransom payments, and claimed that 95 per cent of the money could be traced passing through BTC-e.[42]

Tracing the flow of currencies like Bitcoin from crimes will often lead to an exchange where it disappears in a mass of other transactions. The operators of such exchanges often argue that they are not liable for the origins of the money they receive. 'BTC-e is just a web platform for buying and selling Bitcoin,' Vinnik's lawyer argued. 'As such, it cannot be held responsible for the source of the money used to buy Bitcoin, no more than a bureau de change can be held responsible for exchanging a stolen $100 note into pounds sterling.'[43]

The U.S. now wants to extradite Vinnik to face 21 charges of money laundering and other financial offences. Vinnik, via his lawyer, disputes the facts asserted in the FBI's extradition demand. And his legal headaches continue. France also filed an extradition application, as has Russia, though on much lesser and completely unrelated charges. The latter is reportedly Vinnik's preferred option, and he's requested extradition to his home country.[44]

For the moment, the mystery of the stolen Mt. Gox money remains unsolved. But Mt. Gox, giant a theft as it was, was just the beginning. The hack had revealed a soft underbelly of the international financial system: cryptocurrency exchanges. And over the next few years, this poorly protected store of funds would be the cybercriminals' next billion-dollar target.

In front of a packed press conference, as the photographers' flashes popped and shutters whirred, two young men clad in smart black suits bowed down low behind a bank of microphones, in the traditional Japanese gesture of contrition. Their wrongdoing: losing more than half a billion dollars of customers' money in a cryptocurrency hack that rivalled the massive Mt. Gox break-in.

President Koichiro Wada and Chief Operating Officer Yusuke Otsuka were the leading figures in Coincheck, another Tokyo-based cryptocurrency exchange that had found itself in the hackers' sights. A digital break-in in January 2018 had seen the theft of around $530 million of what are called 'NEM coins', a type of digital currency similar to Bitcoin. Part of Coincheck's mistake was failing to learn the lessons of previous cyberattacks on cryptocurrency exchanges. It had stored all of the NEM coins in a 'hot wallet' – that is, one connected to the Internet and therefore more vulnerable to hacking.[45]

The company pledged to reimburse the 260,000 affected investors out of its own funds. Along with the foundation that runs the NEM currency, Coincheck did its best to prevent the criminals getting away with the cash. The online wallets into which the money had been transferred were marked with a digital tag which read: 'coincheck_stolen_funds_do_not_accept_trades : owner_of_ this_account_is_hacker', so that anyone receiving money from them would, effectively, be tracked as having tainted funds.[46] According to the NEM foundation, this would make the stolen money 'effectively unusable'.[47]

But the hackers worked too quickly for their pursuers: they set up hundreds of wallets, moving the stolen coins too quickly for all the wallets to be tagged with the warning message. And within a week, a site had reportedly been set up on the dark web offering people the chance to buy the stolen NEM coins at a discount.[48] According to Japanese cybersecurity company L Plus, at least 60 per cent of the stolen hoard – more than a quarter of a billion dollars – was laundered in this way and effectively vanished.[49]

As investigators started looking into the hack, South Korean officials reportedly had strong suspicions about who was behind it. In February 2018, just weeks after the hack, an unnamed South Korean source told Reuters that his country's National Intelligence Service believed North Korea was 'possibly' behind the theft.[50] It is far from confirmed, however – if indeed it ever can be, given the difficulty of tracing the money. Subsequent news reports said that the malicious software used to attack Coincheck had been widely available for years, meaning it could have fallen into many hackers' hands, making attribution of the crime yet harder. However, this isn't the only cryptocurrency exchange hack that South Korea has pinned on its northern neighbour.

In December 2017, Seoul blamed North Korea for thefts from two South Korean firms, Bithumb and Youbit, totalling $150 million at the time of reporting. The National Intelligence Service also reportedly blamed North Korea for a hack on another South Korean exchange, Coinis, although it's not known how much was stolen.[51] You could be forgiven for taking such accusations with a pinch of salt, coming as they do from South Korea, which despite recent thawing of diplomatic relations has long had an acrimonious relationship with the North. But they're not alone in attributing cryptocurrency exchange hacks to North Korea. Russian cybersecurity firm Group-IB claims the country's 'Lazarus Group' of government hackers was responsible for a total of $571 million worth of thefts from exchanges in 2017 and 2018, including the giant Coincheck job.[52]

North Korea declined repeated requests for an interview for this book via its UK embassy and website, and has previously denied any involvement in computer hacking attacks. North Korea aside, however, the raiding of cryptocurrency exchanges has proved a highly profitable cash cow for the hackers, from whichever country they come. A report from U.S. cybersecurity company CipherTrace totted up the totals and found that, in just the first nine months of 2018, such hacks netted the criminals $927 million.[53]

That's $2,000 a second.

And it doesn't end there.

Ever enterprising, and flushed with the profits of their success, the hackers have switched tactics: rather than stealing other people's cryptocurrency, they're now making their own.

Remember the Bitcoin mining activity mentioned earlier? It relies on having a computerized miner which goes back through all the transactions in the blockchain record, checking everything is in order and that there are no double spends. These miners are rewarded with a Bitcoin at regular intervals, and with each Bitcoin currently worth thousands of dollars, that's a big incentive.

Mining through Bitcoin's ever-growing transaction history requires serious computational effort. But what if you could trick someone else into using their hardware to do it for you? Hackers have designed malicious software that does exactly that. If you inadvertently install this virus on your computer, it will secretly hijack your machine and use its computing power to mine for cryptocurrency. While you're typing away (or perhaps while you're away from your keyboard, but with your computer still switched on), the software will be running through the block-chain, checking transactions and occasionally rewarding the person who infected you with the prize of a cryptocurrency coin. The only difference you might notice is your laptop's internal cooling fan spinning furiously as it fights to chill the circuits that have been enslaved into working overtime.

It's called 'cryptojacking', and it's a growing business. In January 2019, two researchers from King's College London and Charles III University of Madrid found that a small number of hackers had pocketed $56 million from this kind of activity over ten years.[54]

Looking back over the preceding chapters: during the last decade cybercriminals have dug deeper and deeper into the financial system. They have gone from defrauding credit cards, to stealing directly from bank customers' accounts, to raiding the banks themselves, to effectively creating their own mint (in the form of the cryptojacking attacks that churn out fresh virtual currency).

Enabling this has been an exchange of skills and tools between nation-state hacking groups and organized cybercriminals. In the case of the WannaCry attack, for example, key parts of the virus code were allegedly invented by one set of government hackers (the U.S. National Security Agency), stolen by a crime gang (the

Shadow Brokers) and subsequently picked up and used to devastating effect by another set of government hackers (the North Korean Lazarus Group).

By now perhaps your head is spinning with bank hacks, Bitcoin, ransomware and sanctions-dodging. It's easy to believe that cybercrime operates at a high level, requiring armies of state-funded hackers wrangling complicated viruses.

But it doesn't have to be that way.

The next chapter shows how to make megabucks using just three pieces of information – plus a dose of psychology. As illustrated by the Love Bug virus, the most vulnerable part of our increasingly networked world is the humans who control and use it. And for one very smart group of criminals, this would be the key to a fortune.

FIVE

YOUR DATA FOR SALE

When the hacking of British telecoms firm TalkTalk hit the headlines in October 2015, there was something different about the coverage. Unlike many previous cyber-crimes, this time it was the company itself revealing that it had been attacked. In a rare decision, its then chief executive Baroness Dido Harding toured the nation's newsrooms, scrambling to explain what had happened. Hackers had broken into the company's servers, she said, and stolen swathes of customers' data. She warned that the fallout could affect every single one of TalkTalk's four million customers. The wisdom of her decision to go public in such a major way became a hotly debated topic. In the ensuing weeks and months it would emerge that there were some compelling reasons behind it, and some disastrous consequences too.

Like most journalists, my first indication that TalkTalk was in trouble was their announcement. Unlike other journalists, however, for me this would become far more than a short-lived news event. Through a combination of mistakes, obstinacy and lucky breaks, I would end up deeper into the tale than any other reporter.

In the end, I spent years, off and on, investigating what really happened at TalkTalk. The story I uncovered was far more intriguing, and certainly more worrying, than the here-today-gone-tomorrow newspaper headlines that greeted the initial hack. What I found took me into the heart of the growing and unrestrained illegal trade in personal data, and brought me face to (virtual) face with some of those behind it.

For most of us, that phrase 'personal data' is a vague, hard-to-grasp piece of jargon. For cybercriminals, however, its meaning is crystal clear: personal data is a commodity that's now as valuable as money, because in an act of hacker alchemy, it's getting easier and easier to turn one into the other. To understand why, you have to change how you think about data. You have to embrace, as the hackers have done, a brand-new way of understanding its value. To do so, it helps to understand the full story behind the hacking of TalkTalk.

Mike Rendall was a teen hacker of the first degree. What made him dangerous wasn't just his technical skill, it was that he combined it with a genius for social engineering. It's a tactic we've already covered in this book – the subtle, psychological art of tricking a victim into doing something they shouldn't.

Unlike the hackers we've met so far, though, Rendall didn't just send carefully crafted spoof emails. Instead, he got up close and personal with his social manipulation. He claims he would actually phone companies' call centres directly, pretend to be an employee of the firm, and trick its staff into divulging or changing sensitive customer data that he could then use to hack those customers. It's a technique that requires guts, confidence and an innate grasp of human behaviour. It's also become a common tactic for computer hackers:

'The media usually thinks hacking is down to some group of people in a basement somewhere, typing away,' says Rendall. 'In reality, it's usually a phonecall to a company saying "Hi, I'm from the tech support department, I need a password resetting," and they'll do it for you.'

As he explains, a key tactic was to put the person on the other end of the phone under pressure. 'You basically just have to guilt-trip the employee on the other end into helping you out,' he says.

Rendall and his associates quickly realized that employees responded better to women's requests, so they used computer software to change their voices. Then they took the psychological manipulation up a notch.

> The idea was to have a crying baby sound effect in the background. So you'd call up with your voice changer, you'd act all stressed like you'd had a really stressful day. You'd say, 'I just need this one thing doing.' They can hear the kid in the background. It always gets to them, they want to help you out. It sounds ridiculous at first but it works, like, 80 per cent of the time.

Rendall's particular obsession was hacking Twitter accounts. He'd blag enough information from different sources to break in, take over the account and lock out the real owner. Then, if it was a famous person's account, he'd have some fun tweeting bizarre or inappropriate comments, or doing 'shout-outs' to his friends. If it was a sought-after account (one with few letters, for example, such as @abc) he could sell it for cash among his hacker mates.

I've changed Rendall's name because, like many former criminal hackers, he's now gone straight, taking a university course in cybersecurity and pitching his skills to Britain's growing roster of tech security companies. Back in 2015, however, he was still very much 'on the scene', and in the course of his hacking he and his friends found some serious security holes in the TalkTalk website.

What they'd stumbled on was something that some of TalkTalk's staff already knew, according to a former employee who held a key position in the company's tech team. The TalkTalk website had a chronic issue with what are called 'orphan pages'. The site was regularly updated with new pages, but old, outdated ones were still sitting on the company's computer server. Because there was no link to them from the current TalkTalk site, the company's techies struggled to keep track of these orphans, according to the source. The problem was that each of those outdated pages presented a potential way in for the hackers. That's because the pages might contain old computer code that had become vulnerable to attack. But without any way to know which pages were still live, TalkTalk's techies didn't have a way of updating all the pages to make them secure, let alone deleting them, says the source.

Soon enough, hackers like Rendall discovered this hole in TalkTalk's security. (Baroness Harding, TalkTalk's chief executive at the time, later said that three such vulnerable pages were targeted, which actually belonged to the website of a business that TalkTalk had bought in the past.)[1] Rendall claims he'd publicly highlighted other security flaws in TalkTalk's website, but they had gone unfixed. 'So I thought "Fuck them", their security is their problem,' Rendall told me shortly after the hack.

Rendall watched as news of TalkTalk's weak spot leaked out on the cybercrime underground, and he had a front-row seat as several hackers he knew broke into TalkTalk's website using those vulnerable orphan pages. The tactics they used in order to do so raised yet more troubling concerns about the company's security.

TalkTalk's website, like many, many others, has two sides: a public-facing side, where visitors could find out about broadband deals and so on, and a private, hidden side where sensitive customer and company data was kept. Of course, the two sides have to be linked at some level: for example, a TalkTalk customer would log in on the public-facing side, but once logged in they'd be accessing the private part where all their account information was stored. This bridge between public and private was where the hackers struck.

There's a system that takes website searches from the public side (such as 'Lowest broadband price, Acacia Road, London') and rummages around in the website's private database for the results ('£20 a month'). This system is called SQL (Structured Query Language). If poorly configured, this system is vulnerable to being tricked into revealing information it shouldn't.

For example, if you type in 'Lowest broadband price Acacia Road London', but then add some special characters (such as ; or

/* or @@) at the end, then a badly installed SQL system might get confused by the extra text, and accidentally show you the hidden, private side where the sensitive customer and company info is stored. This may seem crazy but it sometimes works, and it's been a staple in the hacker toolbox for decades. Because it's such an old trick, most websites are well protected against it. TalkTalk, perhaps because of its orphan page problem, wasn't.

It was this hole that the hackers exploited in October 2015, as witnessed by Rendall. What he observed next was a classic, juvenile 'joint enterprise' crime: one kid finds a hole in the fence, dares a few of his mates to go inside, and the rest stand around waiting to see what comes out. What came out, according to later investigations, was tens of thousands of customers' details, including bank account information and partial credit card numbers.

Compared to many other attacks the tactics were very basic, but nonetheless the teen hackers were making hay – stealing data and boasting to each other of their successes. Then someone dropped the ball. One of the less experienced hackers got carried away and started trying to scan TalkTalk's entire network to find more ways into the company's data. This involved inundating TalkTalk's website with requests, and pretty soon the company's systems started to grind to a halt. Its tech security team realized something was wrong.

As the company scrambled to get on top of the problems, things escalated: a ransom demand arrived in Baroness Harding's personal inbox from one of the hackers, who wanted a payment in Bitcoin worth around a quarter of a million pounds. (The extortion attempt was later revealed to have come from Daniel Kelley, then aged sixteen and living in Llanelli in South Wales. He would later be sentenced to four years in a youth offenders institution for this and other hacking offences.)[2] This seemed partly to explain the company's decision to go public – to neutralize the extortionist's threat. TalkTalk's PR team, however, claimed the motivation was to inform customers promptly. Whatever the explanation, and however well intentioned, the decision to hit the newsrooms would go on to have seriously damaging ramifications for many TalkTalk customers.

As the chief executive toured the TV studios to warn of the attack, the police were closing in on the juvenile hackers behind it. Their investigation was helped by the fact that the young thieves weren't exactly the most professional bunch. Some of them had boasted about their escapades on Twitter, for example, before panicking and deleting their tweets. I was able to make contact with several of them using secure messaging software. And if a journalist can find you, the chances are the police aren't far behind.

Within days, arrests were made across the UK – one of which apparently occurred while I was chatting to the arrestee online. Predictably, the culprits turned out to be, in many people's eyes, shockingly young. 'Babyface "Hacker"' was the headline in the *Daily Mail* newspaper, emblazoned next to a photo of a fifteen-year-old suspect who'd been arrested in Northern Ireland. He turned out to be Aaron Sterritt, resident of the seaside town of Larne. He was sentenced to fifty hours of community service and a year's supervision.[3] A sixteen-year-old arrested in East Anglia was named as Elliott Gunton – he was the hacker whom Rendall had seen publicizing the weak spot in TalkTalk's systems. Gunton got a twelve-month rehabilitation order.[4] Matthew Hanley of Tamworth, Staffordshire, who was twenty at the time of the hack, was sentenced to a year in jail for pilfering the personal and financial information of customers. He'd handed the data on to eighteen-year-old Connor Allsopp, also living in Tamworth, who fenced it on to others. Allsopp was jailed for eight months.[5]

TalkTalk was also punished. A year after the hack it was fined £400,000 by the data watchdog the Information Commissioner's Office – close to the maximum fine at that time (TalkTalk paid early and got an £80,000 discount).[6]

In the aftermath of the hack, the wisdom of Baroness Harding's decision to make so many TV appearances became the subject of lively discussion in corporate, tech and PR circles. While some applauded the company for coming clean so promptly, others criticized it. For a start, the chief executive had struggled to explain some of the technical detail of the attack, attracting fire from tech-savvy viewers. Perhaps more crucially, though, at the stage when Harding went public, the company still didn't know how many people had actually been affected. It turned out to be 156,959, of whom a fifth had seen their bank and partial credit card details leaked (which, had it been known at the time, would probably have made it a non-story – in my newsroom, at least). But by announcing that the problem could have affected all of the company's customers, Harding put the frighteners on four million TalkTalk users, and that may have opened the way for even more criminal activity. Thousands of miles away, a highly organized group of criminals, unconnected to the juvenile hackers, had already made a lot of money out of targeting TalkTalk's customers. Now, as the firm's hacking woes hit the headlines, this criminal operation was given a new lease of life.

This is the story-behind-the-story of the TalkTalk hack. It's a tale of how companies send customer data halfway around the world, how it can fall into criminals' control, and how even just a few pieces of it can be manipulated to con victims out of their life savings.

These nuggets of personal data may seem almost worthless, and most of us hand them over to companies without a second thought. But in the wrong hands they can be used against us to devastating effect. This particular crime gang used the data to fuel a well-oiled money-making machine. And I would never have found out about them were it not for a chance encounter with a single victim.

When I first met Tamsin Collison, my day had turned into what was called in our newsroom slang a 'kick-bollock scramble': a hellish shift when you have just a few hours to pull a story together, embrace the latest news lines, and get something coherent on air. I'd been told Collison was a TalkTalk hacking victim, and so I spent a rushed half-hour interviewing her before racing back to the office and incorporating her into my report, as news of the company's battle with the teen hackers came to light. It turned out that in my haste, I'd failed to spot key elements in Collison's story – but that wouldn't emerge until much later. At that moment, all I knew was that she was a 'TalkTalk hack victim', and so I crowbarred her into the report.

And then I made a mistake.

I wrote in my voice-over script that Collison had been given a small compensation payment from TalkTalk. When I phoned her a few days later to follow up, she was distraught and angry. She hadn't accepted the payment, she told me, she'd been offered it, but had refused on principle. It was a one-word mistake, but the impact for her was huge.

I felt ashamed. Collison had given up her time for free to relive a bad experience on camera so I could put it on TV. The least I could do was get the details right, and I hadn't even managed that. I offered to buy her a coffee so I could apologize in person. I also hoped I could find out more about the hack, and maybe push the story forward.

In a more relaxed environment, Collison was able to tell me all the background, and I was able to listen more attentively. As she spoke, I realized the story she was recounting was something altogether different to what I'd thought. It was totally unrelated to the October 2015 attack, and if what Collison was saying was correct, it was much, much more worrying. It was a remarkable tale of a complex, well-rehearsed fraud that had cost her dearly, and many others too. And it perfectly illuminated what can go wrong as a result of companies' growing reliance on their customers' personal data, and the illegal trade that has grown up around it.

Collison was in many ways a model TV interviewee. Well turned-out and in her late forties, she works as a voice-over artist, and in person her mellifluous delivery is mixed with a disarmingly straightforward manner. And unlike many cybercrime victims, she refused to be cowed or feel ashamed – her anger at what had happened drove her to talk when many stayed silent.

She'd been a TalkTalk customer for six years, she told me, and was not happy with the service. She wasn't alone. The company's satisfaction ratings had been below industry average for several years.[7] In May 2015, months before news broke of the teen hack attack, Collison made repeated, fruitless calls to TalkTalk's technical support staff, and with her broadband once again on the blink she decided to cancel her contract. Then on 27 May, she received a call from someone with a heavy Indian accent calling himself 'Shane Williams'. He claimed to work for TalkTalk, and said he could fix her connection problems.

Collison was convinced she was talking to a genuine TalkTalk employee because Shane Williams knew her account number and address. And because she'd had previous dealings with TalkTalk's call centre in India, the man's accent didn't seem incongruous. But Shane Williams was a member of a giant criminal enterprise operating out of a series of fake call centres dotted around India, and Collison was about to be subjected to an intricate and well-crafted confidence trick.

He began by warning her that her computer had been infected with several viruses. As evidence, he gave her instructions which she typed into her computer, bringing up a screen that appeared to show a terrifying list of warnings and errors. The screen Collison was looking at is called Event Viewer; it's a log of everything a Windows computer does in the background. While the list is indeed full of menacing-looking exclamation marks, the vast majority of them are harmless and happen continually on any normal computer. Collison didn't know this, of course. 'I thought the computer was about to blow up,' she later recalled. She was panicked, and the con artist knew it: frightened people are easier to manipulate. After convincing her that her computer was badly broken, the fraudster moved on to the next part of the scam. He emailed her a link to a website which he claimed would fix the computer's problems.

Clicking on the link installed on Collison's computer a piece of software called a Remote Access Tool (or RAT). As the name suggests, this gives the sender of the email the ability to remotely control the recipient's computer. Such software is often used legitimately in large companies to help IT support staff fix employees' problems without having to attend in person.

Still believing she was talking with a TalkTalk employee, Collison followed his instructions to install the software. Unknown to her, the scammer was now able to see everything that happened on her computer, and anything she typed on the keyboard.

Now Shane Williams had some good news for Collison: she was entitled to compensation, he said. He transferred her to yet another 'TalkTalk employee' in India who would help her with her refund. This new employee gave his name as 'Patrick Anderson'. (The use of English names is not uncommon: call centres outside the UK began using such names as they increasingly serviced British customers, in an attempt to make callers feel more comfortable.) Patrick Anderson sent Collison a link to a website where she could claim her £200 compensation. It looked like the TalkTalk website, and featured the logos of all the British banks. Clicking on her bank's logo, Collison was confronted with a website that looked like her online banking login page. In reality, it was another fake set up by the scammers. (Websites can cost only few pounds to register, and creating a convincing-looking fake bank site is quick work for a web designer.) Anderson told her to log into her bank account.

'Don't tell me your password, just type it in,' he told her. This one comment alone did a lot to win Collison's trust, as it echoed precisely the safety advice she'd heard from legitimate sources, telling her not to divulge her details.

But of course, the scammer didn't need her to tell him the password. Thanks to the Remote Access Tool that she had unwittingly installed, as Collison typed in the requested characters from her password, the scammer was able to read them on his screen. He simply went to the real bank login page and typed her details in.

Thousands of miles away from Collison's London home, Patrick Anderson was inside her bank accounts, staring at a balance of thousands of pounds which Collison had put aside for her tax bill. But spiriting the money away wasn't going to be easy.

In order to transfer the money to another account, the fraudster would need to set up a new payee, and that required access to the card reader issued to UK bank customers like Collison. And besides, a bank transfer would create a breadcrumb trail which may get the scammer caught. Instead, Anderson opted for a more complex, but ultimately safer tactic. He transferred £5,200 from Collison's savings account to her current account, and used the Remote Access Tool to show her the current account on her computer screen.

Seeing the new balance, Collison was furious. 'You've made a mistake,' she told Anderson, chastising him for overpaying her by £5,000. At which point he went into what she described as an 'Oscar-winning meltdown performance', explaining between sobs that the mistake would cost him his job, his family and his home. By this time, Collison had been on the phone for several hours with what she still believed was TalkTalk's customer services team, and she wanted the quickest way to get rid of them. She offered to transfer the money back, but Anderson said this would expose his error to his bosses.

Instead, he told Collison she needed to send the money to a colleague of his in a different TalkTalk office, who would deposit the cash in TalkTalk's systems and hide the error. He gave Collison the name of a man, 'Sohail Hussain', whom he said was in Bangkok. He talked her through the process of transferring cash via MoneyGram (all you need is a name and a city), and urged her to make the transfer quickly.

So Collison went to the bank, then to the post office, and sent £5,000 to a man she'd never met, 6,000 miles away.

I know what you're thinking, because everyone thinks it at this point in Collison's story. Her behaviour seems inexplicably foolhardy. It is painfully easy for you to rewind through the events and find all the moments when she could have spotted the crime. But there are three factors to keep in mind: first, you, the reader, have the benefit of following the story, knowing from the beginning that it's a scam. It is impossible for you to put yourself in Collison's place, as someone not only ignorant of the fraud but who'd been worked on for several hours by professional crooks.

Second, Collison, by her own admission, is not web-savvy. Anyone who has dealt with a panicked IT emergency call from a relative knows how easy it is to be blinded by technology.

Third, she was exposed to a modern twist on a classic confidence trick. Con artists only need two things: a way to contact their victim, and something to win their confidence. In the old days of doorstep scams, the way to contact the victim was the doorbell, and the confidence-winner was the clipboard and the smart uniform. The doorbell rings, and a polite man in a utility company uniform tells you there's an urgent issue with your gas supply. You let him in, go to make him a cup of tea and the next thing you know, he's vanished along with the family silver.

In the cybercrime era, the tactics are the same but the tools are different. The way to contact the victim is via phone or email, and the confidence-winner is the stolen account number. But there's another, deeper reason why the particular scam executed on Collison worked so effectively.

In his book *The Big Con*, David W. Maurer describes the world of the late nineteenth- and early twentieth-century 'grifters' – confidence tricksters who marauded across the U.S. exploiting the emerging, cash-rich society that flourished before the Great Depression brought the gravy train to a halt.[8] During this time, the confidence trick developed into an intricate art form. It was fictionalized in the film *The Sting*, but in real life these same tricks were used to net crime gangs profits that would be worth millions in today's money. As Maurer explains, Big Con games relied on the creation of a fantasy world in which the victim was convinced they were part of an organized scheme that would result in a big payout. Vital to the trick was 'roping the mark', in which the victim (the 'mark') was transferred from dealing with one person to another, creating the illusion of a legitimate, organized business. As Collison was passed down the line of fake TalkTalk workers, she was simply a mark being roped, a victim being fooled into thinking she was dealing with a large, organized and legitimate operation.

Another vital step in the Big Con game is called 'putting the mark on the send'. Once a gang was sure that the victim was ready to be swindled, they gave them the opportunity to escape; to go home or stay in a hotel, for example. Often they would give the victim a small but significant portion of the gang's money to go away with.

It was a gamble for the crooks, but this psychological trick had the effect of reassuring the mark that they weren't about to be scammed. After all, the victim would think, why would a bunch of thieves let me walk away, especially with a few thousand dollars of their money? By making Collison think he'd overpaid her by £5,000, Anderson was putting her on a version of 'the send'. She was convinced she was dealing with the real TalkTalk call centre. And it couldn't be a scam, she reasoned, because as far as she was concerned she'd just been handed £5,000 of someone else's money. It was Patrick Anderson's mistake, she thought, and he, not she, was the victim.

As a result of these mind games, thousands of miles away in Bangkok, a man called Sohail Hussain was suddenly £5,000 richer.

This was the story Collison told me over coffee. The con had been a surreal episode lasting just a few hours, but she'd been swindled out of a substantial chunk of her savings. And as I was later to discover, she was far from alone.

Over the last few years, dozens of victims' experiences have filtered out through the media, all telling almost identical stories. One British law firm alone was acting for around twenty TalkTalk customers who between them lost almost £100,000. They're part of a very modern crime wave: cybercrime now accounts for more than half of all offences reported to the Crime Survey for England and Wales, with fraud costing British businesses more than £1 billion every year.[9]

But Collison's story also threw up some tantalizing potential leads. This kind of scamming requires an up-close-and-personal approach, and it's very difficult not to leave a trace. The thieves had sent her emails, made phonecalls and transferred money. Surely, I thought, there would be some telltale clue I could unearth to find out more about the people who had ripped Collison off.

But as I questioned her, the answers were depressing.

Were there any clues on her computer? No, she said, she'd had it wiped.

What about the emails? No, she'd deleted them too.

The Remote Access Tool? All details vanished when the computer was wiped.

In fact, Collison had only one, solitary lead: written on a piece of paper was an Indian mobile number, stored on her phone after a call from Patrick Anderson. I'd love to claim that I had access to some super-advanced investigative journalism tools that helped me trace the number. But the truth is that I simply typed it into Facebook.

In those days, even if someone hadn't made their mobile number public on their Facebook account, you could still search for a number and it would throw up accounts that it was linked to (in the wake of the Cambridge Analytica scandal, this 'feature' was withdrawn). When I typed in the number, what came up was a picture of a slender young Asian man with the account name Shoaib Khan. He said he was 22 and lived in Kolkata. His timeline was a string of selfies: smoking a cigarette on a night out, posing with an expensive car, handling a huge snake at the zoo and, in one intriguing shot, standing in what looked like a call centre.

I harvested as much as I could, then called the number. A voice answered with an Indian accent and said, 'Hello, TalkTalk

speaking.' I told him my computer needed fixing and he said
he'd call back. I then asked a colleague in India to call the same
number from an Indian mobile. My colleague called me back a
few minutes later, and told me the man who answered had identified himself as Shoaib Khan. This, it seemed, was the true face
of Patrick Anderson.

I never heard back from Khan, and when I phoned the number
a few days later, another voice answered and claimed to have
nothing to do with him. But the Facebook account was still open,
and it yielded up some crucial evidence. Khan had a friend called
Sohail Hussain – the same name to which Tamsin Collison had
been told to send her £5,000. Furthermore, on 25 May 2015,
two days before Collison unwittingly transferred her money to
Thailand, Hussain had flown to Bangkok: 'Going for a business
meeting,' read his Facebook status update. Hussain then posted
photos of what looked like a leisurely holiday in Thailand before
returning to Kolkata. Two months later, Khan's status update
showed him hitting the casino, under the hashtag 'winning'.

Khan and Hussain, it seemed, were the men behind the scam
that fleeced Collison. After a great many conversations with the
in-house lawyers, my bosses gave me the go-ahead to broadcast.

The day before we aired the story in December 2015, I contacted
Khan and Hussain through Facebook, presented our evidence and
invited their comment. When I woke up the next morning, their
Facebook profiles were gone and have never returned.

Putting their faces on TV news and outing them as the men
behind the con was the single most satisfying moment in my time
as a journalist.[10] It also went a long way to making up to Tamsin
Collison for my mistake in saying she'd accepted TalkTalk's compensation payment. But the initial follow-up was disappointing.
After the story was broadcast I attempted to contact Kolkata
police, with no success. I helped Collison update her report on
Action Fraud, the UK police's help centre for fraud victims, which
also received no follow-up. I was contacted by several Indian men
following the report, all of whom claimed to know of the gang,

and who gave me snippets of information. But none could provide enough evidence to move the story on significantly. Some claimed that Hussain and Khan had fled town. After six months of working on it on and off, the trail went cold and the story slipped down my to-do list.

Then more than a year later, on 18 January 2017, a message arrived in my Facebook inbox from a man in India: 'Hi sir I need to talk to you. Its emergency.'

The sender claimed to have vital information about the TalkTalk scammers. I was initially dismissive, assuming it would be yet another false lead. I was wrong. The man who contacted me said he knew Khan and Hussain. 'They're my bosses,' he wrote. I shortly received another message from another Indian sender, who also claimed to have worked for Khan and Hussain. They'd seen my TV report, they said, and recognized their employers when Khan and Hussain's Facebook photos appeared on screen.

Over the next few hours the two sources mapped out the inside story of the criminal network that had been used to scam Collison and the many, many other victims. It was a brilliantly well-planned and efficient fraud operation, running on an incredible scale. The two had worked alongside dozens of others in a call centre in a central Indian city, they said. As many as sixty employees worked in shifts, where they were told they would be helping TalkTalk customers. They described how the employees, hired from ads in local newspapers and on social media, made 10,000 rupees per month (roughly £120) from making calls. The aim, they explained, was to convince customers to install software – the same Remote Access Tool that Collison had been tricked into downloading. They were paid a bonus each time they did so.

Each employee made thousands of calls per day using automated software, the whistle-blowers told me, but many either went to an answerphone or were not connected. Only a handful of those who answered ended up installing the virus, but with each victim potentially worth thousands of pounds, the business proved lucrative enough for those who ran it.

On the surface, the call centre presented itself as entirely legitimate: it had machines for automatically dialling TalkTalk customers' numbers, training for its staff and even scripts that the employees were told to read out when talking to customers. When the two whistle-blowers sent me copies of those scripts they matched, almost word for word, what had been said to Tamsin Collison over the phone some eighteen months earlier.

It was all there: the call-centre workers were told how to bring up Event Viewer and trick the TalkTalk customer into thinking their computer was infected, just as Collison had been. They were given instructions on how to install the Remote Access Tool, the backdoor access that allowed Collison's money to be stolen. And most chilling of all, the scripts directly addressed how to deal with anyone suspicious of a scam. They contained a list in pidgin English of answers to questions that sceptical customers might ask. Number eight of which read (*sic*):

'Why I Trust on You?'
  'Answer: OK I will give you your talk talk account number and you can match it with your talk talk bill . . . that is very confidential number no one have this A/C no in the whole world expect you and talk talk.'

Did the employees of the call centre know they were involved in a scam? After all, there were telltale signs: anyone using Event Viewer would soon realize it's not an indication of an infected computer, and if you tell someone it is, you're lying to them. Perhaps some employees simply didn't care. Work isn't always easy to come by in India, and for a fairly decent wage, a bonus and the chance to break into the country's burgeoning call-centre industry, some workers might be happy not to ask questions.

In the case of the two I communicated with, they insisted they had no idea they were part of a criminal enterprise. They expressed remorse for what had been done to TalkTalk customers, some of whom, they claimed, had been reduced to tears during the scam calls. The pair even tried to share with me the phone numbers of TalkTalk customers they had recently called, requesting that I phone them to warn them off the fraud.

Both have now left the call centre (and in the interests of full disclosure, I made a payment of £250 to one of them, to pay for transport to and accommodation in a safe place following his communications with me). They were soon joined by more whistle-blowers. In the end, five seemingly separate sources came forward to say they either worked for or were trained by the gang, or had identified Khan within the organization. All the whistle-blowers claimed they only realized they were part of a scam after seeing my report. And who knows? This might just be true. After all, they and everyone else working in their call centre could claim innocence, thanks to an inspired business decision by the scammers to divide their operation up.

Ingeniously, the operation was split across two offices: one in central India where the whistle-blowers worked, the other in Kolkata. The job of the central India office was to call the customers and convince them to install the Remote Access Tool. Once this was complete, the customer's call would be transferred to the Kolkata office from where the RAT would then be used to carry out the bank account hacking. This would be handled by a different, smaller and more skilled team. When Tamsin was transferred to Patrick Anderson, who would 'handle her refund', she was being transferred from the bigger, central Indian call centre to the smaller Kolkata office.

For the con artists, this astute decision solved two problems at once: the low-level employees in the first office took on the donkey work of calling customers, whittling them down and leaving the smaller, senior team free to work on those primed for the con. And second, it minimized the gang's chances of getting caught, as it reduced the number of people aware of the full scale of the operation. The low-level employees were told they were working on behalf of TalkTalk, and while it's hard to imagine they didn't suspect wrongdoing, it would be easy to look the other way as they had no involvement in the final theft.

But in all of this, there's a big, as-yet unanswered question: where did the scam call centre get all those TalkTalk customers' details from? This is where the worrying questions start about the vulnerability of our personal data once it enters an internationally connected system.

As stated earlier, TalkTalk had a poor standing in customer satisfaction rankings, and in 2011 it hired Wipro, an Indian outsourcing company, to help improve matters.[11] Wipro is a giant company with more than 170,000 employees worldwide, part of India's huge and growing 'Business Process Outsourcing', or BPO, industry. It's why British customers often find themselves speaking with Indian operatives when they call a UK company. Wipro works for many British firms, and the vast majority have reported no problems with its services. This wasn't true, it seems, in TalkTalk's case.

In January 2016, news began to leak out about arrests in Kolkata. Three employees at Wipro's office (where TalkTalk's calls were being handled) were arrested in connection with selling TalkTalk customer data. The full story can now be told, thanks to former TalkTalk staff, sources in Kolkata and publicly released details from UK investigators.

Wipro workers dealing with TalkTalk customers had access to an online system through which engineers' visits could be booked. A customer in the UK who had a tech problem would phone TalkTalk and their call would be answered by a Wipro staffer in Kolkata who would book an engineer. The problem was that when Wipro staff left the company, no one revoked their access to this online engineer-booking system. Their passwords continued to work and so, even after leaving Wipro, they could still log in from the Internet and see details of TalkTalk customers who'd had problems, including their phone numbers and account details.

The UK's Information Commissioner's Office, which fined TalkTalk £100,000 for this breach (separate to the £400,000 fine mentioned earlier), confirmed that three Wipro accounts were used to steal the details of up to 21,000 customers.[12] The stolen data then fell into the hands of Khan and Hussain. According to a source who knows the gang, but did not want his identity revealed, memory sticks full of data were traded for cash at parties in Kolkata. It was then sent to the scam call centre where the whistle-blowers worked. And the gang was almost certainly exploiting data stolen from other companies too: the whistle-blowers said other staff worked a night shift, during which they believed victims were targeted in other countries.

Internal documents from TalkTalk show that the company knew about the problems in September 2014, and by March 2015 had a detailed view of exactly how the scam worked. 'Wipro agents identified as suspects,' the documents state. The company made efforts to close the data-leaking holes, but it was too late: the information was already in the scammers' hands.

TalkTalk also tried to warn customers several times, according to the documents. But clearly no warnings reached Tamsin Collison, or they weren't effective enough.

Throughout my investigation into the TalkTalk hack, Collison was a patient source of information and encouragement, jokingly signing off her emails as 'Watson' to my Sherlock. While it may have been cathartic for her to find out so much information about those who swindled her, the crime affected her in very material ways beyond just the loss of £5,000, which she never recovered.

During the scam, the criminals told her they would send someone round in person to fix her connection. She believes a member of the gang called at her flat while she was away. The thought of her name and address being known to criminals, and the prospect of further visits, made her feel increasingly uneasy about being in the property. She'd been thinking of moving for some time, she says, and the feeling of violation after the fraud made her mind up. She moved to another area of London. At the same time, the whistle-blowers claim, Khan and Hussain were setting up their second scam call centre.

Baroness Dido Harding, who has now left TalkTalk and works at NHS Improvement, declined to be interviewed for this book.

TalkTalk said it takes its responsibility to protect its customers very seriously. In the wake of the cyberattack it launched a 'Beat the Scammers' campaign to educate customers. The company also says it now proactively blocks over ninety million scam and nuisance calls a month.

Wipro did not respond to multiple requests for comment.

It's hard to overstate the impact of the TalkTalk hack on corporate Britain. Chief executives up and down the country winced as its CEO was repeatedly grilled on TV. Keen to avoid the same fate, they have in some cases boosted cybersecurity, and in others paid lip service to the importance of the issue.

The story of the Wipro leak and its attendant scam may be an extreme example, but it taps into a more troubling vein: the security of the global personal data industry. As margins shrink in data-driven businesses, the urge to drive down costs means many are contracting out the work of data storage, processing and customer service.

Business Process Outsourcing reportedly generates revenues of almost $150 billion in India alone, with giants like TCS, Infosys and Wipro vying for trade.[13] In order to make it work, personal data on UK customers often has to be routed (albeit virtually) to overseas call centres, and episodes like the leak at Wipro raise serious questions about how safely this can be done.

I spoke with one source who claimed to be a former long-term Wipro employee. He was stunned that such a breach could happen. He described the company as 'obsessive' about data security. He suggested that an operation to steal data and feed it out would have taken considerable planning. Yet the fact that it happened in a company of this size implies that any firm may be vulnerable, given a sufficiently determined adversary. And that's because the market is there for even the slightest bit of data.

What's amazing in the TalkTalk story is how much money the gang managed to make with so little. In some cases all they had was their victim's name, phone number and account number. Millions of those can be stored on a memory stick the size of a fingernail. Yet hacker alchemy can turn such thin pickings into a profitable scam big enough to run several call centres. Personal data is lucrative, sought-after and hard to protect.

Of course, it's one thing having access to all this stolen information. It's another thing fencing it on. The crooks who stole TalkTalk customer records in India were fortunate to have a network of criminals living in the same city who would happily buy the data and exploit it. What if you don't live near such nefarious individuals or, more likely, you don't even know any? Many of us have access to confidential information at work that would probably be worth something to someone, somewhere. How easily could we leak it and get paid for it?

The answer, thanks to the Internet, is very easily indeed.

On the surface, Intel Cutout looked like a normal website forum. There were different sections for different interest groups, and a healthy amount of discussion between its several thousand users. What was different was the type of thing being discussed: Intel Cutout was a haven for hackers, leakers and data traders of all stripes. At one point, someone posted what appeared to be the home addresses, email addresses and personal phone numbers of senior Facebook staff, including Mark Zuckerberg.

Often the information was publicly available for free, so the site's users would simply point people in the right direction by giving them a link where it could be downloaded. Among the forums, however, were offers to sell exactly the kind of insider corporate data that had proved so lucrative in the hands of the Indian fraud gang targeting TalkTalk's customers.

In 2018, tech security firm Digital Shadows recorded a post on Intel Cutout by a user called 'cys' titled 'selling insider access to an enterprise company'. The user posted some links to what they said was proof of their claim. 'It's a mortgage company,' the user said. Digital Shadows was unable to verify the claim, but it was among several found on various sites selling insider access to everything from banks to pharmaceutical companies.[14]

The original Intel Cutout collapsed after it was hit by police, who found a flaw in the website's code. But the site is now back under the banner Intel Cutout Reloaded, and its owner (who also ran the previous version) spoke to me anonymously through encrypted chat. 'It's like a hydra,' he wrote. 'For every time they attack we grow back. I'd like [Intel Cutout Reloaded] to be better than it ever was.'

I asked him about the sale of corporate data, including sensitive customer information. He insisted that much of the data is already publicly available and that his site simply points people towards it. He also claimed a moral justification for the site: 'Exposing government corruption. That's a big thing for us. People deserve to know what their leaders are doing behind their backs. While they can find this info on their own, we make it much easier to find such things.'

It was hard to assess this claim. When I visited the site's 'government leaks' section it was overrun with posts advertising recreational drugs and one (very probably fake) offering the services of a hitman, prices starting from $10,000.

The boss of Intel Cutout Reloaded also claimed that, even if personal data is sold, he and the others running the site get no money. 'We're a non-profit,' he wrote. 'People can sell whatever they like to each other but we get no cut. Money would corrupt our values.'

It was a surprising comment from someone running an illicit data website, so I responded: 'When you talk about corrupting values, I think a lot of people would find that confusing – after all, you're facilitating the exchange of stolen information.'

'Well the values we stand by are free speech,' he replied. He claimed that once information is hacked, its eventual publication is inevitable. 'If someone has access to such data then the source of it is already compromised and it will become public elsewhere regardless.'

Intel Cutout Reloaded's owners may not be making any money out of the site, but some of their users almost certainly are. That's because, in some ways, the dynamics behind Intel Cutout Reloaded are very similar to those driving one of the first e-commerce businesses ever created: eBay.

Prior to the emergence of online auction sites such as eBay, your ability to sell goods was in many cases linked to your ability to find a physical market. eBay created an easily accessible global marketplace in everything, even things that might have been considered worthless before. Suddenly those four Nissan Micra hubcaps that had sat at the back of your garage could be turned into cash. Not much cash, admittedly, but some at least. Almost everything could potentially be put up for sale and found a value.

Likewise, personal data that might previously have seemed worthless can now be valued and sold easily through sites such as Intel Cutout. Take, for example, a list of passwords. Devoid of any other information, such a list may seem worthless. Not so. Ranked in order, it gives a potential hacker a handy guide to the most common passwords. If they're going to try hacking into someone's account, they can start with the most common one, and work their way down.

What's being sold on Intel Cutout and other such sites is different to what's on eBay, however, in a single but vitally important respect: the hackers are selling data, and not material objects. As a result, most of us have a hard time understanding how to value it. Up until now, much of our conception of a raw commodity's value has been tied up with its scarcity. During a drought the cost of crops goes up. When oil producers limit supply, the price rises. Gold is expensive because there's not much of it and it's pretty difficult to get it out of the ground.

Data doesn't work like that. It's not finite, for a start – there's an almost infinite supply being constantly created. According to the traditional scarcity model, that should mean it decreases in value the more of it there is. But the odd thing about data is that each individual nugget of it increases in value when it's connected to another piece. The more of it that's created, the more valuable it all becomes.

As a simple thought experiment, imagine I want to set up a social networking website. I want to sell advertising on the site for, say, £10 per advert, but the advertisers will only pay me if they know their ads are going to appeal to at least two people on my site. So I invite my two best friends to join. One of them likes cheese, the other likes motorbikes. That's not enough to get the advertisers interested. But it turns out they both like jazz. So at least I can sell advertising to a jazz record label and make £10.

Then my friends sign up two more people. It turns out one of the new joiners likes cheese, the other likes motorbikes, and they both like brogues. So now I can sell ad space to cheese makers, motorbike brands and shoe shops, as well the jazz record label. That's £40. I've doubled my number of users, but when I add their pieces of data together, I'm making four times the money.

This is what's called the 'network effect'. Data nuggets and the connections between them are the basis of our emerging information economy. Put simply, this means that instead of increasing in value in a straight line, data businesses can potentially grow exponentially.

If you want to see how this works at scale, look at Twitter. In essence, all the company owns are its users' tweets and the connections between them. Yet it's valued at $28 billion.

The worth of data is hard for many of us to comprehend, having grown up in a system that values raw materials relative to their supply and demand. It also explains why we give away our personal data so easily, despite the consequences illustrated by the (admittedly extreme) TalkTalk story. For us, these nuggets of data might seem worthless, because most of us are unaware of the giant and growing hinterland of companies aggregating this information, making new connections from it and selling those connections on. As usual, the techies are way ahead of us, and hackers are no exception. They've long seen the merit in combining stolen data. For example, imagine if the Indian scammers had been able to supplement their stolen list of TalkTalk customers' names, phone numbers and account numbers with, say, a list of email addresses and the most common passwords used by Brits aged 55 and over? This is the market in which sites like Intel Cutout Reloaded operate – a global scene of cybercriminals eager to get their hands on as many data stores as possible, and with myriad ways to monetize the links they find.

Of course, Intel Cutout Reloaded and other such sites are potentially breaking multiple laws in multiple countries. They're facilitating a trade in stolen data, and their operators are absolutely aware of this. How, you may be asking yourself, can such sites exist? The answer is that they don't appear on the World Wide Web that many of us use. Intel Cut Out Reloaded and the others are hidden away from most people's view, on a shadowy yet fascinating area of the Internet called the 'dark web'.

It's a haven for criminals, drug dealers and data traders, as well as a vital tool for freedom fighters, journalists and whistleblowers. It exists thanks to the creation of the ultimate online invisibility cloak. The behaviour of those who hide behind it is having an impact around the world. And perhaps most remarkable of all, this invisibility cloak was designed and built by the u.s. military.

SIX

BEYOND THE DARK WEB

As the World Wide Web boomed during the 1990s, one group watched with particular interest. Military and intelligence specialists in the U.S. government had long understood the value of new technology in the exercise of soft power: from establishing Voice of America radio in the 1940s to smuggling photocopiers to anti-Soviet pamphleteers during the Cold War.[1] But their interest in communications technology went beyond propaganda. Spycraft often relies on moving data around securely, as illustrated by the classic James Bond plot: he sneaks into the villain's lair, copies the top-secret plans, makes an audacious escape and hands the dossier to his bosses. Stripped of his Walther PPK and his Aston Martin, Bond is essentially a criminally inclined FedEx driver.

Some in the U.S. military and intelligence community looked at the emerging Internet through this lens, seeing its potential as a way to allow agents in the field to communicate with their commanders. But the spooks faced a problem: the Internet as it was originally built is very bad at keeping secrets, and the reason for that lies in the very way the Internet and World Wide Web function.

As we saw in an earlier chapter, the Internet and the Web are two separate but related technologies. The Internet came first, linking up computers around the world into a spider's web of connections. If any one intermediate computer fails, there are multiple other routes through the maze. To make the system work, each computer has a unique address. Computers relaying messages to one another use these Internet Protocol (or 'IP') addresses to work out where the message should go. Therefore, it's very important that the IP addresses are viewable by everyone carrying messages around the system.

For example, if I want to visit the BBC website, my computer sends a request to my Internet provider, which contains my IP address and also the IP address of the BBC website's servers. My Internet provider can see both of the addresses, as can every other intermediary along the way as they send my request to the BBC. And when the BBC sends its website pages back to me, it can also see my IP address, so it knows where to send the content.

And that's where it gets tricky for the spies. Imagine I'm a CIA operative visiting a terrorism discussion website. I really don't want every Tom, Dick and Harry handling my requests to see my originating IP address, as it could reveal my CIA credentials. And I really, really don't want the terrorism website owners to see it.

The solution the Americans concocted was a work of genius: a way of using the existing Internet while hiding in plain sight. It was elegant, robust and easy to deploy. But it would go on to create an underworld that would cause millions of dollars of economic damage to the society it was meant to help protect. As a result, it would create a paradox at the heart of U.S. government, whereby one branch poured resources into a new technology that created massive headaches for another branch of the same government. The U.S. military was about to unleash the dark web.

First, they invented a special Internet browser. It looks like normal browsers such as Chrome or Firefox, but in the background it behaves very differently. When you use this browser to send a request for a website, it wraps it inside three layers of encryption.

When your request hits the first intermediary (let's say it's your Internet provider), the first layer of encryption is removed. But that doesn't reveal the IP address of your eventual destination; it simply sets up the next hop in the chain.

The next intermediary is allowed to unwrap the second layer of encryption. Again, this doesn't reveal the final destination, but simply sets up another hop.

When the third intermediary unwraps the last layer of encryption, the destination address is revealed and the request can be sent to the website. But – and this is the key point – neither the destination website nor the final intermediary knows where the original request came from.

In summary: the first link in the chain knows where you came from but not where you're going; the final link in the chain knows where you're going but not where you came from; and the middle links don't know either. Because no single party has the full picture, users of this browser can surf the Web with anonymity.

This threefold encryption tech was called 'onion routing', in reference to the layers of an onion, and was developed from 1995 onwards by the U.S. Naval Research Laboratory.[2] The NRL is an institution with a long and illustrious history of working on new technology, having helped out with everything from atomic weapons to the development of the Global Positioning System (GPS).[3] Its employees are not necessarily military officers – they're equally likely to be civilians, including mathematicians and physicists. The team who came up with onion routing were cut from just such cloth. The system they created meant that spies and others could piggyback on the existing Internet infrastructure, while dodging the surveillance applied to everyone else.

But once again, there was a snag. When you actually use this kind of three-layer encryption to surf the Web, it stands out like a sore thumb to anyone handling the traffic. It's easy for intermediary computers, and their owners, to single it out for extra scrutiny. Even if they can't crack the encryption immediately, they can beaver away at it over time, and the U.S. military didn't like that prospect.

In short, the U.S. spooks had invented a top-quality digital cloak to hide under, but it was made of neon fabric so bright that everyone could spot it. But what if everyone were wearing a neon cloak? That would make it impossible to spot the spies. If the NRL could somehow get onion routing adopted by the masses, then the spooks could slip in and hide among the crowd. To do this, the U.S. Navy techies needed a partner to help spread the word. And in an ironic twist they got one thanks to a man who'd been a thorn in the side of the U.S. government for decades: John Perry Barlow, lyricist for the band the Grateful Dead, Internet libertarian and co-founder of the Electronic Frontier Foundation (EFF). It was to this group that the NRL went for help in spreading the use of its new, online invisibility cloak. It's not as crazy as it sounds: the EFF supported freedom of speech and privacy, and the tech the NRL had created could prove invaluable in protecting whistle-blowers and dissidents as they moved around the Web – not to mention protecting ordinary users from the kind of online surveillance (both commercial and governmental) that is now near ubiquitous. Nonetheless, one can only imagine what those early meetings were like, as the NRL scientists from Washington, DC, rubbed shoulders with the anti-establishment EFF from San Francisco.

Working together, in 2003 the two organizations publicly released the code for Tor, as the triple-encryption onion routing system became known. They also made the code available for continuous public scrutiny. This so-called 'open source' approach was an important decision, as it countered the inevitable suspicion that any privacy technology invented by the U.S. military must be vulnerable to some kind of state surveillance. The Tor Project, which now oversees the software, actively invites techies to find problems in the code and report them, ensuring trust in the system. Today the Project estimates that more than two million people use the Tor browser so that they can visit websites without fear of being surveilled along the way.[4] People in repressive regimes from China to Iran try to use it to look at websites their governments would like to censor. Journalists use it to handle sensitive sources.

So far, so good. But that's not the story of the dark web that most people have heard. What about the drugs, guns, child abuse and financial crime? If the dark web is such a worthy tool for getting round censorship and surveillance, why does it have such a bad reputation? It's because of a feature that the developers of Tor built in from the early days of their experiment.

Using the Tor browser doesn't only allow you to visit normal websites like the BBC and CNN without being tracked. It also allows you to visit a special network of websites that are only viewable if you're using Tor. If you try to visit these sites using a normal browser you'll see an error message. That's because these special websites check whether their visitors are using Tor, and won't reveal their content to those who aren't. Most sites, of course, want to be found, so they make sure services like Google can see them. For dark website owners, it's exactly the opposite. These sites are called Hidden Services, and when you hear about the dark web being used for drugs, guns and images of child sexual abuse, it's these sites that are being referred to.

Just as the Internet and the World Wide Web operate on two different levels, so does the dark web. There is the triple-encrypted onion routing Internet system that you can use to visit normal sites while avoiding surveillance, but there is also the hidden web of sites to which it grants access. This twofold aspect has created a continual headache for supporters of Tor. They try their hardest to flag up the civil liberties case for surveillance-dodging onion routing (a service called SecureDrop, for example, is used by many big news outlets worldwide to link journalists with sources under the blanket of Tor).[5] But then the media (myself included) also frequently point to the mass of criminality that thrives on the dark web sites.

The awkward truth is, it didn't have to be this way. It might have been possible for the NRL to create the eminently defensible surveillance-avoiding onion routing, leaving out the ability to create the dark web sites that hide within it. They could have created Jekyll without conjuring up Hyde.

So why did Tor's creators do it?

Paul Syverson was one of the original team behind onion routing's development. He still works at the U.S. Naval Research

Laboratory, but he's no buttoned-up military type. His profile photo shows a stubbly, cheery character in a collarless shirt. He signs off his emails with 'aloha', and in our phone conversation he came across as a charming example of the breed of techies who forget their differences under the banner of computer code. Talking to him, the idea of meetings between the Navy folks and the Electronic Frontier Foundation didn't seem so weird.

I asked Syverson why they'd opted to create the Hidden Services sites, when it seemed so obvious they'd be used for criminality. He outlined some solid technical reasons: notably, if you don't have Hidden Services, then at some point you have to 'pop out' of Tor into the open Internet, at which point you're vulnerable to surveillance once more. If you keep the destination website hidden within Tor, you never have to tip your hand. But he then went on to give a more philosophical, and far more intriguing defence:

> Any time you have a new technology, the people on the fringes of society are often the people to explore it early on.
>
> I remember reading about how, in the early part of the previous century in Detroit, the police were very disturbed because criminals had this technology [which meant] when the police would show up at a crime scene, the criminals had just vanished. They had this nifty new technology called an 'automobile', and the police didn't have them.

Thank goodness, his argument goes, that we didn't ban cars.

There's an immediate problem with Syverson's rationale because it assumes technology is always neutral. What about a car that can hide its number plates from CCTV cameras and automatically deletes any DNA traces? If the technology you invent is so tailor-made for crime, how far can you push the technology-is-neutral argument? What's striking is that, in effect, Syverson and his Tor colleagues made a bet on humanity. They believed that although early adopters may exploit technology for antisocial aims, in the end, good will prevail.

Seen through this lens, the dark web is nothing less than a giant experiment in human behaviour. We've been handed a government-funded, top-quality invisibility cloak that allows us to operate online with impunity and to express ourselves, seemingly without fear of judgement. And what we do with that power of invisibility says as much about us, as humans, as it does about technology. Deep down, given a free choice and with no one watching, would you be good or bad?

As you'll see, the ensuing years of dark web evolution were as much a laboratory of ethics as they were of technology.

For years, the dark web trundled away in the background. But it became a global news story in mid-2011, thanks to a site that would become an iconic tale of extreme Internet libertarianism, unrestrained crime and police corruption. It would put the dark web on the map for good.

On 1 March 2011, an anonymous post appeared on a Bitcoin discussion forum:

Hi everyone, Silk Road is into it's [sic] third week after launch and I am very pleased with the results. There are several sellers and buyers finding mutually agreeable prices, and as of today, 28 transactions have been made![6]

It was a humble start for what would become the world's biggest dark web marketplace, eventually conducting 40,000 transactions a month and making headline news around the world.

Silk Road was a groundbreaking synthesis of two radical new technologies that happened to coincide with perfect timing. The dark web created a freely available, anonymized web publishing system where laws could be ignored under the cover of encryption; and Bitcoin seemingly gave its users an equally secretive method of payment. Just as credit cards had led to explosive growth in the Web, so Bitcoin was fuelling Silk Road's expansion.

By the time I visited the site in August 2011, it was a thriving community of illegal traders, mostly touting drugs. The site itself looked like a stripped-back version of eBay or Amazon. Dark web sites are often built using the same software as normal sites, and look no different. There was a list of products on the left-hand side, grouped into different types of drugs (stimulants, depressants, dissociatives). I'd installed the Tor browser to explore Silk Road for research on a story about it, but I soon began scanning other dark web sites. It wasn't easy because, as explained earlier, normal search engines don't work on the dark web. Links to other underground sites were shared in discussion forums on a digital word-of-mouth basis.

As I surfed, I felt a wave of nostalgia. This was what the Web used to be like. I'd worked for an Internet company during the late 1990s in the days when Google was unknown, and at that time, even though the Web was growing rapidly, it still felt as though you could get around all the major sites in a week or two by following links organically from site to site. In the ensuing years, the Web had boomed and was now almost unimaginable without search engines, which function as intermediaries between you and an online territory too vast to navigate alone. By contrast, the dark web seemed like a small, exclusive club – and exploring it was exciting.

Nonetheless, after we broadcast our story on Silk Road I believed, as did many, that the dark web and Bitcoin were crazy fringe experiments that probably wouldn't amount to much. Not for the first time, I was wrong.

Meanwhile, Silk Road was expanding rapidly, and it wasn't just journalists who were taking note.

In June 2011, U.S. Democratic Senator Charles Schumer held a press conference, lambasting Silk Road and calling for authorities to shut it down.[7] It would take two and a half years and multiple law enforcement operations to finally take out the site, but by that time the genie was out of the bottle, and it wouldn't return.

For its part, Silk Road claimed an intriguing *raison d'être*. The harm from drugs, the site's proponents argued, came mostly from two sources: first, the violence of drug gangs; and second, drugs that were dangerously tainted or sold without proper guidance (about safe dosage, for example). Operating online, they argued, solved the first problem because buyers and sellers never met, leaving no chance for violence. Postal services were used to dispatch the drugs and, incredibly, that often worked, with careful packaging used to conceal the true nature of the contents. But Silk Road also had an answer to the problem of tainted or mis-sold drugs, thanks to a feature it borrowed from the legitimate e-commerce world. Users of the site could leave reviews and ratings for sellers, just like on sites such as eBay. They could report bad experiences and, the argument went, dangerous sellers could be weeded out. Once logged into the site, a prospective buyer could click onto a seller's profile and immediately see a star rating for them, along with comments from previous buyers about the quality of the products, plus a 'stealth rating' as to how well they packaged the goods to avoid postal checks. There was even a doctor who contributed to the site's forum, issuing safety advice under the pseudonym Doctor X (who turned out to be a genial Spanish physician with an expertise in treating drug users).[8]

Of course, Silk Road's harm-reduction arguments only stretched so far: first, they conveniently ignored the violence that happens further up the chain of drug dealing, from slavery in the poppy fields to extortion in the shipyards. And second, harm isn't only caused by badly cut or poorly administered drugs: it's perfectly possible to ruin your life with carefully measured doses of top-quality heroin.

Nonetheless, for its users, Silk Road was pushing at an open door with these pro-drug claims, which were given extra force because they were backed by a charismatic leader who sat at the very top of the heap: the boss of Silk Road, who went by the pseudonym Dread Pirate Roberts.

The name alone was steeped in enigmatic backstory. It comes from a character in the 1987 fantasy film *The Princess Bride*. Dread Pirate Roberts was an identity which, according to the movie script, was handed down from pirate to pirate, an immortal persona belonging to multiple people.

The name suggested to Silk Road's users, and very probably to law enforcement too, that no sole individual controlled this massive online market, but instead a revolving team was running the site. In fact, Silk Road was indeed the creation of just one man. Furthermore, he genuinely believed in the libertarian ideals he was using to defend the drug trade. But as his business grew, he was increasingly dragged into the violent, lawless world of drug dealing. According to insiders on the site, it wasn't long before Dread Pirate Roberts abandoned his liberal notions and reverted to the dog-eat-dog morals of the underworld.

Early on in its evolution, a Silk Road user named 'Chronicpain' had begun helping out Dread Pirate Roberts. In real life, Chronicpain is Curtis Green, a barrel-chested American with an infectious laugh who seems to love recounting the drama of his involvement with the site. He belongs to a peculiar strain of cybercriminals I've interviewed: people who've inarguably been involved in very dodgy enterprises, but have somehow bounced along and come through it not only with their confidence intact, but with a story to tell that sets them up with a career.

Green says he joined the site because he was interested in drug harm reduction. He says he only ever helped with technical issues, and never had access to its accounts. Nonetheless, he was an administrator of a rapidly growing criminal enterprise. In the FBI's view Chronicpain was a senior member of the operation, and they saw him as a potential way into Silk Road.

One morning in January 2013, Green answered a knock on his door, and accepted from what looked like a postman a package which he soon discovered contained a kilogram of high-quality cocaine. Green claims he never ordered it, but on the basis that he'd received illegal drugs, FBI agents burst in moments later and took him off for questioning. Faced with a hefty jail sentence, Green agreed to cooperate with the Feds, but there was a problem: the police interrogation had taken Green away from his Silk Road duties for too long, and Dread Pirate Roberts (DPR) had become suspicious. At the same time, someone had started pilfering Bitcoins from Silk Road customers' funds. Believing (correctly, but for the wrong reasons) that Chronicpain had betrayed him, DPR decided to have him killed. It was a striking turnaround for someone who'd espoused dark web drug trading as a violence-free solution.

DPR tasked another close adviser, whom he knew on Silk Road by the pseudonym Nob, to arrange the hit. Nob had also become a senior administrator on the site, counselling DPR as the site's boss battled scammers and attackers. Nob claimed to have underworld connections. Initially DPR tasked him to find someone to give Chronicpain a roughing up. But as paranoia kicked in, DPR decided more drastic action was needed. He wrote a series of online messages to Nob:

> ok, so can you change the order to execute rather than torture?
>   Never killed a man or had one killed before, but it is the right move in this case
>   how much will it cost?
>   ballpark?
>   less than $100k?[9]

Nob agreed to find someone to carry out the execution. But unfortunately for DPR, in reality Nob wasn't a drug runner with underworld connections. He was in fact an undercover U.S. Drug Enforcement Agency officer who was part of a task force that had been circling and gradually infiltrating Silk Road.

The FBI now had a problem. Nob had agreed to get the murder done, and DPR demanded photographic evidence. The solution was for law enforcement officials to fake Curtis Green's death.

'They waterboarded me,' recalls Green. 'It was a fake water-board, I guess you call it a dunking, which was traumatic. Even though it was fake, you have to kind of be there to understand.' He goes on,

> They took pictures of them killing me, basically. And then later on, noticed they didn't take pictures of me being dead. So me and my wife at home staged photos of me being dead. I got some soup and put it all over me, [so] it looked like I had thrown up. It looked pretty realistic, and I lay down on the floor in a weird position, eyes kind of half open. It looked like I had died. They were pretty darn good photos.

With Green on their side, the FBI had turned a key member of Silk Road. Multiple law enforcement agencies were now involved in the task force and were edging closer to its shadowy boss. But one of the biggest factors in the capture of Dread Pirate Roberts came down to a very basic principle of online life: the Internet never forgets.

For humans, time and relevance are often bound together. Mundane events become less important to us as they fade into the past. Computers don't think like that; for them, time is merely another data field. For a machine something done or said many years ago, no matter how inconsequential to us, is as relevant as what happened in the last minute. And more importantly, it can all be retrieved instantly. We all make mistakes in our past: moments that we're not proud of and would rather forget. But as we digitize our world, our ability to put the past behind us diminishes, and for the man behind Silk Road, that would have disastrous consequences.

Years before the arrest that would eventually take down the world's biggest dark web site, in January 2011 a user calling himself 'altoid' had posted on an online drug forum, directing readers to a blog about Silk Road. It was almost certainly the first time the site had been mentioned online. The FBI found this post, started looking for other postings by the same pseudonym and came across one from later that year (ironically, it was asking for IT help). This time, the post contained an email address: altoid was asking people to contact him at rossulbricht@gmail.com.[10]

The FBI served Google with a warrant, asking for all the IP addresses that had logged into that Gmail account, and discovered repeated access from an Internet cafe in Hickory Street in San Francisco (it seems the owner of the world's biggest dark web site had neglected to use Tor, the dark web software, to access his Gmail account). Meanwhile, the FBI had gained another new lead. They had visited Silk Road and refreshed the page again and again, analysing the site's code and the Tor connection in the hope of finding a clue. Through this painstaking process they had found out the location of the computer server where the Silk Road website was stored. They requested a copy of the server's contents and gained a treasure trove of information.

The owner of Silk Road had been careful to log into the server using a Virtual Private Network (VPN), a system that promises to hide a user's true location. But the FBI simply subpoenaed the VPN company and discovered (even though the Silk Road owner had tried to delete them) records showing a login from Laguna Street, 150 metres away from Hickory Street, the address from which the Gmail address was being logged into.

The net was closing in on the FBI's suspect.

But the final piece of the jigsaw was, as cops are fond of saying, 'down to good, solid police work'. In July 2013, U.S. Customs seized a package inbound from Canada containing fake ID documents. The recipient was one Ross Ulbricht with an address in San Francisco. Dread Pirate Roberts had been unmasked. Law enforcement had confirmed his name, and perhaps more importantly, discovered his address.

Behind his Silk Road persona, 29-year-old Ulbricht appeared a sunny, intelligent and handsome young man. He was raised in Austin, Texas, and had graduated from the state's university with a physics degree. In an online video apparently made before Silk

Road's creation, he chatted eruditely about his desire to change the world. It was a goal he would achieve, though almost certainly not in the way anyone expected.

According to FBI documents published when Ulbricht was arrested, between February 2011 and July 2013 there were approximately 1.2 million transactions completed on Silk Road, across almost a million user accounts. Based on Bitcoin's value at the time of Ulbricht's arrest, the site made around $1.2 billion in revenue and $79.8 million in commissions.[11] Dread Pirate Roberts sat at the heart of a sprawling and immensely profitable drug empire.

The police began a surveillance operation on the San Fransisco addresses and discovered that Ulbricht used a local library. To swoop in and arrest him looked like an easy option, but in order to make a prosecution stick, law enforcement needed to catch Ulbricht red-handed, grabbing him – and his laptop – while he was logged into Silk Road's servers as Dread Pirate Roberts. There was a considerable risk that DPR had his laptop rigged so that when he closed the lid, the contents would be encrypted. If Ulbricht had even a few seconds' warning of his arrest, he might kill the evidence and undo months of police work.

On 1 October 2013, undercover FBI agents followed him to the library, one of whom sat opposite Ulbricht as he opened his laptop and logged in. At that moment, Ulbricht was distracted by a loud argument between two library users (in reality, also undercover cops). Across the table, the agent seized Ulbricht's laptop and handed it off to a colleague, still unlocked and showing Ulbricht logged into the Dread Pirate Roberts master account on Silk Road.[12]

On 29 May 2015, Ross Ulbricht was sentenced to life in prison for distributing narcotics, engaging in a criminal enterprise, computer hacking, money laundering and trafficking false identity documents.[13] His mother continues to campaign hard for his release, alleging that critical exonerating evidence was prevented from being shown in court, and that her son's sentence is disproportionate. Curtis Green ultimately ended up serving two days in prison, with four years of supervised release. However, there were no charges against Ulbricht related to the hiring of a hitman to kill him.

But there was a remarkable postscript to the takedown of Silk Road. A few months after Ulbricht's sentencing there was another court appearance. This time it was Carl Force, the undercover DEA agent who'd masqueraded as Nob, the 'drug smuggler with underworld connections' who organized Curtis Green's 'execution'. Wrapped up in his undercover identity, Force had gone haywire. Not only had he stolen $700,000 from the site and extorted Ulbricht for tens of thousands of dollars more, he'd also offered through another online identity to sell Ulbricht leaked information on the law enforcement investigation into Silk Road.

In addition, according to the U.S. Department of Justice: 'Force also admitted to entering into a $240,000 contract with 20th Century Fox Film Studios related to a film concerning the government's investigation into the Silk Road.'[14] He and a Secret Service agent, Shaun Bridges, were each jailed for six years. Bridges had stolen $820,000 from Silk Road's coffers.[15] It was an ignoble epilogue to a multi-agency law enforcement investigation that spanned years and took down a criminal website that considered itself beyond the law.

One of the most remarkable things about the whole Silk Road story is that, at the time of writing, no one has yet turned it into a Hollywood movie. But in real life, no sooner was Ulbricht arrested than the sequel to Silk Road began.

Within a month of the demise of the original site, Silk Road 2.0 was up and running, with its owner promising new and improved security. That turned out to be a rash claim – its owner was arrested in November 2014 – but it didn't stop the emergence of a slew of copycat sites. Law enforcement had cut off one of the Hydra's heads, but the publicity around Silk Road ensured a constant flow of successors.

Even though they could not be found using traditional search engines, links to the new marketplaces began to appear on discussion sites dedicated to the dark web. No doubt spurred on by the millions of dollars Silk Road had made in commission, the glut of new dark web sites vied for supremacy, among them Black Market Reloaded, Sheep Market, Evolution, Russian Anonymous Marketplace and dozens more. Almost universally, their layout looked practically identical to that of Silk Road – after all, they weren't competing for who had the flashiest design, but were fighting over something much more important: trust. As the dark web morphed in the following years, this single issue would become the key battleground for both the cybercriminals and the police who hunted them.

Many users of the original Silk Road had, at heart, put their faith in Dread Pirate Roberts, whose self-confident leadership had convinced them the site was secure. The longer Silk Road survived, the more convincing his argument became. Then came Ulbricht's arrest. Dark web users would no longer place their faith in the abilities of one person (or even persona). They started demanding credible solutions to a fundamental problem that the criminal dark web sites faced all along: in a world inhabited by crooks, how can you create the trust that underpins trade?

The systems the sites came up with once again mirrored those of the legitimate e-commerce websites. In addition to user reviews, many of the new dark web marketplaces now adopted an escrow system (first trialled by Silk Road). Buyers and sellers would agree a transaction, and the money would be paid into a Bitcoin wallet owned by the dark web site, only to be released once the deal was fulfilled. It was a dark web twist on the 'money back guarantee' offered by sites like eBay. It also gave the underground sites a handy source of revenue, because they took a percentage of the escrow transactions.

And it wasn't just illegal drugs and hacked information being traded as the dark web flourished. It had been long assumed its anonymity made it a natural home for paedophile networks, but few really knew the scale of child sexual abuse activity until in 2015 a group of researchers at Portsmouth University set out to get an overview of the world of hidden sites. They signed up to become one of the computers carrying dark web traffic, a so-called 'node'. There is no vetting procedure for such nodes: anyone who installs the right software and waits long enough will find themselves a conduit for dark web traffic. As the information flowed across their machine, the university's researchers gradually built up a picture of many of the hidden sites that make up the dark web.

When the researchers pulled together their figures, they made a disturbing discovery: they stated more than 80 per cent of dark web traffic was going to sites which had names that left the researchers in little doubt that they were being used to peddle sexual abuse material, much of it related to children.[16] For the lead researcher, Gareth Owenson, the discovery was very uncomfortable.

> Our initial hopes were that we might find out that it was largely used for what it was claimed, for some of the reasons it was promoted as being used for [such as avoiding censorship]. We probably suspected deep down that drugs may be by far the most popular category. We knew that there would be some child abuse sites. We certainly didn't expect to see the quantity we found, and to say we were stunned would be pretty accurate.

There are alternative explanations for why Owenson and his team found so much traffic going to such sites: law enforcement, for example, often visit them as part of their investigations. In addition, anti-child-abuse campaigners sometimes inundate the sites with traffic to try and knock them offline – such floods of malicious traffic could be misinterpreted as genuine visits. And it's worth remembering that the entire dark web represents only a tiny fraction of the Internet, and so in terms of total volume, there is almost certainly far more of this material on the open web. Experts from the UK's Internet Watch Foundation, a body funded by tech companies and the European Union to find and remove such material, say they are equally engaged with finding child sexual abuse content on sites on the open, non-dark web.[17]

For their part, many dark web site owners themselves often do not want to host child sexual abuse material. Their reasons are as much prosaic as moral. Any site hosting this kind of material quickly appears on the radars of law enforcement agencies worldwide, not to mention scores of vigilante hackers. Even in the morally bankrupt world of online crime, many crooks consider dealing in child abuse beyond the pale. Dark web sites don't have extensive terms and conditions for their users, but 'no child porn' is a very common entry.

Yet, ironically, the more scarce and toxic child sexual abuse material is, the more lucrative it becomes. How lucrative is hard to say, because it's an area that investigative journalists find almost impossible to explore. There are many links on the dark web that appear to lead to images of child sexual abuse, but investigating them without breaking the law is almost impossible. Even accidentally stumbling on such images is a crime, because as soon as the image appears on your screen you've committed an offence, whether you intended to call it up or not. There are good reasons for this harsh legal approach: no one wants a world in which 'research' can be used as cover by paedophiles. However, it raises the risk that without rigorous journalistic interrogation, online paedophilia can be used as a bogeyman by law enforcement (sometimes in pursuit of budget) and government (sometimes in pursuit of regulation).

By 2016 there were estimated to be upwards of 40,000 dark web sites, and around two million people using the Tor browser – although not all, of course, were using it to visit criminal dark web sites. Ever since the former NSA contractor Edward Snowden had revealed the scale of U.S. and UK governments' online surveillance in June 2013, usage of Tor has been growing among those wishing to reclaim their digital privacy.[18]

Among the criminal dark web users, though, drugs were still a key driver. Bitcoin ATMs were popping up in corner-shops and cafes where cash could be converted into the digital currency. The Tor browser took only a few minutes to download and install. Arguably, it was now easier to obtain drugs than it had ever been. Word of the narcotic nirvana spread across college campuses and pounding nightclubs (assisted, of course, by coverage from journalists, which helped raise awareness of the dark web drug trade).

The Global Drug Survey, a study of 100,000 self-selecting participants, found record numbers using the dark web. One in ten users bought through encrypted marketplaces and, of them, one in twenty had never used drugs prior to finding the dark web's e-commerce wonderland.[19] But for some, the boom was proving fatal, and the casualties were starting to mount up.

Brothers Jacques and Torin Lakeman were aged nineteen and twenty when they travelled to Manchester to attend a football match together in late 2014. Inseparable as children, they'd moved out of the family home on the Isle of Man a few years before and were looking forward to a reunion. To liven up their night, Torin had bought powdered ecstasy on the dark web.

Their father Ray bursts with pride when talking about his two boys. He brings up a YouTube video of them playing in a band, and waxes lyrical about their musical talents and where they hoped it might take them. But as he recounts what happened next, Ray Lakeman's voice quietens.

He tried to call Torin and Jacques after the match, but there was no answer. As the hours ticked by he made the series of phonecalls every parent dreads: the police, then local hotels they might have checked into, then hospitals. By the time two officers called at his house, he and his wife had begun to fear the worst. The police told the couple that their only sons had been found dead in a hotel near Manchester. Staff had found the room locked. It seemed the brothers had died quickly, not even able to reach the door, let alone call for help. Toxicology reports revealed they'd taken five or six times the fatal dose of the drug.

As Ray Lakeman struggled to cope with the loss of his only kids, he also fought to understand the new, anonymizing tech that had made obtaining the ecstasy relatively easy. He now campaigns for Anyone's Child, a charity calling for drugs to be legally regulated rather than outlawed.

When police investigated the Lakeman brothers' deaths, they discovered that Torin had bought the drugs from a dark web dealer called Stone Island, but with only this pseudonym to go on, the police told Ray they were unlikely to make much progress in tracking him down. Eighteen months later, however, Stone Island was brought to justice, and the facts around his case illuminate just how lucrative the dark web drug trade had become in the years after Silk Road's dramatic rise and fall.

In May 2016, UK Border Force officials intercepted two parcels on their way from Holland to Portsmouth. They looked like boxes containing jigsaws, but inside was a different kind of puzzle for the police investigators: 11,000 ecstasy tablets.

Police removed the drugs, switched the tablets for harmless pills and an undercover officer delivered the parcel to its destination: a terraced house in a sleepy street a mile or so from Portsmouth Harbour. Once the parcel had been taken in, an arrest team swooped. Running out of the back door, they found 24-year-old Kurt Lai Lan, the true face of the dark web drug dealer known as Stone Island.

As police uncovered the details of Lai Lan's finances, it became clear just how profitable his dark web drug trading had been. There was a Harrods account showing hundreds of pounds spent in its perfume department. Three hundred thousand pounds was discovered in a Bitcoin wallet. He'd recently placed an order for an £80,000 Mercedes. In the bedroom of the little Portsmouth house there were boxes and boxes of high-end shoes from the likes of Gucci and Louboutin, many still in their wrappers. It seemed that as the Lakeman brothers died in a Manchester hotel room, Kurt Lai Lan was stockpiling designer footwear he hardly, if ever, wore. The prosecution could not prove that he sold the brothers their fatal dose of ecstasy, however, and Lai Lan's lawyer argued there was no 'causal link' to their deaths. On other charges though, Lai Lan was sentenced to sixteen years in prison.[20]

But convictions like this one did little to deter other dark web dealers, who were perhaps more impressed by Lai Lan's Harrods lifestyle than his jail sentence. Even as Lai Lan began his prison term, dealers were embracing a new drug that would prove very popular on the dark web and, for some, fatal in the real world.

Fentanyl is a synthetic opioid, meaning it's made in a lab but aims to replicate the effects of the opium poppy's by-products. It's a hundred times more potent than morphine, meaning the chances of an overdose are terrifyingly high, especially given the dealers' tactic of slipping it into other products such as ecstasy.[21] In addition, chemists have tinkered with the formula to produce dozens of strains, each with a different degree of potency, making safe dosage a game of Russian roulette.

The fentanyl craze on the dark web took place within the context of a much wider opioid abuse problem, particularly in the u.s., with pharmaceutical companies pushing powerful pain-killers, creating addicts who sought out illegal sources when their legitimately prescribed supply ran out. The UK wasn't immune either: 75 people died from overdoses of the drug in 2017, even as deaths from related narcotics like heroin and morphine declined.[22]

Dark web vendors continued to cash in. Tech security company Flashpoint found that mentions of fentanyl rose twentyfold on the dark web in the two years to March 2017.[23]

As fentanyl sales increased, some dealers became increasingly callous in their efforts to profit from the boom. Dark web marketplaces allowed anyone to set up shop, hiding behind compelling sales pitches, bargain basement prices and eye-catching brand names.

Among them was a vendor called 'Savage Henry'. On one of the main dark web marketplaces during this era, he offered

'China White', another name for fentanyl, alongside tempting user reviews. Savage Henry looked as reputable as any other vendor, and soon attracted buyers. In reality, the two people behind the operation were dangerously incompetent criminals who, it seems, knew that fentanyl was killing people but carried on regardless. When police raided the squalid flat used by Ross Brennan and Aarron Gledhill, they found a copy of a book called *Chemistry for Dummies*. The pair had apparently used it to work out how to mix the drug with other narcotics such as crystal meth and cocaine.

Four people who bought from Brennan and Gledhill died, according to prosecutors. During the investigation police found a Skype message in which Brennan told Gledhill he knew there were 'bodies out there on me'. But in an echo of the Lakeman brothers' case, no direct link between the defendants and the deaths could be proven and they were not prosecuted in connection with them.

Both men pleaded guilty to offences of importing and supplying drugs. Brennan was jailed for thirteen years, Gledhill for three years and nine months.[24]

It would be wrong to paint the cases of the Lakeman brothers and Brennan and Gledhill's fentanyl factory as typical. For many drug users the dark web was and still is a place where they can find a reliable dealer selling high-quality narcotics and get their weekend off to a flying start. But it's also fair to say that with a cornucopia of sites and growing competition for buyers, there were plenty of dealers prepared to sell dangerous drugs to make a fast buck with fatal consequences. In the end, several of the main dark web marketplaces added fentanyl to their list of banned products – perhaps out of moral repugnance, but perhaps because a dead customer isn't as profitable as a live one.[25]

Nonetheless, by 2017 law enforcement agencies around the world were facing a chaotic problem: in the four years since the demise of Silk Road, sites on the dark web were continuing to trade with seeming impunity.

Law enforcement needed a new approach, and if they were going to do serious damage to the criminal underworld they would need to hit the issue of trust that has threaded its way through this whole chapter. Dark web sites had succeeded in building it up – could the police knock it down?

Bas Doorn now runs a tech security company in the Netherlands called Keyn that aims to replace passwords with something more effective and less tempting for thieves. He's thirty years old but looks barely out of college. He would have looked even younger when he first started working as an intern for the Dutch National Prosecutor's office in 2014, in the wake of the Silk Road takedown. In person, he seems more likely to be running an artisanal coffee shop or an indie record label than investigating cybercriminals.

With a degree in information technology and a masters in criminology, Doorn had been researching the shifting scene of the dark web marketplaces. He'd watched the previous take-downs, including the original Silk Road bust, and noticed a depressing trend: as each site got raided by police, users would simply switch to the next biggest marketplace. Doorn called it the 'waterbed effect': jump on one bit, and you simply move the problem elsewhere. If Doorn and his colleagues wanted to under-mine the trust that the dark web had built up, they'd have to hit multiple parts of the waterbed at once – perhaps even causing it to spring a leak.

In 2016, by far the largest dark web marketplace was AlphaBay. Its name was a riff on one of the world's biggest e-commerce sites, and its aspirations were no less grand. AlphaBay was a sprawling den of every kind of illegal product, and key to its success was that it combined two of the biggest drivers of dark web crime: drugs and stolen data. AlphaBay was where traders in hacked databases and forged identity documents rubbed shoulders with heroin dealers. And it had also proved remarkably resilient for its estimated 400,000 users, staying online for two years – a long time in the dark web world.[26]

But AlphaBay's days were numbered. Once again, it was a relatively simple slip-up that led to the site's demise; and just like Silk Road it was a mistakenly revealed email address that helped lead police to their target.

The FBI had been making test purchases on AlphaBay, hoping they could track the site's owners through the communications being sent. New users received a welcome email, and when FBI agents dug into the data behind the message they discovered an email address. It belonged to a Canadian called Alexandre Cazes. He had a high-profile lifestyle, with a fleet of luxury cars, millions of dollars dotted around various accounts, and a string of properties in Thailand, his adopted home country. With a target in their sights, the FBI began circling AlphaBay.

At the same time, Doorn and his team in the Netherlands had received a lucky break: a tip-off about another dark web site called Hansa which, though not as big as AlphaBay, was a serious contender for the number two spot and had also evaded law enforcement's clutches for several years. The tip-off led the Dutch police to Hansa's computer servers in Germany, and from there local police were able to put names to the site's two administrators.

At this stage, one option was to arrest Hansa's bosses, shut down the site and try to hoover up as much information as possible as the rats left Hansa's sinking ship. But Doorn and his colleagues had a more radical plan. With access to Hansa's servers, and with the site's administrators about to be arrested, it was possible for the Dutch police to take over the entire site.

It was an unprecedented move. Previously, police had infiltrated criminal sites and even taken on senior roles within them. Taking over the entire business was, as far as we're aware, a step into the unknown. Legal approval was granted, but only for a few weeks.

Meanwhile, quite by chance, Doorn learned that the U.S. authorities were preparing to move in on AlphaBay. The Americans had discovered that some of the site's servers were in the Netherlands,

CRIMEDOTCOM   178

and went to the Dutch for permission to access them. Word spread, and when Doorn discovered AlphaBay was about to be closed, a golden opportunity presented itself.

'We hoped that they could do the takedown while we were controlling Hansa market, and that people would flock toward Hansa, being an alternative for AlphaBay,' says Doorn. In short, it was the perfect chance to hit the waterbed in two places at once.

Operation Bayonet was born, and the clock was ticking. The Americans wanted to shut down AlphaBay and the Germans wanted to arrest Hansa's administrators. Doorn and his colleagues needed to create a copy of Hansa and move the entire site to the Netherlands where it could be managed. It wasn't as simple as copying and pasting the code, however. Doorn had to take the site apart and rebuild it. And his team couldn't afford to make any mistakes as they reconstructed Hansa. If the site's users suspected for a moment that something was up (if the site crashed, for example), word would spread like wildfire and the chance to snare thousands of dealers and customers would be lost.

To complicate matters, transactions were being conducted constantly on Hansa, so the switchover between the criminal version and the police re-creation would need to run seamlessly. Any glitches might cause a discrepancy or failed transaction that would raise the alarm.

Doorn battled to understand and re-create the code, and over a fraught two days he and his colleagues gradually moved the entire Hansa website piece by piece onto the Dutch Prosecutor's servers, while its users seemingly remained oblivious.

On 5 July, AlphaBay's owner Cazes was arrested in Bangkok. A week later, he was found dead in his cell. Thai and U.S. police said he had committed suicide.[27] As the news leaked out, panic ensued among AlphaBay's criminal community of buyers and sellers. But as in previous takedowns, many simply switched to the next best option – and for most that meant Hansa.

Thousands flocked to the site, oblivious to the fact they were now conducting their criminal trade on a site controlled by the

Dutch authorities. So large was the influx of Hansa users (an eight-fold increase, according to Europol)[28] that for a short time Doorn had to close it to new members while he desperately tweaked the site's code to handle the traffic. Not only were he and his team running a dark web crime site, they were now optimizing it.

That wasn't their only task as newly installed administrators. Hansa had a helpdesk function whereby users could raise complaints and report faults. To give the impression that the site was functioning as normal, a team of Dutch police were tasked with answering computer support queries known as 'tickets'. 'We had a team that worked on handling tickets,' recalls Doorn. 'People were sending tickets because, for example an order didn't work, or they were complaining that someone wasn't paying, or pointing out some bug. Then we just had to fix it and send them an answer.'

Dutch authorities were also carefully screening every transaction that went through Hansa, aware of the risk that they could be accused of entrapment, or even of enabling a horrific crime while they were in charge of the site.

A full-scale digital surveillance operation was mounted on the thousands of users flocking to the site. Members logging into Hansa had their username and password captured, potentially opening up more lines of inquiry. If those members had ill-advisedly used the same password elsewhere, for example, it might allow law enforcement to apply for access to their other accounts, potentially revealing their real-life identities. In addition, Doorn and his colleagues subtly changed the site's messaging system. Hansa had offered its users inbuilt encryption, so that when they messaged each other about their dealings in drugs or stolen data, their communications would be scrambled by Hansa. Doorn's team turned the encryption off. Anyone who relied on Hansa's encryption to send messages with their home addresses or identities (and that was quite a lot of people) would have those details harvested by the police.

The exercise continued for three weeks before the Dutch team finally let the hammer fall. Joint press conferences were held in the

Netherlands and the u.s., revealing the pincer movement that had snared customers of both AlphaBay and Hansa. For dark web users already spooked by AlphaBay's closure, the fear was palpable. Doubt seeped through the community. If they moved to another site, what's to say it wasn't another law enforcement trap?

The intel gathered by the Dutch investigators was parcelled up and distributed to police forces worldwide. It's not possible to put a number on the convictions that occurred as a result, because many prosecutions are still being conducted, some of which are not solely based on evidence from the joint u.s.–Dutch operation. But it's beyond doubt that Operation Bayonet had (at least temporarily) a devastating effect on dark web users' trust in the criminal marketplaces, and is seen by many as a major victory for the global police effort to tackle online crime. Ironically, though, it may also have driven the crooks towards a new technology that some experts fear may prove even harder for law enforcement to crack.[29]

I met Karen in a church hall in Biggleswade, a small town about an hour's train ride from central London. I needed somewhere quiet for our interview, and on a busy Friday night the local church was the only option. She was nervous, and even though she's in her thirties she brought her dad along for our interview.

Her concerns were understandable: two weeks previously I'd contacted Karen out of the blue to tell her I had her password, credit card number, bank details and home address. It had taken some time to convince her I was a legitimate journalist and not a scam artist. I'd been investigating where crime had moved after the dark web takedowns, and the trail had led me to a new type of secure technology.

After Operation Bayonet, the cybercriminals didn't simply shut up shop. Instead, they moved with the times, and embraced the mobile phone revolution. A new breed of highly secure phone apps has become the next outlet for traders who might previously have turned to the dark web. There are still plenty of dark web sites, but the vendors who inhabit them have changed their tactics. Increasingly they are used simply as shopfronts where goods are advertised. The actual deals are often now done through apps. The crooks feel more comfortable using them because they contain a new form of encryption.

Before we continue with Karen's story, now is a good a time to talk about how encryption works. You're probably using it already without even knowing it.

The best way to think about encryption is through the analogy of padlocks and keys. If I want to send you a secret message, I put it in a box, padlock it and send it to you. But then, of course, I also need to send you the key to unlock it, and that's where the risks come. No matter how strong I make the padlock, if the key gets intercepted en route, then it's game over for our secret communication. Furthermore, even if the key reaches you safely, I'm reliant on you to keep it safe and not get burgled or somehow coerced into surrendering it.

The challenge of how to swap keys safely has been a thorn in the side of privacy obsessives for years. The solution came, like many pivotal tech developments, from a change of outlook as much as a change of technology. Instead of sending you the key, what if I send you the open padlock? Under this system, you put your secret message in the box, lock it with my padlock and send it back to me. Anyone intercepting the box won't be able to unlock it. And because I hang on to the key at all times, I can be sure it hasn't been lost, copied or stolen. Likewise, when I want to respond to your message, you send me an open padlock, I use it to lock my response in a box and send it to you. You unlock it with your key, safe in the knowledge that it's never left your possession. What's more, I can hand out as many duplicate padlocks as I like, because I know there's only one key for them and it's always in my hands. I can give out my padlocks on the street if I want to, with my home address attached. Suddenly anyone can send messages to me securely.

The more astute reader will have spotted a flaw in this scheme. If someone can intercept the padlocked box, can't they sculpt a key to fit the lock? In the physical world that's certainly a risk. Given enough time a good locksmith can make a new key for most locks. But in the world of computers, things work differently.

In the tech world, the keys and padlocks are just strings of numbers. When my computer receives the locked box from you, it takes the number representing the padlock, and combines it with the number representing my key. The encryption software checks the result, and if it's correct, it unlocks the box, unscrambling the message. Sure, someone might intercept the locked box, pull out the padlock number and start trying different combinations of key numbers to get the right answer. Good luck to them. Even the most basic encryption keys are now so complex they're hundreds of digits long. There are so many possible combinations that even the most powerful computers would take a very, very long time to try them all. In short: by the time you break the code, it's too late. Used correctly, such encryption technology is close to uncrackable. This neat solution to secrecy is called 'public key' encryption, and it was such a leap forward that when it was made available to the public, the man behind it was immediately put under criminal investigation.

In 1991, an American named Phil Zimmermann created a program that harnessed the padlock-led encryption system. In the spirit of self-deprecating techies' humour he called it Pretty Good Privacy or PGP. At the time, this kind of strong encryption tech was so potent that the u.s. government regarded it as a form of weapon and, as such, it was controlled under the Arms Export Act. So when the code for PGP started turning up in foreign countries, the u.s. Customs Service went after Zimmermann.

The charges were eventually dropped, however, and PGP became free for anyone to use.[30] But it was fiddly. Users needed to have software to create their digital padlock and key combinations. They needed to store their private key securely and distribute their public padlock code widely. And in order to send messages to others, they needed to download their public padlock code. All in all, it was a faff. Tech security folks loved the idea of public key encryption, but making it work on a wide scale was a nightmare. And as time went on, most people didn't feel the need to bother dealing with encryption, because they had a far more convenient security solution: they thought they could rely on someone else to do the work.

People sending messages through Gmail, Facebook, Twitter and other services were given the impression that encryption was all taken care of. That's because the tech companies promised they would encrypt the message from the sender to their servers, and then protect it again from their servers to the recipient, so that no one could intercept it en route. Of course, the tech companies also kept a copy of the message on their server, but it was under lock and key, they said, and only someone with a proper warrant could come and get it. The tech companies fostered an atmosphere of trust, and as a result they sat in the middle of millions of conversations, holding a master key.

That atmosphere of trust began to dissolve after the Snowden leaks. In 2013, the former National Security Agency contractor-turned-whistle-blower revealed that tech companies had been used, secretly but legally, by the u.s. government to give unprecedented access to the communications of some of their billions of users.[31] Overnight, the drawbacks of trusting a central key-holder were exposed. For the tech companies, it was traumatic. On the one hand, their legal counsels were telling them they needed to comply with secret government orders for interception; but from a PR perspective, their users were now angry and distrustful.

For some tech firms the solution to this dilemma was to remove themselves from the equation, and to do so they turned to the kind of public key encryption Phil Zimmermann had worked on. Using mobile phone apps, the tech companies (notably WhatsApp, now owned by Facebook, and Apple's iMessage) implemented a system whereby users stored their own keys to their own communications. Using this 'end-to-end encryption', no longer would the tech company sit in the middle with a skeleton key to unlock all the messages when law enforcement came knocking. From now on, the only people who could ever see the messages would be the sender and the recipient. Law enforcement agencies could hit the tech companies with as many warrants as they liked; the tech firms had no way to read the messages, so they could reply to such police inquiries with a polite shrug. If pushed, they would hand over a soup of encrypted data.

Soon, the ability to create end-to-end encrypted apps spread way beyond the big players, spawning a string of apps that you've probably never heard of: Wickr, Dust, Signal, Threema, Silent Phone, Telegram and others. All of them used some twist on end-to-end encryption. For cybercriminals deflated by intrusions into the dark web, this was fertile new territory. End-to-end encryption offered a blanket of secrecy, but without the centralized power-broker that had proved so fatal to Silk Road, AlphaBay and Hansa. What's more, for potential customers the encrypted apps were even easier to find and use than the dark web. They were available in Apple's App Store and Google's Play Store. Anyone could download them for free onto any smartphone in a matter of seconds.

Of course, for many users these apps are not a gateway to crime, but rather a way of communicating conveniently and with less fear of surveillance, which is why they are available in the app stores. But for cybercriminals plying their trade, they have proved a boon. Apps like Telegram contain group conversations where stolen financial information and drugs are being traded. Users can simply search for a group and tap a link to join in the chat, often with no questions asked.

For criminals, it's a perfect combination: they can advertise their wares in these public groups, but do the deals in private behind end-to-end encryption.

It was on such a group that I found Karen's information. There were dozens of sellers offering UK credit card data, and the going rate was around $25 per card. But incredibly, Karen's details were being handed out for free by one criminal as a 'teaser' to promote his business. What he was giving away wasn't just a stolen credit card number. It was Karen's entire digital identity: her full name, email address, mobile number, home address, credit card number with three-digit cvv security code, bank account and sort code and even her mother's maiden name. It was all the information needed to assume her identity, and would allow anyone to pass the checks carried out over the phone by banks, insurers, doctors' surgeries and more.

For my part, I was convinced the information was fake. In all my research on the dark web I'd never seen such valuable personal data being handed out for free. But when I showed it to Karen, her face froze. It turned out that the data was real.

After I contacted Telegram, they deleted the group that was offering Karen's details (nonetheless, I've changed her identity as a precaution). The company also said it carries out proactive searches to prevent such abuse.

Some security researchers believe these encrypted apps could take over from the dark web as the cybercriminals' main sales tool. If this is the case, it potentially poses an even bigger challenge for police than the dark web era. On one level, it's easier for police to track down the people who build these apps because they're often legitimate businesses (the chief executive of Telegram, Pavel Durov, for example, is a public figure who has accounts on social media sites like Instagram and LinkedIn). But when police approach them, even with the right warrants, the app providers can simply shrug their shoulders and point out that users' communications are encrypted beyond even their power to see.

Such encrypted communications technology has come a long way since the creation of the dark web at the turn of the millennium. It started out as an experiment in freedom of expression cooked up by techies. In the eyes of groups like the Electronic Frontier Foundation, dark web technology was a vital tool for fighting censorship and surveillance, and that continues to be true today. But the bald truth is that significant parts of the dark web are dominated by organized cybercrime. As pointed out by Paul Syverson, one of the inventors of dark web software, the first adopters of new technology are often on the fringes of society, criminals among them.

In the next chapter we will see how that same trend played out within another Internet group: so-called 'hacktivists'. The tools pioneered by an online protest movement ended up subsumed into cybercrime. And they would be used to target the very heart of the Internet technology that increasingly keeps modern society running.

SEVEN

THE INTERNET
HATE MACHINE

Peyia is a pretty little town on the west coast of Cyprus, popular with British expats who like the sun, the cheap living and the fact the locals also drive on the left.

It was from here in November 2016 that Daniel Kaye set out to destroy an entire country's Internet connection. Using his mobile phone, he typed in some commands and thousands of miles away phones and laptops started grinding to a halt, starved of the flow of communications that are the lifeblood of modern social and economic existence. Meanwhile, Kaye stuffed $10,000 of cash into his suitcase and set off for the UK.

To understand how this thirty-year-old hacker ended up almost demolishing an entire country's Internet link, and why there are dozens more like him, you have to take a bizarre and occasionally unsettling journey through online trolling, video game culture, juvenile betrayal and the Guy Fawkes-mask-clad hacker movement that came to be known as Anonymous.

The roots of the Anonymous movement lie in a discussion website called 4chan, which launched in 2003. For the uninitiated (and that's most of us) it's a bewildering barrage of infighting, in-jokes and catchy, captioned images called 'memes'. It's mesmerizing to watch, as reams of communication flood across its servers in a blink-and-you-miss-it hurricane of chat.

The site is grouped into different interest categories, but it's the 'random' board that's attracted most attention. Irreverent, capricious and often obscene, this section has become notorious, and was once branded 'the asshole of the Internet'.[1] It's also a bastion of what's called troll culture.

Internet trolling is hard to summarize, and anyone who attempts a definition will almost certainly be attacked by trolls. As Whitney Phillips points out in her book *This Is Why We Can't Have Nice Things*, trolls have a mix of different motivations, and are often resentful at being grouped together.[2] For example, trolls who trick news reporters into covering ridiculous, fake stories might take umbrage at being lumped in with the trolls who hang out on dead teenagers' tribute pages in order to mock their mourners. A fairly common thread, though, is a desire to prick the pomposity of today's 24-hour media culture, particularly news coverage, which many trolls regard as po-faced, shallow and adversarial. It's a view that began to permeate the evolving online counter-culture in places like 4chan.

A key tactic among some in its emerging troll community was the practice of 'life ruin'.[3] A target would be selected, sometimes at random, sometimes with an ostensible justification (a cheating girlfriend, for example), and the group would work as a team to trash the victim's online life. They would find the target's home address, workplace and whatever other personal details they could muster, then use them to sow mayhem. They would publish deeply private information online, send offensive messages to friends, family and workmates, and take over social media accounts. For some 4chan users, the goal was to trick or hack the victim into surrendering sexual photos of themselves. These could then be used for blackmail or shared among the group for kicks.

Of course, such trolling is much easier if you can do it anonymously, particularly if you're a fairly benign person who'd never dream of doing such horrible things in the physical world. Hiding behind a mask not only gives the troll a level of safety from counter-attack, it also helps disassociate a vicious, online identity from the ethics of the offline world.

In this context, 4chan made an important decision early on to introduce anonymity by default, whereby comments on the site were made under the user name 'Anonymous'. This proved controversial, and its opponents began referring to the Anonymous users as though they were a single entity ('Anonymous is trying to take over this discussion,' for example). As a result, Anonymous began to be perceived as a sort of hive mind with a single voice.[4] Again, this would seep into the DNA of the movement as it evolved.

As Anonymous grew in numbers and its attacks increased, the media began to take note, and in July 2007 a Fox TV News affiliate aired a report which branded the group and its life-ruining tactics an 'Internet hate machine' (a piece of fear-inducing hyperbole that, ironically, was probably lapped up by the troll community on 4chan).[5] But truly mainstream news coverage came largely thanks to a now-infamous video in which Hollywood actor Tom Cruise talks in apparently bizarre, rambling terms about Scientology. Filmed for a 2004 Church of Scientology event and leaked illicitly, the clip was uploaded to YouTube in January 2008 and subsequently shared by media outlets.[6] It was hugely embarrassing for the Church, which made a considerable effort to have the video removed from the Internet.[7] However, copies of the film proliferated online, seemingly in proportion to the Scientologists' attempts to stamp it out.

Over on 4chan, some of the users who were now banded together as 'Anonymous' watched the media storm with glee and quickly began to coalesce around a fresh target for life ruin: this time, an entire institution would feel the force of 4chan's online army. Many 4chan users knew the Church of Scientology defended itself robustly and was not afraid of taking legal action against those who attacked it. But they felt a safety in numbers, particularly as they believed their identity was hidden behind the mass-movement banner of Anonymous. Their campaign against Scientology included a trick that some in the group had been honing over years: the Distributed Denial of Service, or DDOS, attack. The theory behind it is simple: websites are stored on central computers called servers. When you visit a website, the server sends you a copy of the relevant web page. But if enough users all request the same page at the same time, the server cannot handle the influx and stops working, potentially rendering the whole site inaccessible for everyone.

Among more proficient cybercriminals, DDOS is barely considered to be hacking. Merely visiting a website is not illegal and doing so en masse is often referred to as a 'digital sit-in protest'. Certainly in the early Anonymous days, that's how it was used.

It doesn't take many people to shut down a small website with a DDOS attack, particularly if they use special software to automate and multiply their requests. Soon, attacks were being mounted on Scientology's online estate to force its websites offline.[8] But the main reason 'Op Chanology', as the attack became known, made the news was because of a decision among the hive mind of 4chan to take the protest to the streets.

On prearranged dates from early 2008 onwards, noisy demonstrations were held outside Scientology churches, including those in the UK, Australia, the U.S. and Canada. Hundreds turned up, with Anonymous protesters' numbers swelled by anti-Scientology campaigners.[9] Fearing identification by the Church of Scientology, most of the protesters wore masks, with many opting for the now-famous grinning Guy Fawkes image featured in the 2006 movie *V for Vendetta* (even before the protests, the mask had slipped into 4chan culture as one of its catchy meme cartoons). All this created the perfect opportunity for the broadcast media, who suddenly had something to point their cameras at, rather than having to make TV news out of an obscure online spat between Anonymous and Scientologists. But when reporters at the demonstrations asked to speak to an organizer, no one could really tell them who was in charge.

Also useful for the media coverage was the Church of Scientology's predictably vigorous reaction. Its spokesperson branded Anonymous demonstrators 'cyberterrorists' motivated by 'religious bigotry'.[10] It's hard to imagine the protesters not basking in such condemnation. But what they didn't realize was that, as they battled Scientology, they were in fact fighting an adversary that perfectly exposed Anonymous's own weaknesses.

Anonymous was a group riven by two fundamental, inter-linked faultlines: paranoia and a phobia of having their real-world identities exposed. These faultlines sprang from the backbiting bitchiness of 4chan, a community where anyone could suddenly become a target of attacks. Life ruin could just as quickly be meted out to long-term members of the group. Trusted friends could become traitors in seconds. This paranoia fed the need for anonymity. Yet the inability to truly know anyone, in turn, fed the paranoia.

It was a downward spiral, and the Church of Scientology's unflinching pursuit of its critics pushed Anonymous further into it, fuelling the paranoia and making anonymity a critical yet vulnerable asset. Anonymous may have believed it was battling an evil foe in Scientology, but at the same time, Anonymous's own Achilles heel was becoming ever more exposed.

Spurred by the success of Op Chanology, the 'Anons' were looking for their next big cause, and they got it thanks to someone whose legacy is woven through online history.

In November 2010, WikiLeaks founder Julian Assange announced the release of more than 250,000 cables sent between American embassies worldwide.[11] It was a huge trove of data, embarrassing not only to the U.S. for exposing its candid views on world affairs, but to the governments whose dirty laundry was suddenly aired in public. Some even argue the release of the cables kick-started the Arab Spring uprisings, with anti-government feeling in Tunisia stoked by revelations in the leaked documents about its president's use of power.[12]

After the leaks, a series of financial institutions, notably PayPal, refused to continue processing donation payments to WikiLeaks on the basis that it had breached their rules.[13] Anonymous went into action to punish those it felt had wronged Assange's site. Among the tactics were the DDoS attacks that had proved so successful against the Church of Scientology. But this time there was a difference. A piece of software was gaining prominence that would allow anyone to sign up to the emerging online insurrection.

The Low Orbit Ion Canon, or LOIC, named after a computer game weapon, was a fairly simple piece of software that could be used to synchronize requests for website pages. Simply enter the name or IP address of the website you wanted to hit, and press 'Go' (or, as the LOIC software slang put it: 'IMMA CHARGIN MAH LAZER'). LOIC would then bombard the target site with requests, and if enough people joined in, the website would go down.

LOIC had been used in previous Anonymous campaigns, including against the Church of Scientology.[14] But with Op Payback, as the PayPal attacks were known, it received widespread adoption: suddenly, anyone could be part of Anonymous's online army. As a result, some saw Anonymous's behaviour in the context of other insurgent movements. Carole Cadwalladr in *The Guardian* compared it with al-Qaeda, as a loose, amorphous 'un-organisation' with a motivating ideology but no command structure.[15]

For many of those who took part in the attacks there was an equally powerful force driving the dynamics of Anonymous: the world of computer gaming.

Unlike in the early days of solitary entertainment, today's games are often played online against a field of potentially thousands of opponents, all linked together over the Internet. The way these games work sheds light on how hacker movements can come together. At their heart is a swarm mentality. Each player is out for the best score for themselves, but working together in ad hoc or loosely organized teams can yield better results for all. The question is, who to team up with?

On joining a game, players are often presented with a list of the nicknames (or 'handles') other players are using, and a seasoned gamer will quickly spot the experienced players, teaming together with some, while attacking others. The swarm mentality of gaming teaches people to come together for short periods, for limited, common objectives, on the basis of nothing but a recognizable nickname. It's exactly the same dynamic that helped feed online attack swarms such as Anonymous, as its members coalesced around a target, often following the lead of pseudonymous colleagues in Internet chatrooms.

Among a generation of people raised in this gaming milieu, Anonymous found fertile ground. The prospect of downloading a bit of software like LOIC and swarming collectively onto a target with a bunch of unidentified co-conspirators came naturally. And Anonymous's campaigns were getting results, even against the might of international payment companies. At first, the attacks just took down the PayPal blog, but in December 2010 the main PayPal site was hit. The protesters claim they took the site entirely offline. PayPal said they only slightly slowed it down.[16] Either way, it reportedly cost the firm £3.5 million in damage, and news outlets around the world were reporting Anonymous's successes against PayPal and others.[17] The group seemed to be coming from everywhere and nowhere at once, creating a terrifying new adversary.

Anonymous's online chatrooms (now running independently of 4chan) fuelled the impression of an ad hoc army that anyone could join, giving newcomers easy-to-follow instructions on how to download the LOIC software. Behind the scenes, the truth was a little different.

Companies like PayPal are almost entirely reliant on online access, and as such, they invest big sums into making sure their websites are a lot better protected than those of, say, the Church of Scientology. To knock over such a site requires more than a few hundred users using DDOS software like the Low Orbit Ion Canon.

To take on such big targets, Anonymous needed help, and the source of that help pointed to a troubling new direction: a merger of so-called 'hacktivism' with traditional, dyed-in-the-wool cybercrime. According to security researchers, among the inner circle of Anonymous were several members who had access to networks of ten of thousands of computers that had been infected with viruses.[18] The majority of these computers' owners were almost certainly unaware they had been infected. They may have clicked on a malicious email, or perhaps visited a website that downloaded the virus onto their machine. As a result, they'd been secretly (and illegally) recruited into a slave army of machines across the world. These so-called 'botnets' of infected computers could be used as a souped-up version of the LOIC software, flooding even the more resilient websites with enough requests to knock them over.

The botnet owners joined Anonymous's fight, and the attacks on PayPal would almost certainly have failed without their assistance, as Parmy Olson argues in *We Are Anonymous*, a book which offers an unrivalled inside view of the movement.[19] In reality, the idea of Anonymous as a leaderless 'citizen army' was wrong. The serious firepower was largely being directed by a small cadre of people, reliant on a hard core of cybercriminals. This fact was not known to the vast majority of Anonymous followers as they celebrated their successful, supposedly collective attacks; and among the noise it wasn't well covered in the media. But it wasn't only Anonymous supporters and the media who paid undue attention to the low-level LOIC users. Prosecutors around the world pursued people who had downloaded and used the software. This came as a shock, because many Anonymous members didn't believe they were committing an offence by simply using LOIC to lob requests at a website. And even among those who did, they didn't think the police would bother to pursue it. These beliefs were actively fostered in Anonymous chatrooms, where new members were encouraged to join the attacks.[20]

In fact some jurisdictions, including the UK and the U.S., decided that launching DDOS attacks was a crime. Efforts to punish offenders were considerably helped by a feature of LOIC software that, once again, was conveniently brushed over by Anonymous promoters. If used unwisely, LOIC revealed the user's IP address, which could in turn be used to trace the person's physical address. Dozens were arrested around the world. One twenty-year-old

American student was sentenced to a year in prison after prose-cutors successfully argued he'd caused $20,000 of damage to the Church of Scientology by taking part in the Anonymous attacks.[21] He later said he'd downloaded the LOIC software and forgotten about it, leaving it running for days.

In the end, Anonymous fell foul of the issue that eventually afflicts many grassroots movements: stamina. Upswells of opinion can bring together masses of people with impressive speed – as with the Occupy movement, for example – but as they sweep up multiple viewpoints, the effort to please all sides can create a fatal lack of focus, dissipating the harnessed energy. So it was with Anonymous. Often a bitchy, amorphous community, it struggled to replicate the successes of Op Payback and Op Chanology.

But as the movement fractured into infighting and intrigue, a splinter group was forming that pursued a radical shift in tactics. Together they would not only harness the media-savvy, asymmetric guerrilla warfare of Anonymous, but create a perfect distillation of the multiple personalities that make up a computer hacker.

Aaron Barr had a simple plan: de-anonymize Anonymous.

As the boss of HBGary Federal, a new tech security company, Barr was targeting U.S. government organizations for lucrative cybersecurity contracts. He hit upon a plan to gain publicity by showing how to expose the true identities of key members of Anonymous, the group that was making headlines around the world. He would gradually infiltrate the group through its online conversations, carefully logging their user names, the times they appeared and disappeared from chatrooms, and any information they shared about themselves. He would then try to match them to Facebook profiles, which sometimes led to much more personal information and, eventually, a real-life identity.

After months of work, by February 2011 Barr had assembled a dossier of information and scheduled a meeting with the FBI. Eager to go public, he arranged a talk at a conference where he would announce his results, and ahead of it he told certain media outlets about his research. The ensuing articles suggested Barr might have enough information on the Anons to get some of them arrested (though he also said he wouldn't give specifics to the police).[22] His boasts caught the eye of some of Anonymous's most dangerous members.

As a whole, Anonymous can't accurately be described as a hacking group, because much of its activity was based around the kind of digital sit-ins that brought down PayPal and others. Many Anons didn't perceive themselves as hackers and some were bemused when the media labelled them as such. But among the group were some with high-level technical skills, one of whom was a hacker nicknamed 'Sabu'. He had first emerged onto the scene at the turn of the millennium, reportedly taking part in a number of attacks with a focus on u.s. foreign policy.[23] He'd been quiet since then, but as Anonymous activity ramped up in late 2010, he re-entered the fray. On joining Anonymous chatrooms he'd quickly zeroed in on two other skilled hackers nicknamed Tflow and Kayla.

Tflow had more in common with Sabu than just hacking prowess: both took a rigorous approach to their privacy and security, never giving out personal information about themselves that could be used to identify them. Kayla couldn't have been more different. She seemed to be liberal with her personal details, describing herself as a teenage girl who'd been taught to hack by her father, and who worked part-time in a beauty salon.[24] She insisted Kayla was her real name, and seemed to delight in revealing the minutiae of her life, littered with precisely the kind of emojis and cartoonish slang beloved of teenagers. When it came to hacking, though, Kayla was a dangerous individual who obsessively scanned websites for any hole and wormed her way inside.[25]

Left to their own devices (or more accurately, others' devices), Kayla, Tflow and Sabu would have been a highly effective set of cybercriminals. But they almost certainly wouldn't have attracted the international publicity they later gained. For that, they needed the extra element added by a fourth member of the group.

Topiary took his hacker handle from an obscure, unfinished movie by the cult director Shane Carruth.[26] That decision alone provides an insight into his personality: cultured, esoterically referential and wilfully bizarre. Unlike the others, he wasn't a technically skilled hacker, but he had another talent that would pull them all into the very centre of the spotlight.

Like many Anons, Topiary got his start on the discussion site 4chan, where he wrote fiction, looked up recipes, chatted and recorded prank calls that he would upload for others' entertainment. Soon he would broadcast the calls live online, taking suggestions from listeners. As Anonymous grew in size, it created a chatroom where members of the media could join and ask questions. It wasn't a comfortable experience for journalists, who were struggling to understand a digital insurgency that communicated in 4chan-speak and constantly pranked reporters with misleading information. But it was far more forgiving than the chatrooms the Anons themselves inhabited.

When Topiary joined Anonymous, he found his niche in these public-facing arenas – his prank-call experiences having given him the gift of the gab (online, at least). He understood the community, its memes and its style innately. He was witty, quick and full of ideas, and soon started rising up the ad hoc seniority levels that existed even within the supposedly leaderless world of Anonymous.

It's hard to overstate how impressive such a rise was. The chatrooms Topiary inhabited were, particularly in Anonymous's heyday, a continuous, bewildering torrent of words. The larger rooms might contain hundreds of members all furiously typing simultaneously. To break through that noise and establish a reputation required continuous focus, with a keen grasp of the group dynamic and how to catch its attention. Topiary was a master.

From early on, Anonymous members knew the value of PR. Attention-grabbing press releases and, later, slick videos accompanied major attacks by the group. Topiary was invited into a special chatroom to help draft the text, along with the sardonic messages that would be posted on the front pages of websites the group hacked into. Soon Topiary began acting as a spokesperson, working with Kayla and others, according to U.S. investigators.[27]

It was around this time they heard about Aaron Barr's work to unmask Anonymous members. Furious at his claims, Topiary, Sabu and their co-conspirators went to work, crawling all over HBGary Federal's website to find a way in. For a company that worked in the security field, it turned out to have some major holes.

It was Super Bowl Sunday in February 2011. Millions in the U.S. and around the world were settling down to watch the game. Aaron Barr was just a day away from his meeting with the FBI, where he planned to talk about his work de-anonymizing Anonymous members. Little did he know that, as the Super Bowl kicked off, for him a far more dramatic event was about to unfold. Barr was to be the subject of a globally publicized 'life ruin' exercise that would eventually destroy his entire company.

Sabu and his hacking group had found a way into HBGary Federal's systems, thanks in part to the same kind of low-level SQL injection attack used by the TalkTalk hackers discussed earlier. The hackers pulled out encrypted passwords for Barr and his colleagues and managed to break the encryption. This eventually gave them access to the company's email accounts, where they found some deeply sensitive information. The documents seemed to show HBGary Federal had discussed a strategy to discredit WikiLeaks by mounting a disinformation campaign about the site and launching cyberattacks on its infrastructure. Not only was HBGary Federal trying to identify Anonymous members, but it also seemed to be engaged in a smear campaign. And thanks to Sabu, Tflow and the others, the hacking team had found them out – helped by the fact that Barr used the same password across many accounts.[28] What happened next is a chilling demonstration of hacker tactics at their most ruthless. Knowing that swathes of damaging information from HBGary Federal were ready for imminent release, Topiary contacted Barr in a chatroom. Barr used the pseudonym CogAnon, under which he'd pretended to be an Anonymous supporter. For the next few minutes, Topiary toyed with his victim, dropping hints about what was going to happen, all the while simultaneously mocking Barr in a separate chatroom with Sabu, Kayla and Tflow.

After he chatted with Topiary via his pseudonym, a creeping realization swept over Barr. He discovered he was locked out of his email and Twitter accounts. All of a sudden, the chief executive was losing control of his company's IT, and as he fought to regain control he found himself repeatedly outflanked by his attackers. HBGary had expected pushback from Anonymous when they went public with their de-anonymizing research, but nothing had prepared them for this. Back in the chatroom, Topiary stretched out the agony: 'something will be happening tonight. How available are you throughout the evening?' As Olson wrote in *We Are Anonymous*: 'he wanted Barr to have a front-row seat to the end of his career.'[29]

As the Super Bowl kicked off, Topiary and his team went into action. The whirlwind was unleashed on multiple fronts. Barr's Twitter account was defaced; his profile photo had the word 'nigger' scrawled across it, and the hackers used his account to tweet 'Sup motherfuckers, I'm CEO of a shitty company and I'm a media-whoring cunt.'[30] HBGary Federal's website was defaced and, in an insulting irony, used to share a link where tens of thousands of emails Barr had sent and received could be downloaded, along with those of his colleagues.[31] Barr's mobile phone and social security numbers ended up being publicized.[32] As he frantically fought to regain control of his business, abusive and mocking messages flooded into his phone. His hacked Twitter account was used to publish Barr's home address, and within two days Barr reportedly decided to move away with his wife and two children for their safety.[33]

Before doing so, he had logged back into the chatroom, partly to see if he could talk the group round and control the damage. Topiary's response was blunt – a quote from a 4chan meme he says Barr had used himself: 'Die in a fire. You're done.'

Within weeks, Barr announced he was leaving HBGary Federal.[34] The company's name quickly became a byword for unscrupulous dealings, and soon after it closed its doors for good.

The destruction of HBGary Federal was the opening salvo in a sprawling hacking campaign by a group that would come to be known as LulzSec (lulz being 4chan-slang for laughs, generally at someone else's expense – usually someone whom the group considered worthy of ridicule). Its membership varied, but at its heart were always Sabu, Tflow, Kayla and Topiary. Media management was key, and Topiary knew how to build an audience: releasing teasing information bit by bit. Time and again his witty, occasionally sarcastic voice could be heard. But Topiary was far from just a PR man for the group. As their targets increased in size and number, he took a key role in harvesting and organizing the sensitive information they'd pilfered, according to U.S. investigators.[35]

And there was no shortage of work to do as the targets mounted up throughout 2011: U.S. TV network Fox was hit in May, and the profiles and names of 73,000 X Factor contestants were published.[36] The same month another U.S. TV company, PBS, had its website hacked by LulzSec, which was then used to publish a bizarre story about the murdered rap artist Tupac being found alive in New Zealand.[37] Sony Pictures Entertainment's systems were hacked in June, with LulzSec claiming to have the private details of more than a million people, including passwords, email addresses and home addresses (Sony claimed it was 37,500 people).[38] Hacks were mounted against video game companies, the NHS, the Arizona State Police – the group even launched a DDoS attack on the public website of the CIA, taking it offline for several hours.[39]

LulzSec's hacks were so frequent and various it's hard to draw together a comprehensive list: every official document seems to run with different ones. That's partly because, as time went on, LulzSec's members weren't necessarily doing all the hacking themselves. Their fame meant they were tipped off to security flaws by their followers, and in some cases, hacked information was fed to them.[40]

However they got it, the extensive, strategic leaking of data was what made LulzSec different to Anonymous, and it brought the group global fame. They weren't just taking down websites, they were breaking in, stealing personal and sensitive information and then smearing snippets (and sometimes swathes) of it online for all to see. And unlike many hacking groups of the past, LulzSec's members, notably Sabu and Topiary, were on Twitter to answer questions. Hacking had always happened in the shadows, but LulzSec were conducting their affairs in the full glare of publicity. The media had a field day. 'We're kind of like a rock band,' Topiary said in one private chat that was later leaked online.[41]

Yet internally, the group was struggling with tensions: for Tflow, the aim was always to expose security weaknesses in the organizations they attacked; for Sabu, there was often a political motivation; for Topiary, it was more about the lulz. This three-way split often pulled them in different directions, but it may also account for their success. Their personality profiles neatly mirrored the mix of hacker DNA described earlier in this book: Tflow represented the rigorous, technocratic ethos of the early Massachusetts Institute of Technology groups; Sabu seemed to embody the high-minded, freedom-fighting outlook of John Perry Barlow and the Electronic Frontier Foundation; and Topiary represented the subversive spirit of the Texan hackers the Cult of the Dead Cow. Perhaps this was the secret of LulzSec's meteoric rise.

But to quote the classic sci-fi movie *Blade Runner*: 'The light that burns twice as bright burns half as long.' LulzSec's days were coming to an end, and its demise would come about thanks to a combination of infighting, betrayal and armchair detective work.

Jennifer Emick was a journalist covering alternative religions for a website when she first attended an Anonymous protest outside a Scientology church in San Francisco in spring 2008. She was swept up by the exuberance, quickly moving beyond just writing about it to becoming an active Anonymous supporter.

A mother in her mid-thirties at the time, Emick didn't match the archetypal 4chan user's profile, but she immersed herself in the febrile world of Anonymous. As the movement morphed in the wake of the attacks against the Church of Scientology, PayPal and others, however, Emick started to see troubling signs. She worried that people were being wrongly assured that using LOIC software for DDoS attacks was safe, when in fact it could expose them to arrest. She saw evidence of mob rule. She feared young people were being pulled into criminal hacking. The final straw for her came when Anonymous members leaked data on Sony Pictures Entertainment executives, including their home addresses, their children's names and even details of which schools the children attended.

'That infuriated me,' she says, claiming it marked an aggressive change in the group's atmosphere. 'It just accelerated from there, everything became fair game.'

Emick says she decided to give Anonymous's leaders a 'dose of their own medicine' by de-anonymizing them – the same tactic Barr had attempted, although for Emick, the results would be far less catastrophic. In her sights was the man she regarded as at the apex of everything she disliked about the emerging face of Anonymous: Sabu.

To get the evidence she needed, Emick identified someone she described as a 'weak link' in Anonymous, a member who had access to LulzSec's chats. She used fake personas to trick that person into leaking records of the team's online conversations. Within the stream of LulzSec's comments she found a website that Sabu had inadvertently mentioned. This led Emick to a Facebook page. Staring back at her was the true face of Sabu, the seasoned, elite hacker. Hector Xavier Monsegur was a 29-year-old unemployed man living in a housing estate in New York, where he looked after several young family members.

Emick released her revelations in March 2011 under her security company name, Backtrace.[42] The problem was, she'd also guessed at the identities of other key members of LulzSec and got some of them wrong. And her research was just one of many reports that claimed to have successfully outed Anonymous members. For many, including LulzSec itself, her findings went unnoticed and the group carried on. But the FBI didn't ignore the research. Emick was spot on when it came to Sabu; in fact, law enforcement had already started closing in on LulzSec's tech guru themselves.

It would take until 7 June 2011 for the FBI to finally knock at Hector Xavier Monsegur's door on the sixth floor of the Jacob Riis complex in New York. Confronted by the police, the super-hacker who'd evaded detection for more than a decade and openly mocked the authorities agreed to cooperate 'immediately', according to court documents.[43] The FBI wanted to charge him with credit card fraud, among other crimes. Threatened with jail time that would take him away from his young family, Monsegur capitulated.

The FBI didn't want him to stop hacking. Instead, they wanted him to keep working with LulzSec while they monitored the group, hoping to snare all the members. So after interviews with the FBI and a brief court appearance, Sabu returned to his computer and rejoined LulzSec, initially blaming his absence on his grandmother's death (though later switching stories to say it was the anniversary of her funeral). Suspicion flickered briefly through the group, but by this time, a sense of fatalism seems to have set in. They were in so deep, with so many crimes behind them, there didn't seem any point in stopping.

Meanwhile, Emick and the FBI were not the only ones on LulzSec's tail.

The UK's Metropolitan Police were dealing with multiple strands of cybercrime during 2011. Forced to rank them in order of danger, they probably wouldn't have put LulzSec near the top. That changed when LulzSec announced a DDOS attack on the Serious Organised Crime Agency (SOCA). Hitting media companies was one thing, but the UK government has a legal obligation to keep its agencies running, and an attack on the SOCA website, although it didn't massively disrupt police business, was not to be taken lightly.

The task of hunting LulzSec fell to the relatively newly created Police Central e-Crime Unit (PCEU), described by its then-boss Charlie McMurdie as the 'cyber Sweeney', in homage to the 1970s police drama about Scotland Yard's Flying Squad. Like their TV namesakes, the unit's officers were keen to launch successful raids on unsuspecting offenders, and when it came to LulzSec's SOCA attack, it took them only a few hours to find the right door to knock on.

Their investigation zeroed in on a small suburban house in Wickford, Essex, where they found nineteen-year-old Ryan Cleary. He'd been one of the Anonymous members running the group's 'botnets' of virus-infected computers.[44]

Leads from the Cleary investigation, along with other digital forensic evidence, led the Met to their next target: Topiary. It turned out that he lived on an island in the Shetland archipelago, far off the very northern tip of Scotland. On the rare occasions when they make the news, the Shetland Islands usually appear alongside the word 'windswept'. Their population is 23,000 and their main economic activity is fishing, notably herring and mackerel.[45] It was an unlikely location for a member of a globally famous hacking group. It was also a faff to get to from London, and for the PCEU team sent to arrest him, the logistical problems were about to get much worse.

Ordinarily, there are daily ferries to the Shetlands. But the Met Police had managed to choose the worst possible time to try to visit: the one week in 25 years when the Tall Ships Race was being held around the islands. All ferries were suspended. The police hunted for other options. At one point, there was talk of requesting help from a Royal Navy ship so its helicopter could be used to ferry them out.

The clock was ticking. Due to the international nature of the investigation, the PCeU officers had only a limited amount of time to arrest and charge Topiary, and commercial flights proved too infrequent. In the end, only one option was left: charter a private plane at a cost of around £9,000 – which felt deeply extravagant for officers who normally took the underground to work. Sheepishly, the three-person police team boarded the plush aircraft, furtively taking selfies on the way to send back to their colleagues in London, who sarcastically photoshopped a 'PCeU Airlines' logo onto the plane's interior.

On 27 July, they knocked at the door of a static caravan near Lerwick, and were met by the real-world Topiary. Jake Davis was a polite, softly spoken eighteen-year-old who'd moved to the island with his family more than ten years previously.

One by one, the members of LulzSec were rounded up, and as their real names and addresses became known, the public were once again confronted with the realization that some of the world's biggest companies had been digitally burgled by, in some cases, teenagers working from their bedrooms. I was among the journalists dispatched to knock on the suspects' doors.

Tflow turned out to be Mustafa Al-Bassam, a sixteen-year-old living in a block of flats in south London. When I called at their door, a member of his family told me he was out at college and didn't want to talk. When the police got to Al-Bassam, though, they had more luck. In his jacket pocket they found a piece of paper with a list of the targets the group had attacked in their pre-LulzSec days, including a handy guide as to which member of the team had played what role.

But of all of them, it was Kayla who was the biggest surprise. Online she was a sixteen-year-old schoolgirl whose chats were a pink, sparkly parade of emojis. So it was with some surprise that I knocked on the door of a semi-detached house in Mexborough in northern England to be confronted by a heavy-set,

25-year-old man who shyly leaned out of his kitchen window as he did the washing up and declined my request for an interview. Ryan Ackroyd, a former soldier in the British Army and now unemployed, was the true face of Kayla.[46]

Perhaps it shouldn't come as a surprise that Kayla was really a man. For a start, Anonymous had a set of rules about online life that, although typically sardonic, reveal deep-seated assumptions. Number 29 states: 'All girls are men and all kids are undercover FBI' (and just for good measure, Rule 30 is: 'There are no girls on the Internet').

It is true that the majority of attendees at tech security conferences are men, and the vast majority of those convicted under the UK's Computer Misuse Act are identified as male: in the decade leading up to 2017, 222 offenders out of 265.[47] But the counter-argument is that there's nothing inherently 'male' about tech security and hacking at all. Rather, male dominance has become a self-stoking cycle, with many women finding it an unwelcoming environment, containing few role models to follow.

For hackers like Ackroyd, creating a fully fleshed-out online female persona was a good distraction tactic. His adversaries would instantly assume (correctly) that his entire online edifice was fake, potentially deterring them from looking any more deeply into it for clues as to his real identity. But on a deeper level, despite a culture that was often crass, heteronormative and male-dominated (and where the word 'faggot' was used so commonly it was barely considered an insult), Anonymous and its surroundings was a surprisingly gender-fluid environment. The person who leaked the diplomatic cables and other material to WikiLeaks, for example, was born as Bradley Manning, but later transitioned to become Chelsea Manning. The person who leaked the chat logs to Jennifer Emick, the investigator who outed Sabu, had also transitioned.

In her book, *Hacking Diversity*, Christina Dunbar-Hester quotes a hacker named Salix: 'To me the word "hacker" is about anyone who wants to tear down a system. It's the same with

[my] gender and sexuality – tearing down a system and seeing where I fit in it.'[48]

Away from their carefully crafted online identities, however, the first time LulzSec's members met was in court. Topiary, aka Jake Davis, was sentenced to two years, which he served in a youth offenders institution. Tflow, aka Mustafa Al-Bassam, got a suspended sentence of twenty months and two hundred hours of unpaid work. Kayla, aka Ryan Ackroyd, got thirty months in prison. Ryan Cleary was imprisoned for 32 months.[49] His charges also included possession of child sexual abuse material.[50] Part of his defence was a diagnosis of Asperger's syndrome, indicating an autism diagnosis. This is not uncommon in high-profile cyber-crime cases: British hacker Gary McKinnon also partly relied on an Asperger's syndrome diagnosis in fighting his extradition to the u.s. on charges of hacking into sensitive military systems.[51]

But the cliché of the 'autistic hacker' is, like many aspects of hacker culture, wide of the mark, as illustrated by intriguing research from the University of Bath. Spurred by interest from the uk's National Crime Agency, which had spotted what seemed to be autistic-like traits among some cybercriminals, researchers set out to investigate the links.[52] They recruited 290 tech-savvy participants through online computing forums. They then asked them whether they'd participated in cybercrimes, and also surveyed them to see where they fitted on the spectrum of autistic-like traits.

'Those who had committed cybercrime were the highest in terms of [having] autistic traits,' says lead researcher Mark Brosnan. That might lead you to assume that the link between autism and computer hacking is real. Not quite. Autism is a clinical diagnosis, and merely having autistic traits doesn't necessarily mean you're autistic.

Among those Brosnan surveyed were 25 people with a diagnosis of autism. 'If they had a diagnosis, they were less likely to commit cybercrime,' says Brosnan. 'Autistic people tend to be very honest and trustworthy. Part of what defines autism is a preference for consistency, rigidity, rules and regulations.' Clearly, you don't have to be autistic to be a hacker. But much of the work of hacking is of a type that might appeal to those high on the spectrum: repetitive, highly focused and solitary.

For Cleary and the other British members of LulzSec, it would take until May 2013 for them to be sentenced. In the meantime, the secret story of the group's de facto leader, Monsegur (aka Sabu) and his collaboration with the FBI had emerged. The 'rock star' members of LulzSec were forced to confront betrayal by one of their most trusted members.

In person, Jake Davis is quiet and studious, and rarely swears. It's almost impossible to reconcile his offline personality with the online persona of Topiary, who helped to destroy Aaron Barr's company HBGary Federal in a blaze of obscenities. His initial descent into hacking is easier to understand, however. In the Shetland Islands, this intellectually curious youngster ended up attending knitting classes and learning sheep-herding whistles. A bigger world was waiting online, and Davis found a new audience to impress.

Davis acknowledges that what he and LulzSec did was wrong. But he points out that much of their hacking was low-level, and had their targets employed better security, many of their attacks would have failed. He also seems, in hindsight, to regard LulzSec as a sort of performance art experiment. Certainly, there's a Barnumesque touch to their exploits. And as Davis points out, had the group been financially motivated, they could have used their access and their data far more damagingly. Instead they courted publicity with their lulz and, of course, that's a large part of why they got caught.

Davis is sanguine about Monsegur's betrayal, but is deeply critical of the FBI's decision to allow LulzSec's hacking to continue following the American's arrest.

'The targets increased in volume as the FBI wanted to steer us to hacking more things,' he says.

All of that was directed by the FBI. They were responsible for all those attacks, essentially. Even if we pushed back a bit to Hector [Monsegur] and said 'we don't want to do this,' he would push back to make us do it. Even our tone of voice began to shift in a way that was more prosecutable based on Hector's cooperation.

The FBI declined to comment on his allegations.

It's hard to be precise about how many hacks actually took place during Monsegur's FBI collaboration, because data that was leaked by LulzSec following his arrest may actually have been obtained by the hacking group long before. However, while he was working with the Feds, LulzSec continued to crow about its victories: internal documents from the U.S. Senate were published, several large computer gaming companies were hit, the CIA's website was taken offline with a DDOS attack and, in what was their final and perhaps most infamous attack, LulzSec hacked *The Sun* newspaper's website, posting a fake story claiming that the boss of its owner News Corporation (now News Corp), Rupert Murdoch, had been found dead. All of this took place while the FBI was monitoring Monsegur's activities. For his part, Monsegur has insisted that the FBI was not directing the targets of LulzSec. He told me the group's aggression ramped up partly due to his own anger at the situation in which he found himself.

In May 2014, Monsegur was sentenced. He'd already served seven months in prison after his earlier guilty plea and was given a year of supervised release. The Department of Justice said he had engaged in 'extraordinary cooperation' that enabled the government to 'identify, locate, and arrest eight of his co-conspirators' and prevent or limit more than three hundred cyberattacks as he back-channelled information to his handlers.[53] He now works for a U.S. tech security company. 'I'm over that point in my life [of] trying to be a martyr for anyone's cause,' he writes in an email. 'Life is good, I have no complaints, I do regret some of my actions though I do not regret the consequences.'

Like Monsegur, the other core LulzSec members have also now found themselves fulfilling careers in cybersecurity. Davis is a consultant (he says he met Aaron Barr for drinks recently: 'A very cool guy.' Barr still works for tech companies in the u.s.). Al-Bassam set up a tech business, sold it to Facebook and is completing his doctorate at University College London.[54] According to his social media profile, Ackroyd does cybersecurity training and consultancy.

Galling as it may be for some to see people who went on a cybercrime spree now earning a living from the same industry, many see the sense in hiring ex-hackers to put their skills to good. There's a snag, however: doing tech security jobs for banks, governments and law enforcement (some of the most lucrative contracts) often requires accreditation or vetting. A past conviction for hacking can prevent that from happening.

For its part, the tech industry has also made efforts to divert youngsters away from the path taken by the likes of LulzSec. Companies have introduced so-called 'bug bounty' schemes, whereby hackers can get paid if they do the right thing and inform the company of a tech vulnerability, rather than selling it on or exploiting it themselves. Such schemes can be very rewarding. In 2019, it was revealed that one leading bug bounty hunter had earned $1 million over four years.[55] But no matter how attractive the legitimate side of hacking becomes, there are always those looking to make easier money, and more of it, by illegal means.

As LulzSec faded into history and Anonymous fractured into different geographical focuses, the tactics they'd applied found new life among cybercriminals. Denial of Service attacks on the likes of PayPal and the CIA had shown the power that such approaches could wield. It had been used for political activism and out-of-control pranks, but now it would be used for something far more directly rewarding: making money.

Eight-year-old Harry is showing me around his personal Boeing 767. It's impeccably appointed: the first-class passengers all have flat-bed seats and their own toilets. Business-class fliers have workspaces with tables and chairs.

What's more impressive is that Harry (who's my nephew) built the whole aircraft from scratch in under two hours. Admittedly, there's no chance of you getting a seat on board. Harry's plane exists only in the computerized world of Minecraft.

If you're the parent of young child or an avid gamer yourself, you probably need no introduction to this wildly popular computer game, in which players use an on-screen buddy to construct personal worlds using three-dimensional blocks, painstakingly building everything from jumbo jets to skyscrapers. Originally created by Swedish developers Mojang, the company was bought by Microsoft in 2014. It turned out to be a shrewd investment: within two years, Mojang reported that it had sold more than 100 million copies.[56]

For Harry and other players like him, it's an absorbing digital universe in which to immerse himself and have some fun. But for a set of computer hackers, Minecraft became the driving force for an attack that spread around the world and affected hundreds of thousands of innocent victims. The story behind it demonstrates how the digital sit-in tactics used by the likes of Anonymous have now been turned into a highly refined form of cyberextortion.

After LulzSec's convictions, the group's rock-star-style success spurred a series of imitators.

For all their bravado, however, most of these groups lacked the skill of Sabu, Kayla and Tflow. But there was one tactic that didn't require such high-level ability: the Distributed Denial of Service, or DDOS, attack. With access to enough virus-infected computers, anyone could wield the kind of power that had gained international publicity for Anonymous.

DDOS-for-hire services began popping up all over the place, mainly powered by the same kind of 'botnets' that boosted the Anonymous attacks. These services often went under the guise of legitimate website testing tools – so-called 'stressers' – which can be used by website owners to test their sites' sturdiness. But in the background, these hired guns of the DDOS Wild West would take aim at anyone for the right price. With sufficient Bitcoin and a big enough DDOS attack, a business's website could be taken out for hours at a time, costing it valuable revenue. What's more, these attacks would be almost impossible to trace back to the true source, if done correctly.

A former member of one of the most high-profile of these groups, speaking on condition of anonymity, recounted being approached on an underground forum by a businessman seeking to take out a rival:

> He was asking me about denial of service attacks. He said he owns a big business and one of his competitors is in the same business, and he wants us to take [his competitor's] business down so he could flourish.
>
> He gives me the money, I get the IP address.

The hacker claims he then duly obliged, knocking over the competitor's site. What was most remarkable was his response when I asked which site he'd taken down: 'No idea. I couldn't really read it, it was all in Korean.'

Things had moved a long way from the ideological claims that drove many of the Anonymous DDOS attacks. Now the same tactic was being used for pure profit by hackers who didn't even know who they were attacking. But the DDOS-for-hire businesses had a problem: scale. Creating botnets of a large enough size was difficult, and got progressively harder the more the tech security industry pushed back against the hackers. Thankfully for the cybercriminals, just as traditional botnet creation got more difficult, the Internet developed a new weak spot, in the form of devices that millions of people began plugging into their computers all over the world.

Webcams, speakers, televisions, thermostats, baby monitors, fridges and even sex toys – many of them can now be wired up to the Internet. And for the hackers, this created an explosive growth in what they call the 'attack surface'. Put simply: millions of new devices means millions of new potential ways in. With the birth of this 'Internet of Things', the stage was set for a new cyberwar, and Minecraft would be among the first battlefields.

To understand how a hugely successful construction game became the key arena for a global hacking attack, you need to understand a little of how Minecraft works and why it's been so profitable for so many people. While it's possible to play Minecraft solely on a mobile phone, laptop or games console, sooner or later many players want to take their carefully constructed digital world and put it onto a computer server. This allows them to invite other people in to join the fun, and also means their on-screen universe is safely stored online and won't disappear if they drop their phone down the toilet. These computer servers are not run by the game's developers, Microsoft and Mojang, but by numerous smaller companies. They can make money by charging for entry to the server and selling extras to Minecraft players such as pets or outfits for their on-screen characters.

You may be thinking that this all sounds very far-out and eso-teric. So did I, until I asked how much money a leading Minecraft server company makes.

'About a million-and-a-half dollars a month,' says Robert Coelho, vice president of ProxyPipe, a company that protects Minecraft server businesses from attack.

Minecraft is big business, says Coelho. And it all relies on run-ning and maintaining those computer servers. No servers means no money. If you want to take a rival Minecraft server company out of the game – or, worse, blackmail them for cash – then you need to hit its servers. And the best way to do that is a DDoS attack.

As the game's popularity grew, Minecraft became a minefield of DDoS attacks, with servers hit on a regular basis, according to Coelho. Once a server went down, the players who were using it would often quickly lose patience (a commodity already in short supply among young gamers) and switch to another server, taking a valuable revenue stream with them. After running a Minecraft server himself and witnessing the attacks at first hand, Coelho set up in business helping to protect other server owners. His firm did reasonably well, then one day in 2016, something big hit Coelho's protective software – a powerful new weapon that would change the face of DDOS attacks forever.

The scale of such attacks is measured according to how many junk requests are being aimed at the victims, using the number of gigabits per second, or Gbps. Up until this point, says Coelho, an attack of 40–50 Gbps was considered pretty serious. Suddenly, he started seeing attacks reaching 300 Gbps. 'This was definitely in a class of its own,' he says.

What's more, the attacks seemed timed to cause maximum damage. A server would be taken down for a period of time, then allowed back into life just long enough for users to log back into their Minecraft world before the attacks would knock the server out again. Even the most loyal customers might be driven away in frustration.

The junk requests hitting the servers had to be coming from somewhere. In a traditional DDOS attack, they usually come from computers that have been infected with a virus and harvested into a botnet. But when Coelho started looking into it, he noticed something strange. The requests weren't coming from people's laptops or home computers. Each incoming request comes from an IP address, a device's gateway onto the Internet. Coelho's software was able to record the IP addresses being used to bombard his clients' servers. So, as an experiment, Coelho copied one of the IP addresses that was being used to attack a Minecraft server, pasted it into his web browser and hit 'go'. A live video stream appeared on screen.

'It was a webcam,' he says.

The junk requests that were flooding into Minecraft servers in unprecedented numbers weren't coming from a traditional botnet of infected computers. They were coming from all those new devices being plugged into them. Security cameras, smart TVs,

Internet routers – gadgets around the world had been infected and were being forced into sending droves of malicious traffic to Minecraft servers.[57]

Tech security researchers started looking into what was going on, intrigued by the size of the attack. What they found was deeply worrying. A lot of these gadgets were quite cheap – after all, if you just want a webcam to keep an eye on your cattle shed (which some farmers do), you're not going to splash out on a top-quality version. As a result, many had weak security. Added to which, many owners had not bothered to change the default password on the gadget, seeing little risk (who'd be interested in hacking a cattle-shed webcam?). This meant that not only were these gadgets connected to the Internet, but anyone, anywhere could connect to them directly, control them and make changes to their software.

Someone, somewhere had created a virus to target just such appliances. It was called the 'Mirai worm', after a Japanese anime cartoon, and it spread from device to device, looking for vulnerable gadgets – with some notable exceptions: it was programmed to steer clear of IP addresses linked to the U.S. Department of Defense, for example (clearly, someone had learned the lessons of Gary McKinnon's case).[58] The virus was loaded with 62 default usernames and passwords that are often programmed into devices when they leave the factory ('admin' and 'password', for example).[59] Using these passwords allowed the virus to walk straight into many badly configured gadgets.

From its first tentative steps onto the Internet on 1 August 2016, Mirai spread like wildfire. In ten minutes it had infected 11,000 devices, going on to infect more than 65,000 in under 24 hours, according to an international team of researchers.[60] It eventually infected 600,000 devices around the world – twenty times more than the botnet that helped attack PayPal. Ironically, security cameras were a common target for infection. The virus-infected machines were mainly in Brazil, Colombia and Vietnam, but the targets those machines were forced to attack were worldwide, with America, France and the U.K. worst hit.[61]

But who was behind it? Who stood to gain from such a ferocious and unrestrained attack?

As the worm made the news and security researchers began tracking it, the Minecraft server companies who'd been hit by Mirai started receiving messages immediately after the attacks, offering them 'DDoS mitigation' systems to tackle the problem, says Coelho. It looked a lot like the traditional, Mafia-style protection racket, in which the owner of a recently burned-out shop gets a suspiciously coincidental offer of 'insurance' to protect against future attacks.

The offers in this case were coming from a company called ProTraf Solutions. The company was in competition with ProxyPipe, and Coelho started seeing his customers leach away. He estimates the attacks cost him as much as half a million dollars in lost revenue, plus the time it took him to research and fight the problem. Some of the Minecraft server owners reasoned that, since they were paying for DDoS protection anyway, they would take ProTraf up on its suspiciously timed offer, which was competitively priced. In truth, ProTraf could offer competitive rates because its owners were the men who had created and unleashed the Mirai virus in the first place.

Paras Jha, aged nineteen, and Josiah White, eighteen, had set up ProTraf Solutions in around 2013. White already had history in the world of DDoS-for-hire. Under his hacker handle LiteSpeed he had written new and highly effective software that could automate attacks on websites.[62]

Jha and Coelho already knew each other, and according to someone who knew Jha, part of the motivation for the Mirai worm was to get one over on an old rival by damaging Coelho's business. But Jha also realized it had the added benefit of driving people towards ProTraf Solutions, the legitimate side of his business, which was struggling for cash.

As their botnet grew in power, Jha and White began to rent it out for cash, charging up to $3,000 for access.[63] Jha also made strenuous efforts to throw investigators off the scent, at one point hacking into the computer of an innocent French family in Versailles and using it as a staging post for Mirai. An elite team of French cyberinvestigators raided the house and arrested a nineteen-year-old, only to discover they'd been led down a blind alley.[64] Perhaps because of tricks like this, Jha called himself 'the untouchable hacker god' in online chats. It might have looked that way, but then in September 2016, he and White hit the wrong target.

Security researcher and journalist Brian Krebs runs a blog called Krebs on Security and had been very publicly probing the Mirai group, getting closer to its true owners. In what was presumably an act of revenge, the Mirai worm hit Krebs's site with a 623 Gbps attack, the largest ever publicly recorded.[65] Krebs went on the hunt, eventually identifying Jha and White as the authors of the virus.[66] The FBI weren't far behind, arresting the pair in January 2017 and later sentencing them to five years on probation with 2,500 hours of community service. They were also told to pay $127,000 in restitution.[67]

If you think this was an online spat confined to the world of Minecraft gaming, think again. Not only did Jha and White's version of Mirai infect hundreds of thousands of innocent people's devices, theirs was just the start.

As the authorities closed in on his DDoS-for-hire operation, Jha made another attempt to throw them off the scent. It was a decision prosecutors would later say was 'among the most damaging and significant acts by the Mirai group'.[68] On 30 September 2016, Jha released the source code for Mirai. Now anyone could download it and have full control of tweaking the program. The ensuing years have seen a rash of copycat attacks with devastating consequences. In all, researchers have found 33 different versions mounting attacks around the world.[69]

One of those who took up the weapon was Daniel Kaye, later described by police as 'one of the most significant cybercriminals arrested in the UK.'[70]

Thirty-year-old Kaye reportedly touted his skills as a hacker on the dark web. In 2015, he was contacted by a senior employee of a Liberian telecoms provider called Cellcom. According to UK police, Kaye was paid a $10,000 monthly retainer to attack Lonestar, a rival telecoms company in Liberia. And it seems the Mirai leak allowed Kaye to kick his attacks up a gear. From September 2016, he used his version of the Mirai botnet to bombard Lonestar, which eventually became the most-attacked target among all the Mirai spin-offs.[71] According to the National Crime Agency, 'In November 2016, the traffic from Kaye's botnet was so high in volume that it disabled Internet access across Liberia.'[72]

Others (notably Brian Krebs)[73] have disputed the extent of the outage, but certainly the effect on Lonestar was dramatic, 'resulting in revenue loss of tens of millions in U.S. dollars as customers left the network', according to the NCA. 'Remedial action taken by Lonestar to prevent the attacks incurred costs of approximately $600,000.'[74] It was just one element of Kaye's hacking campaign. He also admitted attacks on Deutsche Telekom that affected a million German customers.[75]

In January 2019, Kaye was jailed for 32 months. Meanwhile, Mirai has continued to evolve, partly because there has been no decrease in the number of cheap, badly protected gadgets in the world. And Mirai is just one part of a DDoS economy that has exploded in size since the days of the Anonymous group's protests. A 2017 report by a group of academics estimated there were ten million Denial of Service incidents per year, an astonishing 30,000 every day.[76] Most leading tech security companies report that the attack sizes are increasing. It's not only gaming businesses like Minecraft on the receiving end, either: any company doing a high-volume, low-margin trade via the Internet is now vulnerable – and that's a large and growing share of the global economy.

The tools refined by Anonymous during its high-profile protests have now been taken up by cybercriminals exploiting them for profit, and this has had serious repercussions for Internet infrastructure. But it's not just online services that are being hit by organized hacking gangs. As the next chapter will show, they are now threatening the power grids on which entire countries rely.

EIGHT

LIGHTS OUT

I n late 2017, staff at several major UK energy companies got an
email from a job hunter with an impressive CV. It boasted of 'over
30 years working for Manufacturers of Industrial Equipment',
but the applicant's current focus was clear: 'Senior Mechanical
Engineer and Ventilation Engineer at a Nuclear Plant'.

The sender claimed to be part of the decommissioning effort
at Dounreay in Scotland, one of the UK's oldest nuclear power
stations. The plant was in the middle of a demolition scheme, and
the job hunter claimed to have worked on the project, describing
their role in detail with all the right technical jargon.

Having read the preceding chapters of this book, you won't
be surprised to learn that the CV was a fake laced with a virus.
It was part of a concerted hacking campaign aimed squarely at
companies serving Britain's energy sector – including its nuclear
installations. At least four key firms would eventually fall victim.
The intruders not only stole sensitive information about the country's energy industry, but according to investigators they also
came a step closer towards being able to disrupt parts of the UK's
power grid.

The targeting of Britain's energy network was perhaps inevitable. In the preceding years, cybercriminals had learned that their
tools could be used to shut down power stations and plunge entire
cities into darkness. Computer hacking had entered what security
researchers call 'kinetic warfare'; digital tools were being used to
degrade and destroy critical installations, and the energy sector
was a key focus. One of the most damaging opening salvos in

this cyberbattle was widely believed to have been fired by the u.s., aimed firmly at crippling the nuclear aspirations of one of its oldest enemies: Iran.

Sergey Ulasen was supposed to be celebrating at a friend's rural wedding reception in June 2010, but he kept sneaking off to answer his phone:

> All the other guests were of course happily celebrating, dancing and drinking far too much, while I was there hanging on the telephone all the time, delivering urgent technical – and psychological – assistance to a dude near Tehran.
> Bubbly girls – bubbly in hand – dressed to the nines kept passing by to and fro . . . wondering what on earth I was doing talking strange things in some strange language in the woods at a wedding.[1]

The 'dude near Tehran' was a client of Ulasen's, and had just given the 28-year-old techie some news that made it hard to focus on the festivities: information about a computer virus that became more intriguing – and troubling – the more he looked at it.

Ulasen worked for VirusBlokAda, a Belarusian antivirus company. You've almost certainly not heard of them – their profile is far smaller than that of global security software giants such as Norton, McAfee and Kaspersky (where Ulasen now works). Yet the fact that VirusBlokAda stood apart from the mainstream would, ironically, put the company at the centre of a giant cyber-security story. That's because VirusBlokAda had customers in Iran. Many of the bigger international players do not supply software to the country, partly due to sanctions.[2] Even without such restrictions, most companies consider trading with the Tehran regime too contentious to risk.

Not so for VirusBlokAda. The company's antivirus software was installed on computers at several Iranian firms, and one of these customers had reached out to Ulasen after coming under attack. At first the effects seemed more annoying than harmful. When the virus infected a machine, it caused the infamous 'Blue Screen of Death' problem, in which a computer using Microsoft's Windows operating system totally seizes up, displaying an error message on a blue screen (hence the name) and requiring a restart to try to fix the problem. But as Ulasen examined the virus, he started to notice some worrying aspects. For a start, it could infect a brand-new, freshly installed version of Windows software. That meant that the virus wasn't exploiting a program that had been installed later on (like Microsoft Word, for example, or Flash Player) as malicious software more often does. Instead, the virus had managed to infect the underlying Windows operating system itself. Not only that, it had found a previously undiscovered hole in the very latest, updated version of Windows (unlike previous viruses such as WannaCry, which were more successful against older, outdated systems).

What Ulasen was looking at was an example of something rare and much sought after: a so-called 'zero day'. It's hacker slang for a new, previously unknown vulnerability in software. It's called a zero day because, once the legitimate cybersecurity industry finds out about it, the clock starts ticking to the time when they fix it and close off the hackers' access. But while the clock stays on zero, the victims are defenceless and the hackers make hay.

Zero days are not easy to find, because security researchers of all stripes, from malicious to benevolent, are constantly crawling across software to reveal weaknesses. Spotting something that everyone else has missed is tricky. It's also potentially very, very lucrative. There is a thriving market of people who want to obtain such zero days so they can exploit them before anyone else finds out about them, and there are broker companies who solicit and buy up new zero days from researchers. One such company is Zerodium. It offers between $2,000 and $2 million for new vulner-abilities. It says its work is entirely above board, and that it uses its research to help government clients.[3] And its million-dollar incentives aren't pie-in-the-sky figures. In September 2017, the company's website published an offer of $1 million to anyone who could find a previously undisclosed flaw in the dark web software Tor. In its Frequently Asked Questions section, Zerodium gave the following justification:

> While Tor network and Tor Browser are fantastic projects that allow legitimate users to improve their privacy and security on the Internet, the Tor network and browser are, in many cases, used by ugly people to conduct activities such as drug trafficking or child abuse. We have launched this special bounty for Tor Browser zero-days to help our government customers fight crime and make the world a better and safer place for all.[4]

Perhaps the company got what it was after. One year after the offer was published, Zerodium's Twitter feed carried a warning that an older version of Tor had now been revealed to contain 'a serious vuln[erability]'.[5] However, the tweet did not reveal whether that bug had come to light as a result of Zerodium's bounty offer. (The company's chief executive Chaouki Bekrar lists his address as Washington, DC. He declined to be interviewed for this book, calling his company's work 'sensitive and secret'.)

Back in his lab in Minsk, Belarus, Sergey Ulasen considered the virus: someone must have either spent a great deal of time on it, or paid an awful lot to someone else to get into Windows in a previously unknown way. (Ulasen didn't know it then, but the virus would eventually be discovered to contain not one, but four zero days – something described by one leading researcher as 'extraordinary and unique').[6]

Ulasen and his team persevered:

> We started more in-depth analysis with my colleagues in the virus lab. This involved lots of heated discussion

and argument, and actually plenty of swearing too – since there's no textbook approach to something like this and we were learning as we went along.

We kept on with it – brainstorming, drawing up schemes, and developing different idea threads. And with each step we were gradually getting more and more queasy as we started to understand just what we were dealing with.[7]

As well as working out how the virus affected the initial victim, Ulasen and his team were interested in how it spread. As we've seen throughout this book, a key hurdle for virus writers is getting people to activate the malicious software, which is often done by by tricking them into clicking on links or attachments.

The writers of the virus under Ulasen's microscope, however, didn't need their victims to click anything. They had found a novel and effective technique. When you plug in a USB memory stick, a little icon appears on your computer screen to show its presence. The hackers had managed to secrete part of their virus code inside the software that creates the icons. Simply inserting a USB stick and looking at its contents could be enough to get infected without clicking on anything.[8] From there, the virus would try to spread to other computers on the same network.

This trick had never been seen before, and for Ulasen and VirusBlokAda, it was a bombshell. On 17 June 2010, they put a note on their company's website warning that the newly discovered virus 'should be added to [the] very dangerous category [because it] causes the risk of a virus epidemic'.[9] Microsoft – whose software the virus exploited – got on board soon after the news went public. They christened the virus 'Stuxnet' after a series of letters in its code.

VirusBlokAda's announcement was picked up by the tech security community, who started to chip away the code. One researcher who took it apart found the terms 'Siemens', 'Wincc' and 'Step7'.[10] To the untrained eye they meant nothing. But to experts in the energy sector, it was deeply concerning. German company Siemens makes software that controls the equipment that runs factories and power stations. Wincc and Step7 are among the names of those esoteric, industry-specific software packages. Their presence wasn't a random inclusion: the virus wouldn't go into full effect unless it found a very specific Siemens software setup on the victim's computer. The message was clear: Stuxnet wasn't a run-of-the-mill virus trying to steal credit card numbers or launch Denial of Service attacks. Whoever had invented it was trying to interfere with physical machinery, and in a factory environment that could be very dangerous indeed – potentially even putting lives at risk.

Others had discovered what Ulasen already knew: that the virus had taken root in Iran. As Stuxnet spread, analysts at Symantec tracked 38,000 infected computers and found that almost two-thirds had Iranian IP addresses. They, too, spotted the targeting of Siemens software, and put two and two together to conclude: 'Stuxnet is a threat targeting a specific industrial control system likely in Iran, such as a gas pipeline or power plant.'[11]

The jigsaw pieces were coming together, but it would take an expert in ICS – Industrial Control Systems – to fully decode the enigma surrounding Stuxnet.

Ralph Langner ran his eponymous company from Hamburg in Germany. Unlike many tech security researchers, he had a deep understanding of power station technology. And usefully, he had to hand some of the actual equipment used in the industry – specifically, the controller units that link the power companies' computers to the hardware in the plant. Langner knew the virus targeted such units via the Siemens software. So he started testing Stuxnet out on them. No one yet knew precisely what effect Stuxnet would have on this equipment. Langner figured that once the virus thought it was connected to the right kit, it would go into effect and reveal its objectives.

But when he ran the virus, nothing happened. In order to get it to 'wake up', Langner and his team had to keep changing the settings on the test industrial controllers they were using as bait. Only when they hit on one exact configuration did Stuxnet go into effect, trying to issue a series of new commands to the equipment.

Langner and his team had unlocked another part of the Stuxnet riddle and made a stunning discovery: Stuxnet wasn't seeking out just *any* power station technology – it was laser-focused, and would only go into action once it found one highly specific configuration.[12]

Stuxnet, Langner realized, was the cyber equivalent of a guided weapon. It was aimed at only one power station in the world.

Iran has the world's fourth-largest proven reserves of crude oil.[13] So it may come as a surprise that during the period leading up the Stuxnet attack it was a net importer of petrol.

Turning crude oil into something that can power a car requires refineries, and due to sanctions and underinvestment, Iran didn't have enough capacity to meet its citizens' demand for petrol, and even had to ration supply in 2009.[14] This made Iran's drive for nuclear power (which had been going on since the 1950s) all the more critical for the country as it struggled with its energy demands. Its leaders repeatedly insisted that their nuclear pro-gramme was aimed at peaceful uses only, but their assurances did little to allay the considerable concerns of the u.s. government and some of its allies that, secretly, Iran also intended to create military nuclear technology.

Matters weren't helped when, in 2002, it was revealed that Iran had started work on a new nuclear site at Natanz, around 100 miles south of the capital Tehran. Iran was a signatory to the Treaty on the Non-Proliferation of Nuclear Weapons and had agreed to allow monitoring by the International Atomic Energy Agency (IAEA), but the agency had not been told of the Natanz facility.[15]

The purpose of the site was uranium enrichment, the process of refining uranium-rich gas by spinning it at high speed inside metal tubes, which separate out the more usable, heavier uranium gases. The extent to which the uranium is enriched is given a percentage. Uranium used in power stations need only be enriched to a few per cent. Weapons-grade uranium needs to be around 85 per cent or more. When inspectors from the IAEA finally got into the Natanz facility they found uranium particles enriched to as much as 70 per cent, raising fears Iran was assembling the ingredients for a nuclear bomb.[16] During these inspections, the IAEA's director general claimed, Iran 'tried to cover up many of their activities'.[17]

There was something especially concerning about the Natanz reactor: key parts of the site were built deep underground. If, as some feared, Natanz was being used to develop weapons-grade material, and if Iran's opponents wanted to stop it, then even the last-ditch option of bombing the plant wouldn't work (and in any case, it would have meant flying hazardous and easily exposed sorties over hostile states).

Instead, Natanz would become the first known instance of a nuclear facility being attacked using purely cyberwarfare tactics. Striking it in this way wouldn't be easy: unlike so many of the targets featured in this book, the plant's enrichment machines were not connected to the Internet. In order to attack them, the hackers would have to jump across what security researchers call an 'air gap', somehow finding a way to physically transport their virus into the facility and onto its computers, from where it could do its damage. And once inside its target, the virus would then have to 'fly blind', operating autonomously to accomplish its work without any guidance or fine-tuning from a human controller.

The solution Stuxnet's designers came up with was elegant: they created a virus that would spread widely – thereby increasing its chances of infecting computer equipment that would end up inside Natanz – but that would only do serious damage once it identified that it was inside the facility. It was like a carpet-bombing campaign where the bombs would only explode when they hit one individual building.

This explained what Ulasen, Langner and the other research-ers had found: a virus programmed to spread from computer to computer, but only to detonate its secret payload when it found exactly the right Siemens industrial setup – the one used at the Natanz nuclear plant.

At least, that was the theory. In reality, things were a bit messier.

Ultimately, more than 100,000 computers ended up being hit by Stuxnet's indiscriminate spread.[18] Many of their owners may have noticed no ill effects, because the full malicious soft-ware never triggered. But nonetheless, they were still infected by a virus smuggled onto their digital property. And as discov-ered by the Iranian companies who contacted Sergey Ulasen, the Belarusian researcher, Stuxnet *did* cause collateral damage even if it wasn't supposed to, crippling some computers with the Blue Screen of Death.

And aside from the practical fallout, there are serious ethical questions around releasing a self-spreading cyberweapon, no matter how much its authors try to limit and focus its impact. Especially when the weapon relies on 'zero day' weaknesses that, instead of being shared with the public so they can pro-tect themselves, have been hoarded and exploited by a country's cyberarmy.

As Kim Zetter wrote in her comprehensive book on Stuxnet, *Countdown to Zero Day*, 'It's a government model that relies on keeping everyone vulnerable so that a targeted few can be attacked – the equivalent of withholding a vaccination from an entire population so that a select few can be infected with a virus.'[19]

The designers of Stuxnet, however, clearly felt that the harm/benefit calculus added up in their favour. Once they'd designed their weapon, all they had to do was get it onto computers some-where near the target. From then on, the virus would spread from machine to machine, waiting until it found the configuration that confirmed it was inside the Natanz plant, and then triggering its payload.

Stuxnet began infecting firms linked to Natanz on 23 June 2009.[20] Its first victims were five companies in Iran that provided services to the country's nuclear industry. All it took was for an engineer from one of those firms to carry an infected USB stick or laptop into Natanz and plug it in, and Stuxnet would be carried across the air gap and begin its work. Inside Natanz, Stuxnet would have uncoiled its code in exactly the way Ralph Langner and his team in Germany had observed, carefully checking the configuration of the computers on which it found itself, looking for the Siemens software, then checking for exactly the right piece of industrial equipment with exactly the right settings.

Stuxnet's code was looking for the units which controlled the spinning of the centrifuges that separated out the uranium gas. The centrifuges were of an old design because Iran was locked out of the modern nuclear power community and could not obtain the latest technology. As a result, they were incredibly sensitive: one senior Iranian nuclear energy official stated that in the past, centrifuges had blown themselves apart simply due to the presence of germs in the machinery.[21] Stuxnet targeted these delicate spinning tubes, periodically speeding them up before suddenly stopping the rotors inside.

The units are supposed to spin at 63,000 revolutions per minute. Any sudden and dramatic changes in speed would almost certainly warp and crack the finely tuned components, eventually inflicting fatal damage and rendering the centrifuges unusable, thereby bringing the plant's uranium enrichment to a shuddering halt.[22] Yet the plant's workers would not see the warning signs, because part of the Stuxnet code manipulated their readouts to fool them into thinking everything was fine, and that the rotor speeds were steady.

Gradually, Stuxnet did its secret work. Throughout late 2009 and early 2010, IAEA inspectors began to notice hundreds of tubes being replaced at Natanz – many more than would usually be subject to wear and tear.[23] Not only was Iran burning through its supplies of centrifuges, it was using up precious stocks of uranium-rich gas as it tried to figure out what was going wrong.

Whoever had launched the attack was crippling a key part of Iran's nuclear infrastructure without a shot being fired – and it turned out they'd almost certainly been at it for some time. As security researchers dug deeper into the code they discovered versions of Stuxnet targeting Natanz going back several years.

These earlier versions showed that the hackers had tried several different destructive tactics, such as over-pressurizing the centrifuges. But they also revealed something else: earlier incarnations of the Stuxnet virus lacked the self-spreading technique of the newer version. The older version would have to be installed directly onto a computer that the attackers knew was going to be taken into the facility. This implies that it needed to be 'walked in' to Natanz by authorized personnel. And compared to later versions, these earlier incarnations of Stuxnet had to be even more perfectly matched to the setup within the refinery in order to be triggered. All of which suggested that at one stage the hackers had been much closer to their target; close enough that they knew a huge amount of detail about the plant, possibly from an inside source. As noted by Ralph Langner: 'Whoever provided the required intelligence may as well know the favorite pizza toppings of the local head of engineering.'[24]

How did the attackers get this level of detail? This is where the story turns from pure cyberattack into more traditional spycraft. Years after Stuxnet was exposed, it was reported that the Netherlands's intelligence agency had a mole working in Iran during Stuxnet's early development (the Dutch government did not comment on the story). According to journalists, the mole had set up a front company offering engineering help to Natanz. The facility's bosses had fallen for the ruse – the spy walked in with the virus, plugged it in, and the rest is history.[25] But it seems that at some stage, those attacking Natanz lost this precious insider access – hence the requirement for the later, self-spreading virus that could be dropped on relevant nearby companies and left to stealthily propagate until it found itself inside the plant.

But who started the whole hacking campaign in the first place? As more and more news of the once-secret operation filtered out, suspicion fell on America. Many had little difficulty in believing that the U.S. was prepared to deploy its high-tech capabilities to hobble Tehran's nuclear ambitions. And as journalists probed the story, there was no shortage of U.S. government sources happy to confirm it, crowing about having hit their old enemy. Of course, none of these sources would go on the record: the U.S. government has never officially acknowledged any role in this attack on Iran's nuclear industry. Nonetheless, thanks to the anonymous briefings given to the media, a picture has gradually emerged of how Stuxnet came to be.

It seems this idea first started under the George W. Bush administration. As researchers looked deeper into the Stuxnet virus, they found code that showed signs of being written as far back as 2005, only a few years after construction work started on Natanz.[26] The *Washington Post*, among others, reported that the U.S. worked with Israel to develop the virus under a programme called Olympic Games. It was continued under the Obama presidency, and some claim he even ramped it up due to Israel's long-held concerns about Iran's power in the region.

As Zetter writes:

> Little progress had been made with Iran via diplomatic channels, and sanctions weren't having much of their desired effect either. And there was concern that the Israelis might take matters into their own hands if the United States didn't show results soon. For these and other reasons, Obama not only decided to reauthorize the digital sabotage program but to accelerate it.[27]

Like the U.S., the Israeli administration has never publicly commented on the affair.

By November 2010, as security researchers published more and more about Stuxnet, its targeting and impact, the engineers at Natanz halted all the facility's centrifuges for six days.[28] Perhaps they'd finally cottoned on to the sophisticated virus that had been lurking inside their computers for years, subtly sabotaging their equipment to make sure it never quite functioned properly. So subtle were Stuxnet's effects, in fact, that there is some debate over its calculable impact on Iran's nuclear enrichment programme. There is some evidence that production actually increased following Stuxnet's discovery, although others argue that this increase took place within a much-limited facility – without the virus, they argue, Iran would have been far further ahead, with more centrifuges and therefore more enriched uranium.[29]

In fact, the aim of the campaign all along seems to have been to degrade Iran's capabilities rather than destroy them. As Langner states: 'The attackers were in a position where they could have broken the victim's neck, but they chose continuous periodical choking instead.'[30]

As they developed their weapon to be more and more effective, the engineers behind Stuxnet had faced a challenge as old as espionage itself: their infiltration campaign may put them in a position to destroy a key part of their enemy's operation, but if they do so, the infiltration will be spotted and blocked. It was the same dilemma that confronted British intelligence chiefs during the Second World War when they used the cracked Enigma code to decipher Nazi military communications. Had they acted aggressively on all their fresh intelligence, the Germans would have realized that the Allies had broken their code, and would have switched to a new form of encryption. In the end, Stuxnet's designers seem to have taken the same decision as Britain: to use their secret tools for a gradual campaign of attrition rather than obvious destruction.

But that wouldn't be how it would remain. The trend had been set – power stations were now another target for cyberattack.

It wasn't long before the hackers' power grid weapons were used as part of a full-scale conflict. This time there would be no subtle, stealthy tweaking of capability. The mission now was not to degrade, but to destroy.

On 23 December 2015, temperatures in Ukraine dropped to the low single figures. The country was gripped by its annual deep freeze. Then just before 4 p.m., in more than a hundred cities, towns and villages, the lights went out.

The country was used to the occasional power cut, but this was different. The outage wasn't caused by a fallen tree or a collapsed, snow-laden cable. The power had been shut off by a sophisticated and well-planned hacking campaign that had been years in the making. Once again, it came as a result of crosspollination between an organized crime group and nation-state hackers, according to investigators who tracked its origins.

In 2007, a piece of malicious software called BlackEnergy appeared on the cybercrime underground.[31] It was, in many ways, a fairly standard piece of criminal software. Spread via spam email, it would infect a victim's computer, then secretly allow that computer to be used to flood a website with junk requests – a classic Distributed Denial of Service attack of the kind covered throughout this book.

But BlackEnergy's designers didn't stop there. The virus transformed into a multi-use hacking tool capable of controlling an entire computer. Security researchers spotted telltale signs that the evolving series of BlackEnergy versions were all crafted by the same hand, including the fact that each new iteration contained references in the code to the fantasy sci-fi series *Dune* – it seemed whoever was coding it was a big fan.[32] Eventually, BlackEnergy was picked up by people who had far more sinister goals than just infecting computers to stage DDOS attacks. They would deploy it right in the middle of a highly active conflict zone.

In February 2014, after Ukrainian protesters deposed the pro-Russian president Viktor Yanukovych, Russian Federation troops entered Ukraine and occupied Crimea, an area in the south with a majority of Russian-speaking inhabitants that had long been a site of tension between the two countries.[33] It began an intense period of armed conflict.

But according to security researchers, the battle wasn't only being waged using physical weapons. From May 2014, the BlackEnergy malware was loaded into documents sent out to targets in Ukraine. Employees in the country's six railway companies received an email attachment on 'security recommendations', which appeared to contain a list of examples of weak passwords. Regional administrators got a PowerPoint presentation allegedly showing details of people suspected of assisting terrorists. Broadcasters were sent documents containing tip-offs about Ukrainian protesters. All the messages, along with many others sent in the same campaign, had BlackEnergy hidden inside.[34]

The virus exploited a common piece of technology called 'macros'. These are bits of computer code that sit inside, for example, Microsoft Word documents or PowerPoint presentations and are often used to automate repetitive tasks. When asked whether to run the macro, if a user clicks 'yes', then their computer can get infected by malicious software hidden inside the macro code – but the victim won't notice anything different in the document they're reading.

This was exactly the trick the hackers used to break into Ukraine's energy grid.

In mid-2015, virus-carrying emails were received by workers at three of Ukraine's energy companies, all of which owned substations that distributed electricity to homes and businesses throughout the country. The hackers' trick worked: some of the recipients ran the macros and got infected with BlackEnergy software.[35] The cyberattackers were now inside a significant part of the country's critical infrastructure, and would spend the next four months positioning themselves to take the substations simultaneously out of action. Usefully for these hackers, there was one major hurdle encountered in the Iranian nuclear facility attack that they wouldn't be facing here.

The Natanz plant was a hard target because of the 'air gap' between its industrial equipment and the Internet. But as power networks have evolved, they have increasingly closed these air gaps. Cybersecurity professionals who work in the energy sector have watched with concern as increasing amounts of the power network are put online. 'It's being driven by commercial factors,' says Andrew Tsonchev, industrial security expert for UK cybersecurity company Darktrace. This growing trend for connection is driven by two main motivations: upkeep, because it allows engineers to 'dial in' remotely to repair and monitor distant bits of equipment, meaning fewer staff can cover more facilities; and data, the lifeblood of so many of today's businesses. 'To be efficient and compete you need data,' says Tsonchev. 'Everyone is obsessed with data: they need telemetry, analysis on how the power is being generated, how the grid is being run. That means that you need to open up pathways between the systems.'

Each of those pathways potentially opens up a fresh line of attack.

Nonetheless, simply breaking into a power company employee's computer isn't quite enough to allow a hacker to immediately turn a country's power off. Companies like those in Ukraine do have some protection against low-level hacking. Their computer systems are divided into two sides: information technology (IT) and operational technology (OT). The IT side is similar to that found in any company: there are normal computers that likely use Microsoft's Windows operating system, loaded with normal programs like Word and Excel. It's the kind of tech we all use, and for the attackers targeting Ukraine, that meant they were able to hack it using the macro trick.

However, OT computers are a different ball game. They have specialist software that controls the giant, complicated pieces of machinery used to generate and control the electricity feeding millions of homes. These are not the kinds of systems most people have any experience using. And they're often bespoke to each power station: just getting to grips with the systems' layouts is a challenge for a hacker, let alone attacking them. Off-the-shelf, automated hacking software won't work, says Tsonchev: 'The attacks have to be custom-made because the systems are custom-made. It's at the very highest end of the challenge spectrum. The only people who can do this are the ones that are incredibly well-funded and talented.'

Unluckily for Ukraine's power companies, it seems the hackers who broke in during 2015 were indeed well-funded and talented. Once they had penetrated the IT system, they spotted something very useful: links from the ordinary, everyday office computers to the powerful, bespoke OT machines.

They began to map out the network and prepare the ground for an attack.

Hackers have been sniffing around the power network for many years – partly, perhaps, out of curiosity, but also with an eye to finding industrial secrets they might be able to sell or otherwise exploit. Recently, however, security researchers have noticed a step change in the kind of activity hitting the energy sector, as one intriguing experiment shows.

In July 2018, Israeli cybersecurity firm Cybereason set up a fake electricity transmission station.[36] They got hold of exactly the kind of OT software used by the big power companies, basing it on conversations they'd had with a large American firm. Within their computers they linked up the components of their fake facility exactly the way it would be set up in a real power substation. And they made it accessible to the Internet, providing a login page of the kind used by engineers who need to remotely control such an operation. To give the hackers a chance, they deliberately set weak passwords on the system.

Of course, Cybereason didn't have access to an actual power station, let alone teams of employees in boiler suits. But any hackers probing the Internet who stumbled on Cybereason's test setup could be convinced that they'd hacked into a real, functioning part of the electricity grid somewhere in the northeastern u.s. The speed with which their phoney power station was discovered and attacked is astonishing.

'Within moments of putting it online we got scanned,' says Israel Barak, Cybereason's chief information security officer. 'It took them five or ten minutes to start looking for login details.'

In only two days, the fake setup was hacked. The firm had a fair idea where the attackers had come from: the software used for the break-in was rife on a particular dark web crime forum called xDedic. Specifically, what that software did was to provide the hackers remote access to and control of the IT parts of Cybereason's fake electricity facility.

Over the next few days, Cybereason's researchers watched as the hackers went to work. What they saw was run-of-the-mill cybercrime. The hackers used their new-found victim computers to generate cryptocurrency (the 'cryptojacking' covered earlier) and to launch flood attacks against other websites. Nothing especially unusual.

Then suddenly there was a change. Cybereason saw a login from a new user. Given the connection to the dark web crime forum, Cybereason assumes that the original hackers had sold their access to someone else, although the company didn't see the actual transaction go down. These new hackers weren't interested in the generic-but-profitable cybercrime being done by the original intruder. As the researchers watched, it became clear they had only one goal in mind: finding a link between the Internet-facing IT parts and the OT computers that controlled the power station (or at least, would have done if this were a real facility).

Within a couple of weeks, the hackers had found the weak point, correctly identifying the computers that linked the IT side with the OT side. Then they stopped.

Cybereason's researchers aren't sure why, but Barak has an idea: 'The attacker might have realized it was a trap. No matter how hard we worked, there were always aspects of a real power facility that we can't create in a lab.'

Cybereason had created a so-called 'honeypot'. It was an experiment that, although yielding fascinating insight into the way cybercriminals hack the energy sector, would never have any real-world effects. Back in Ukraine, however, things were about to get very real-world indeed.

The hackers there were worming their way deeper inside the three Ukrainian power distributors, using tactics very similar to the ones Cybereason had observed. And they'd found the ideal way to cripple the power supply to thousands of homes.

Out in the electrical grid, there are circuit breakers. Much like the ones in your home, when triggered they open a gap in the circuit and stop the power flow. Unlike the ones in your house, the power station breakers are enormous. In order to cut off the power from the distributors to their customers and plunge them into darkness, the hackers would need to open these breakers. The units themselves are dotted around Ukraine, miles from the power station itself. But they were remotely controlled from within the three power companies using a Human–Machine Interface computer, or HMI. This was the key link between the IT side and the OT side that controlled the machinery.

The hackers gained access to this HMI computer using passwords they'd stolen as they hacked into the power company employees' machines. They now had control of the breakers out in the field and could shut off the power supply whenever they wanted.

By 23 December 2015, the scene was set. At 3.35 p.m., around an hour before sunset, the hackers went into action, hitting all three power providers within the space of half an hour.[37] Workers at one facility, Prykarpattyaoblenergo, reportedly watched as, on one of their computers, the mouse cursor moved across the screen without their control, edging towards the HMI controls.[38] The phantom hand then opened the power breakers one by one, cutting the power to hundreds of thousands of homes.

The engineers immediately tried to close the breakers to re-establish the power, but the hackers were one step ahead of them, ready with the first of a series of intricately planned countermeasures that demonstrate the complexity of the attack.

The hackers had realized that the breakers communicated with the power company's computers using special boxes called serial-to-Ethernet devices (which change signals from the power breakers into traffic that can be sent over the Internet). Immediately after beginning their attack, the hackers sent out a fake update to these boxes. When they received the update, the serial-to-Ethernet boxes installed it, and were immediately disabled. So when the station engineers tried to contact the boxes to close the breakers and turn the power back on, the boxes were no longer listening.[39] With no ability to remotely close the breakers, the station would have to send out engineers to physically re-establish the power, a massive headache that extended the power outage by hours.

But when the power station's staff picked up the phones to call for help, they were hit with another of the hackers' countermeasures. The cybercriminals had cut off the phone lines.

Critical bits of infrastructure like power companies and air traffic control towers have to have their own, independent, reliable supply of energy in case anything goes wrong. This is known as the Uninterruptible Power Supply or UPS. In the event of a power outage, this backup supply kicks in. In the case of the Ukrainian power distributors, the phone system was connected to this UPS, so it should have remained usable even during the outage. The hackers had spotted this and disabled the UPS. Engineers in the power companies now struggled to make a call, let alone reassert control of their facility.

By now, temperatures in Ukraine had dropped to six degrees Celsius. With the power off, more than a hundred cities, towns and villages were plunged into darkness, with 186 more experiencing partial blackouts. Around 225,000 people were without power. Yet if worried residents wanted to call the company to find out what was going on or report the problem, they were out of luck, thanks to another of the hackers' tricks: they had used computer software to inundate the help centre of one of the power companies with phonecalls, effectively jamming the switchboard.[40]

And there was one, final insult still to come. The hackers knew that, after a time, the stations' engineers would reboot the computer system to try to get everything back on track, so they secreted an unpleasant surprise for them. They reprogrammed the companies' computers so that, once restarted, they would run a program called KillDisk. As the name suggests, this software effectively wipes the entire computer clean, rendering it unusable. As the power stations' staff hit the reset button, hoping to end the nightmare and get back on their feet, they wiped every single computer they touched.[41]

The power stations were out of action for three hours, and it took several hours more to reconnect the supply. Throughout the country, lights went out and electrical heating systems ground to a halt. Residents reached for candles and blankets, still unaware of the true cause of the outage.

As the scale of the attacks on Ukraine's power stations became clear, and as the news emerged that it had been carried out by a hack, waves of concern spread across the tech security industry and some parts of the energy sector, which at this time could have been forgiven for believing it was above the fray of cybercrime. One night without power may not sound too bad, but what worried observers was the potential that this kind of hack signalled. The attack was unprecedented and raised a frightening vision of a world in which hackers can disable a country's power grid at will.

Yet far from backing off as their work was revealed, the hackers came back almost exactly a year later with an even more powerful weapon, once again targeting Ukrainian power stations.

Like BlackEnergy, Crash Override was a virus aimed at damaging power stations and plunging Ukraine into the dark. Yet this time, it featured software that could automatically control what the virus did. It was something that could, like Stuxnet, 'fly blind' within a power station without relying on a human controller. This time, the virus hit a single power station rather than the three targeted in the previous attack. But that's no reason to be relieved: the station it infected was a major transmission site that, according to reporting in *Wired* magazine, carried 200 megawatts of power – a greater total electric load than all the distribution stations knocked out in the 2015 attack combined.[42]

The Ukrainian incidents didn't just demonstrate how easily some power networks could be attacked. Taking place during the middle of such a fierce territorial dispute, they tapped into a wider fear about how new tactics of cyberwarfare are being tested in areas already embroiled in conflict.

'The gloves are off. This is a place where you can do your worst without retaliation or prosecution,' Kenneth Geers, a NATO ambassador who focuses on cybersecurity, told *Wired* journalist Andy Greenberg for an extensive article on the attacks. 'Ukraine is not France or Germany. A lot of Americans can't find it on a map, so you can practice there.'[43]

Many in the military and intelligence community have long known that the future of cybertactics is their use as a so-called 'force multiplier': a way of augmenting the kinetic conflict being waged in places like Ukraine. The problem is that, for the moment at least, the global political, diplomatic and legal spheres are struggling to understand how such tactics fit into traditional warfare and its associated rules of engagement. The concern is that in this digital no-man's-land, new techniques will be tested and refined with little regard to the collateral damage or the wider future ramifications.

Some laid the blame for the Ukrainian power hacks in both 2015 and 2016 at the door of the Russian government. Without referring directly to the power outages, a statement shortly after the 2016 attack from the office of Ukraine's president, Petro Poroshenko, claimed his country's 'investigation of a number of incidents indicated the complicity directly or indirectly of Russian security services waging a cyber war against our country'.[44] More specifically, researchers found circumstantial evidence of links to Russia: the original BlackEnergy virus was accompanied by a help page written in Russian, for example.[45] U.S. security firm FireEye claimed to have traced a key feature of the intruders' tactics to a presentation given at a Russian hacker conference.[46] The flood of automated calls that inundated one of the power station's help-lines in 2015 allegedly originated in Russia.[47] Security researchers also make the obvious point that, of all countries in the world, it's Russia that's deep in conflict with Ukraine. Who else, they argue, would have an interest in crippling the country's power grid?

It seems the British government isn't quite so sure. In October 2018, the National Cyber Security Centre issued a press release about Russian cyberattacks. It listed the hacker groups the Centre claims are part of Russia's military intelligence unit. Sure enough, among them were BlackEnergy and Sandworm, two names widely implicated in the Ukrainian attacks. Yet the release stopped short of directly linking them to the 2015 and 2016 power grid hacks.[48]

Some British security researchers, however, firmly believe that Russian hackers are not only hitting power stations, but have already targeted the UK, infiltrating a series of companies that have key roles in supporting the country's energy network. The attacks, they claim, took the hackers worryingly close to the heart of the UK's nuclear infrastructure.

In February 2018, tech security firm Secureworks was called in to help a British company that supplies equipment and services to the country's oil and gas sector.

Secureworks quickly discovered that the victim's network had been hacked and likely been used to send convincing phishing emails similar to the one described at the beginning of this chapter, which appeared to come from a nuclear industry employee. Not only was the company itself a target of the hackers, but it may have been used to snare more victims.

More targets emerged. In April, investigations identified another company serving the oil and gas industry affected by the same campaign, findings that in turn led Secureworks to two more victims. The firms were all key suppliers to Britain's energy sector, including its nuclear facilities. (Secureworks declined to name any of the victims, citing client confidentiality.)

The targets had all been hit with the same malicious software, and it wasn't new to Secureworks' researchers. They, along with other tech security firms, had been tracking it since as long ago as 2010, watching it develop and crop up in multiple companies often linked to the energy industry. Because it always seems to be used in the same way, and because its current version has not been seen for sale on the cybercrime underground, researchers believe it's under the control of a single group. Now, that same group was striking hard at the UK. One of their tricks was to hack into the servers of a U.S. publisher called CFE Media, which produces specialist publications for engineers. They planted infected files that would be downloaded by visitors to the company's online magazines.

This is called a watering-hole attack – rather than pursuing individual quarry, you poison the water they all feed on. 'You're hitting a community of interest,' says Rafe Pilling, an information security researcher with Secureworks. Using this tactic, the hacker doesn't know who'll get infected, but chances are it will be someone useful to their aims.

The hack worked. During summer 2016, visitors to the website of *Consulting-Specifying Engineer* magazine whose computers weren't protected found themselves unwittingly sending their Windows username and password to a server run by the hackers.[49] These details could then potentially be used to log into engineers' work computers, giving the hackers a stepping stone towards their targets in the energy sector.

CFE Media declined to comment on the incident for this book.

Secureworks started to see other signs that the intruders were advanced operators – including the use of a tactic available only to the world's most well-resourced hackers. It exploits the frequent updates that our computers' software carries out. Whether it's iTunes, Flash Player or Java, something always seems to need an update. To hack their victims, the attackers intercepted these update requests and hijacked them, delivering instead an update that was laced with infected files. To do so, the hackers had to tap into the Internet router that sits between the victim and the Internet. Just like a home user, a company connects to the Web via a router, and if you can hack that box, you can spot the update requests as they pass through – and manipulate them.

This interception trick was first revealed to the public by Edward Snowden, the American intelligence contractor-turned-whistle-blower who leaked documents in 2013. He detailed the u.s. National Security Agency's use of it under the name Quantum Insert. Such a tactic requires serious online firepower. The hackers are, in effect, in a race with the world's foremost software companies to see who can deliver their update package first. Winning that race requires skill, speed and resources only available to the world's best.

'It's what most nation-state level groups would do,' says Don Smith, Secureworks' technology director. 'You need big "pipes" [a fast Internet connection to the hacked router]. You're trying to get your answer back faster than the legitimate update provider.'

By now it was becoming clear that companies in the UK energy market were being hit by a player with major resources. And when Secureworks dug into what the attackers were after, they became even more concerned. They found traces of the kind of documents the hackers were stealing: sensitive information not only about the victim companies themselves, but about the wider UK power sector that those companies supported.

In a normal hacking incident, tech security companies are sometimes prepared to let the attackers keep operating for a limited time. There are good reasons for this: it means researchers can track their tactics, get a full picture of how far they've infiltrated their victims' systems and gather data so they can spot them again in future. Not so in this case. Such was the apprehensiveness over the victims' links to critical UK energy infrastructure that Secureworks moved in quickly to shut the attackers out. But the hackers weren't going to give up without a fight.

'They knew we were systematically evicting them,' recalls Smith. 'They did not want to let go of what they had. At one point we saw [the hackers uploading] fresh malware that had been compiled the night before. It was cat and mouse between attacker and defender.'

Eventually, Secureworks succeeded. By this time, they had identified four companies serving Britain's oil, gas and nuclear industries that had been infected with the same strain of malicious software – but researchers feared that they were seeing only a fraction of a much wider hacking campaign.

Like those who investigated the power station attacks in Ukraine, Secureworks found evidence they claim points to Russian involvement. They believe the virus they found is the tool of a single hacker group whose goal is 'to gather intelligence on the energy sector (particularly in Europe) to assist Russian government and corporate decision-making, and to gain access to energy-linked ICS [Industrial Control Systems]'.[50]

The Russian government did not respond to requests for an interview for this book made via its London embassy and directly to its foreign ministry.

Secureworks researchers are clear that at no point did they believe the hackers were about to launch the kind of ruinous attacks inflicted on Ukraine. Britain's power grid was not on the verge of being switched off. Rather, their belief is that what they witnessed were spying exercises. But of course, that intelligence could one day be used in an attack.

Pilling, Secureworks information security researcher, says:

You've probably got two arms to this thing. Espionage, for example collecting information that informs policy and decision-making at political levels. And the other one potentially is some kind of pre-positioning of capability to do something Ukrainian-style in the UK in the event of such circumstances that might merit it.

Hacker tactics have moved a long way. From simple mischief or money-making (or a combination of both), in the last few years they've had bigger and more significant impacts on our lives. And now, hackers are not just threatening the infrastructure that helps us survive, but are manipulating what we see and hear. It's a confluence of criminal hacking and influence management that has been brewing for years.

NINE

WEAPONIZING DATA

I t's perception management using global journalism for ammunition. A new field of propaganda.' These are the words of Jake Davis, aka Topiary, one of the founding members of the LulzSec hacking group. As described earlier, Davis and his fellow hackers formed a splinter group from the Anonymous movement and went on a spree in 2011, breaking into the UK's Serious Organised Crime Agency, the Sony Corporation, the NHS and many others.

While less skilled than some of the hackers in this book, Davis and LulzSec were key contributors to a pivotal evolution of cybercrime: a turn away from straightforward money-making and spycraft and towards hacking as a method of information warfare. Rather than simply dumping stolen data online, hackers have learned to weaponize this information by editorializing it. They pick and choose the most damaging details and release them strategically so as to inflict the maximum damage on their target. Not content with this, they are now co-opting journalists to make sure of the most destructive headlines.

They may not have known it, but groups like LulzSec helped sow the seeds of these developments. They showed how the timing of an attack, the strategic leaking of data and above all the careful use of the news media could generate global publicity and create devastating consequences for their victims.

The quote above is from an interview I carried out with Davis in 2018, long after LulzSec was taken down and he was convicted. It's a bleak but fair summation of how this area of cybercrime has evolved in the years since LulzSec's heyday. The lessons of their hacks and those of others have seeped deep into the cyber-crime community, and led to consequences far greater than the corporate havoc wreaked by the likes of Davis and his associates.

This chapter looks at several incidents covering a range of tactics and motivations. The hacks are disparate, but they have one thing in common: the attempted – and often successful – destruction of a target through data leaks. The mix of strategies involved shows a building convergence of hacking, trolling, journalism and the highly strategic use of stolen information.

MASTERING THE MEDIA

Prior to his days in LulzSec, while growing up in the tiny Scottish island community of the Shetlands, Davis experienced what many shy-but-witty youngsters feel – the drive to win popularity by making people laugh. His early forays into online discussion boards saw him making prank calls for a global audience. 'I felt it was like taking up a microphone and putting on this character,' he recalls. 'There's a sense of freedom. That was my only outlet. All my energy didn't go into clubbing or getting wasted, it went into this performance.'

He went on to cut his teeth in the whirlwind of Anonymous's chatrooms, and learned how to make his voice heard as the movement took shape. As the spin-off group LulzSec emerged, Davis harnessed his ability to gather a crowd, drawing attention to the group's increasingly daring exploits. On occasions, he flagged LulzSec's upcoming hacks like a circus ringmaster, sometimes giving a countdown to when the next leak of stolen data would be revealed.[1] Press interest quickly followed, and so began a symbiotic relationship, with media attention feeding LulzSec and the group reciprocating by giving the media ever more outrageous hacking behaviour on which to report. This reached its height on 19 July 2011, when LulzSec hacked into the servers of *The Sun* newspaper and replaced its front page with a story claiming Rupert Murdoch, head of *The Sun*'s owner, News Corporation, had been found dead.[2]

There were jokes-within-jokes: the article claimed Murdoch was discovered in his 'famous topiary garden' (a reference to Davis's hacker handle). But there was an even deeper dimension to the gag. Davis planned to use their hacking of *The Sun* to subvert another branch of the Murdoch empire: Sky News.

> We replaced the front page with a fake news article. Then when Sky News started reporting on it live on the 10.45 p.m. 'next day's papers' show we changed the website so it redirected to our Twitter account live, and so the news reporter would say 'Oh no, the website seems to have changed.' We wanted to be absurdist and outrageous.

What's remarkable is that Davis and his co-conspirators knew so much about Sky News – a channel which, although influential, probably isn't must-watch viewing for the kind of hacker crowd that made up most of Anonymous. The timing of its late-night newspaper review is something even dedicated Sky News viewers might struggle to remember. Not only did Davis and his buddies know exactly when this relatively obscure news segment went on air, they were prepared to risk going to jail to hijack it.

Perhaps their innate grasp of media machination shouldn't come as a surprise. Davis and his cohort were raised in the era of 24-hour news and constant data flows, and he was deeply interested in how such streams of information could be manipulated.

> There was inspiration from [1980s faux-animation newsreader] Max Headroom, taking over TV transmissions, making something there that's not supposed to be there, and subverting reality. When you're seventeen or eighteen and you've got *The Matrix* and *1984* flying through your head you think, 'This is great, we can subvert the Internet so it doesn't act the way people want it to act.'

Understanding news media so you can subvert it to your own ends has a very long history in Internet trolling. In one infamous case in 2007, trolls picked up on an old news story about children in Zambia allegedly getting high by inhaling a mixture of fermented urine and faeces, nicknamed 'Jenkem'. It was a bizarre story, and some of the trolls clearly found it hilarious. They encouraged each other to hype up Jenkem as a potential threat to local schools in America. Remarkably, despite the lack of evidence, one police force in Florida took the alert seriously and, in turn, some local news outlets began reporting the danger of Jenkem to children.[3]

In her book on trolling, *This Is Why We Can't Have Nice Things*, Whitney Phillips describes this tactic as 'media fuckery':

> By reporting on the story (or nonstory, as the case may be), media outlets give the trolls what they want, namely, exposure and laughs, and participating media get what they want, namely, a story and eyeballs to commodify through advertisements. In this way, each camp ends up benefiting the other.[4]

Incidents such as the Jenkem hoax and LulzSec's manipulation of the Murdoch publications sent out a clear message to trolls and hackers alike: there's fun to be had in taking on big media interests and winning, and there's power to be gained by controlling the feed of information and watching your story make headlines.

This was taken to a destructive level in February 2011 when, as described earlier, LulzSec hacked into u.s. tech security firm HBGary Federal, hitting the headlines by exposing the company's shady dealings. As HBGary Federal was reduced to ashes and its chief executive forced to resign, it became clear that if hackers learned how to master the media, they could break an organization apart.

LEAKING STRATEGICALLY

On 19 July 2015, the website of U.S.-based tech security journalist Brian Krebs – whom we met earlier when he exposed the Mirai group – carried a worldwide scoop. 'Online Cheating Site Ashley Madison Hacked', read the title.[5]

Krebs wrote that a hacker or hackers operating under the name Impact Team claimed to have copied the dating website's user databases, financial records 'and other proprietary information'. Immediately, it was worldwide news, partly due to the irresistibly salacious nature of the target. Ashley Madison was a site offering to hook users up for extramarital affairs. It was owned by Avid Life Media, which ran other sites including Cougar Life (for older women seeking 'energetic younger men') and Established Men (connecting 'young, beautiful women' with 'successful men').[6] Its chief executive Noel Biderman seemed to play up to the moral outrage his sites provoked, appearing on TV programmes to defend the businesses, and harvesting useful publicity as a result.

Impact Team released samples of the stolen data (I've referred below to the hackers as a group, but it's possible it was an individual). Their motive for the hack is implied by a shocking allegation made about the company's practices. Avid Life Media's sites offered to completely erase users' profile information for a $19 fee – something a cheating spouse might consider a worthwhile payment to cover their tracks. Impact Team claimed that in fact the company retained users' details including their real name and address.

The hackers made a simple threat, published in Brian Krebs's online report:

> Take Ashley Madison and Established Men offline permanently in all forms, or we will release all customer records, including profiles with all the customers' secret sexual fantasies and matching credit card transactions, real names

and addresses, and employee documents and emails. The other websites may stay online . . .

With over 37 million members, mostly from the u.s. and Canada, a significant percentage of the population is about to have a very bad day, including many rich and powerful people.[7]

The statement also had a blunt message for the site's users, who may have felt they were innocent people caught in the crossfire: 'Too bad for those men, they're cheating dirtbags and deserve no such discretion.'

There were some intriguing aspects to the hack and those behind it: Krebs never revealed where the initial announcement was made by Impact Team. No one had heard of the hackers before, and no attacks have since been claimed under that name. Whoever was behind it was competent: they wiped the leaked data clean of a lot of the telltale fingerprints that had identified hackers in previous incidents. Meanwhile, Ashley Madison and Established Men stayed obstinately online. Perhaps Avid Life Media thought the hackers were making idle threats. If so, it was a miscalculation. After waiting almost a month, on 16 August, Impact Team ran out of patience and dumped more than thirty million records online for all to see.

Once again, they had a message for the people whose details they'd just exposed in the database: 'Find yourself in here? It was [Avid Life Media] that failed you and lied to you. Prosecute them and claim damages. Then move on with your life. Learn your lesson and make amends. Embarrassing now, but you'll get over it.'[8]

The media had a field day. The database was extremely large and unwieldy, but once downloaded and formatted, it did indeed contain users' real names and email addresses, as the hackers had promised. It also contained deeply sensitive information on their sexual orientations and preferences. A feeding frenzy began. Journalists combed the records for government, police and military email addresses. The leaked information also included IP records, so people could be traced back to the computer they were using when they logged in, potentially revealing their workplace.

Eventually the entire database was posted online and anyone, anywhere in the world could simply enter an email address into a website and find out if it was in the Ashley Madison files. Famously, an Australian radio station, Nova FM, staged a phone-in programme in which listeners could call in with their partner's email address and find out, live on air, whether they were on the list.[9] The stunt was halted, seemingly after only one call, during which the hosts suddenly realized the ramifications of informing a woman that her husband's name was on the leaked database. 'Oh, I don't know if we should have done that,' said one of the presenters immediately after the caller had hung up, furious. 'That hasn't left me with a good feeling.'

As far as many were concerned, however, more than thirty million people had just been publicly outed as 'cheats' and 'love rats', and they deserved everything that was coming to them. The problem was that many of the headlines were wrong. And it's possible that a very small number of people may have died as a result.

The truth about Ashley Madison and its sister websites was that people could very easily register using someone else's email address (as a prank, for example). The sites didn't send an email to check whether the address's owner really wanted to sign up. In effect, this meant that anyone could be enrolled without their knowledge – their email address would be stored in Ashley Madison's database even if they'd never heard of the site, let alone used it.

I knew about this issue, because two months earlier I'd downloaded the profiles of four million people leaked from a different sex hook-up website. Adult Friend Finder claims it is 'the world's largest sex and swinger community'.[10] In early 2015, as part of my dark web research, I discovered an anonymous user on a forum called 'Hell' who'd made available millions of records hacked from the site. Doubting the information was real, I downloaded it in a series of spreadsheets, and was suddenly confronted with the sexual peccadilloes of millions of people, as well as their email addresses and usernames. I stored them on an encrypted USB stick to keep them safe.

I still wasn't sure if the information was authentic, so I set about emailing people on the list, which was obviously quite a tricky task; I worried that my email could be read by the person's partner or spouse, who wouldn't take kindly to finding out about their loved one's use of a site like Adult Friend Finder. Nonetheless, I managed to confirm that the data was genuine, and that many users were appalled to find out it had been leaked. In some cases they'd been told their data had been deleted, yet here it was for all to see. (After my story was broadcast, the site promised a comprehensive investigation and pledged to take 'appropriate steps' to protect its customers.)[11] But among the people I contacted, I discovered that some had been signed up by friends as a joke, because Adult Friend Finder used the same sign-up system as Ashley Madison, meaning anyone's email address could end up on the database without their knowledge.

To be clear: when I broke the story, my reporting described the people whose details were leaked as 'users' and 'members' of Adult Friend Finder, which in hindsight was a mistake. But there was a big difference between my story about Adult Friend Finder and the Ashley Madison hack. In the latter case, not only were millions of people being potentially misreported as 'members' or 'users' of the site, but because the hackers had leaked the database online, personal details could be looked up with a simple Internet search (as opposed to the stolen Adult Friend Finder data, which was only accessible through the dark web).

Arguably, misidentifying every person listed in the Ashley Madison database as a 'user' of the site had extremely serious consequences. Whether or not the people whose names appeared on the database had, in fact, used Ashley Madison, the shame of merely appearing on the list – or even fearing they might have – led some to take their own lives. A Baptist pastor in New Orleans committed suicide. His name was in the Ashley Madison leak, and according to his family he mentioned this in his suicide note.[12] A police captain in San Antonio also took his own life. He'd been experiencing serious problems at work and when his computer was seized, even though it was unrelated to the hack and his email address was not on the Ashley Madison list, his family says he feared the leaked data would be used to incriminate him.[13] Canadian police also reported two suicides they said were linked to the Ashley Madison leak, but no further details were released.

Perhaps the saddest aspect is that there was an easy way to work out which people on the database were actively using Ashley Madison. Like many dating sites, it operated on a free-to-browse, pay-to-message model. The leaked data recorded when someone had made a payment, and therefore by stripping out only those accounts with a payment history, it was possible to work out a truer number of actual 'users'. It turned out to be a far lower figure than the headlines suggested. In my analysis of the 1.2 million UK records in the database, I found that only 12,000 had made payments.[14] But this analysis took me three days of wrangling the giant database. By the time I had done so, the misleading headlines about tens of millions of 'users' had become an accepted truth.

Meanwhile, as Avid Life Media reeled under the global publicity storm, the hackers were preparing another body blow for the company. On 20 August, a few days after the 'user' database was leaked, the hackers published Avid Life Media's corporate emails, along with more company documents. These revealed stunning information about the company's internal practices. Avid Life Media had created 'chatbots' – automated software that would converse with newly active users of the site, presumably in an effort to get them to pay in order to continue the conversation. Some publications put the number of these so-called 'fembots' at 70,000.[15]

If true, the allegations were an insight into the cynical view the company took of its users, many of whom stood little chance of ever finding a date through the site (partly because the hacked data reportedly revealed, perhaps predictably, that the majority of users were male: around 30 million of the 37 million total).[16] Eight days later, Noel Biderman, Avid Life Media's chief executive, quit.

Remarkably, the hack didn't kill the business: all three sites are still operating, albeit under a different company. So the hackers only partially achieved their objectives. But on a deeper level, there was something striking about how the Ashley Madison hackers went about releasing their stolen information, especially in light of the strategic-leaking lessons of groups like LulzSec.

The attackers revealed the 'user' database first, then waited a few days before leaking the company's emails, which got far less publicity. I found this odd, because I suspect most journalists would have been more interested in the company emails. When assessing a story, journalists are often looking for what's called 'institutional failure'. Put simply: while a bad person doing a bad thing might be enough for a story, a person who's supposed to be good but does a bad thing is almost certainly news. In this context, Ashley Madison's user database was far less newsworthy than its corporate emails. The database showed ostensibly bad people ('love rats') doing a bad thing (extramarital affairs). The emails showed supposedly responsible people (corporate executives of a major international company) allegedly doing a bad thing (filling the dating site with fake 'bot' accounts).

The Ashley Madison hackers thought differently. They didn't necessarily care about the corporate failure, as journalists would. They wanted to do the maximum damage to the company in the shortest amount of time by gaining the most headlines. And they had available to them an option that would be beyond the appetite of most journalists: publicly releasing the incredibly sensitive user data.

The hackers' sequencing decisions may have been different to journalists', but nonetheless they'd mastered a key tactic of news media. Rather than dump all the data at once (as hackers had often done previously), they drip-fed increasingly damaging information. As one seasoned reporter put it to me: 'some of these hackers would make great news editors. They can filter and assess loads of information and pick just the right bit to leak at just the right time.'

In short: the hackers set the agenda, and the media followed.

LEAKING STRATEGICALLY AND HARNESSING THE MEDIA

Several months before Ashley Madison's name was dragged through the mud, the Guardians of Peace group broke into Sony Pictures Entertainment's computer systems.

The process of the hack and its alleged links to the North Korean government were described in an earlier chapter, but it is now time to consider a whole other side to the story: how the hackers stage-managed the leaking of the data.[17] Guardians of Peace (GOP) stole an estimated 38 million files from the entertainment giant over the course of three months before breaking cover and beginning to wipe Sony employees' computers with their virus.[18] They started by leaking a few unreleased films, but that was just a taster of what was to come. By the time they went public in November 2014, the group reportedly had everything from private emails to employees' social security numbers and medical records, and even the aliases that celebrities used when they checked into hotels.[19]

Like those who attacked Ashley Madison, the GOP hackers set out to carefully drip-feed this trove of stolen data to ensure maximum damage. But unlike Impact Team, they didn't just wait for the news media to pick up the stories: they actively prompted them.

Hi, I am the boss of G.O.P.

A few days ago, we told you the fact that we had released Sony Pictures films including *Annie*, *Fury* and *Still Alice* to the Web.

Those can be easily obtained through Internet search.
For this time, we are about to release Sony Pictures data
to the Web. The volume of the data is under 100 Terabytes.

This email arrived on a Saturday morning, 29 November, in the personal inbox of Kevin Roose, who at the time was a senior editor on a news website called Fusion.net. The email included a link to a site where the data could be downloaded, and a password to unlock the files. Roose wasn't alone. Emails arrived in the inboxes of editors at Gawker, BuzzFeed, The Verge and others.[20] The names of these relatively new online publications may be unfamiliar to some, but they had one thing in common: a reputation for publishing quickly and a knack of garnering mass attention for juicy content.

What the journalists found when they clicked on the links in the email was a goldmine of sensitive corporate information. It included a spreadsheet of Sony employees' salaries – including its top executives' pay – as well as a list of who had been fired that year, with reasons for their termination. As the journalists trawled through the data, the steady drumbeat of damaging stories began. 'Hacked Documents Reveal a Hollywood Studio's Stunning Gender Pay Gap' was among Roose's headlines.[21]

By targeting individual journalists and offering them an exclusive first look, the hackers made sure their leaks appeared in key publications. Once the stories appeared in one outlet, it became harder and harder for others not to report on them. And this was just the start. The hackers would go on to stage eight releases of information (compared to two in the Ashley Madison hack), each more damaging than the last. They carved the stolen data into rough chunks, safe in the knowledge that once it was released, an army of journalists and bloggers would do the work of digging through it to find the individual stories.

On 8 December came the most damaging leak yet: 5,000 emails sent by the co-chairperson of Sony Pictures Entertainment Amy Pascal, one of the most powerful people in the film business. A prolific communicator, she sent messages on her smartphone day and night. She had been part of a conversation in which Angelina Jolie was described as a 'spoiled brat'. She joked about the kind of movies Barack Obama might like, including *12 Years a Slave* and *The Butler* – both films about African American experiences.[22]

For the preceding fortnight, ever since the hack was exposed, Pascal had been trying to deal with a nightmare combination: the destruction of her company's computer systems by hackers and the incessant leaking of highly sensitive company data. Now she was thrown into the fray on a personal level, forced to apologize as every unguarded email came back to haunt her.

This move, more than any others, showed just how astute the hackers' grasp of news management had become. As Sony Pictures' co-chairperson and a hugely well-connected Hollywood player, Pascal took a key role in trying to limit the damage from the hack, attempting to reassure people both inside the company and outside it. All the time she was trying to smooth things over, the hackers knew she was standing on a trapdoor, and on 8 December, they let her drop.

Some spoke out against the reporting of the hacked material. Aaron Sorkin, whose scriptwriting includes hugely successful TV shows *The West Wing* and *The Newsroom*, argued that the media were playing into the hackers' hands by picking up the goodies laid out for them and publicizing the leaks. 'If you close your eyes you can imagine the hackers sitting in a room, combing through the documents to find the ones that will draw the most blood,' he wrote in the *New York Times*. 'And in a room next door are American journalists doing the same thing.'[23]

He called for more solidarity from Hollywood, but major studios reportedly declined to come to Sony's aid. In the dog-eat-dog world of entertainment media, they seemingly regarded Sony as a competitor and worthy of limited sympathy at best.

Meanwhile, news outlets defended their coverage by claiming the stories were in the public interest. WikiLeaks, which published a full searchable archive of the leaks in April 2015, said the documents offered 'a rare insight into the inner workings of a large, secretive multinational corporation' and that 'behind the scenes this is an influential corporation, with ties to the White House . . . with an ability to impact laws and policies, and with connections to the u.s. military-industrial complex.'[24]

But for others, their interest was far less high-minded. When WikiLeaks published the data, Gawker's attitude seemed to sum it up: 'We're taking this opportunity to enthusiastically dig through Sony's cybertrash.'[25]

Sony's lawyers contacted publications to try to stop the use of the leaks. Bloomberg reported being told by Sony: 'We are writing to ensure that you are aware that [Sony Pictures Entertainment] does not consent to your possession, review, copying, dissemination, publication, uploading, downloading or making any use of the stolen information.' The message warned that publications may be held responsible for damage and losses 'to Sony Pictures Entertainment or others'.[26]

Similar legal tactics had also been tried by Ashley Madison's owner, Avid Life Media. Its lawyers had issued 'takedown notices' to sites publishing the stolen data, claiming the content of the leaks was actually the company's intellectual property and thus any media outlets using the leaked data were infringing their rights.[27] Such legal threats had limited effect in Ashley Madison's case, and didn't do much for Sony either. The feeding frenzy was in full flow.

A few days later the hackers were back with yet more leaks, and this time, in a tactic reminiscent of the showboating promotion of LulzSec by Jake Davis, aka Topiary, they promised a 'Christmas gift' still to come. Once again, they fulfilled their promise. On 16 December, they leaked thousands of emails from Sony's co-chairman and chief executive Michael Lynton. 'Just the thing everyone in Hollywood has been waiting for,' entertainment website The Deadline gleefully reported.[28] In the end, the content of Lynton's emails was largely overshadowed by unfolding events: the following day, Sony cancelled the cinema release of *The Interview*, the film the hackers said was the cause of their rage (due to its depiction of North Korean leader Kim Jong-un). The hack cost Pascal her job, and Sony an estimated $15 million to fix the damage.[29] (The company did not respond to requests for comment for this book.)

It's impossible to know whether hacktivist activity like Topiary's hype-machine directly influenced the behaviour of those who hacked Sony and Ashley Madison. But it's hard not to notice significant echoes in how the leaks were handled. In the Sony case, however, there was the added tactic of direct exhortations to the media to cover the story. And from the point of view of news-cycle management, the Sony hackers handled their campaign brilliantly: first they leaked the unreleased movies online, raising awareness of the hack among the general public. Then they drip-fed increasingly damaging content about the company – targeting smaller, hungrier publications first. They continued to grow the story, gradually drawing the firm's two most senior employees into the fray before dispatching them too. Compared to the simplicity of previous hack-and-dump exercises, it was positively Machiavellian.

The Sony and Ashley Madison cases must be seen in a wider context of leaks and news media. In the ensuing years there were signs that traditional journalism, as it battled for attention in a noisy world, was increasingly willing to report on hacked information from sources that were not just anonymous, but totally opaque.

THE INTERFLORA OF DATA LEAKS

On 3 April 2016, *The Guardian*'s website carried a major story. It alleged that a close friend of Vladimir Putin was at the centre of a scheme to hide money from Russian banks by placing it in offshore tax havens (Putin's spokesman told *The Guardian* its story was an 'undisguised, paid-for hack job').[30] More stories quickly tumbled out, incriminating the rich and powerful in schemes to conceal money from the tax authorities. At the heart of it all was a giant leak of data from a previously obscure Panamanian law firm called Mossack Fonseca, so *The Guardian* branded its stories 'the Panama Papers'.

The Guardian's opening story was bold and significant, but the timing was odd. It landed at 6.50 p.m. on a Sunday evening, arguably one of the worst times to break a story: too late to lead the weekend's agenda, but also at risk of being forgotten in Monday morning's rush of new stories. But *The Guardian* wasn't necessarily in charge of the timings – because it was only one of a consortium of publications around the world who were simultaneously running stories from the same huge stash of leaked data.

Mossack Fonseca, it turned out, was at the centre of a global empire servicing clients in countries from Andorra to Zimbabwe. According to the leaks, it had around 14,000 customers whom it assisted in ways many found deeply unethical. It helped members of China's ruling politburo secrete their wealth; it worked with people who'd had sanctions imposed on them, helping them to set up companies in tax havens; Europol reportedly reckoned 3,469 names in the leaked documents matched suspected criminals on its records.[31]

Using offshore tax havens isn't necessarily illegal, but the stream of revelations described by the Panama Papers had serious consequences for entrenched interests the world over. In Iceland, the prime minister resigned after it emerged he'd failed to declare his interest in one of the country's banks.[32] In Spain, the industry minister resigned after admitting mistakes as he attempted to account for his role as the director of a Bahamian firm.[33] In the UK, several Conservative party donors' tax affairs were exposed, leading to accusations of hypocrisy on the part of then prime minister David Cameron, who had pledged to crack down on tax avoidance.[34]

Mossack Fonseca closed its doors in March 2018 citing 'irreversible damage' from the leaks.[35] But the story of the Panama

Papers was more than just a set of corruption investigations. The way it emerged, and how it was coordinated and spread around the world, was among the most notable aspects of the whole episode.

The leak came via *Süddeutsche Zeitung*, a venerable German publication with a significant history of investigative journalism. Several of its reporters had received an anonymous message from someone who claimed to have data from Mossack Fonseca.[36] Some suspect it was an insider from the company, but the leaker's identity has never been revealed. He later told journalists his motivation was to expose injustice.

As the data started to arrive, the *Süddeutsche Zeitung* journalists realized they had a scoop of global proportions. There were around 11.5 million documents. Not only would they need help wrangling all the material, but to get maximum impact it would need to appear simultaneously in publications around the world, where journalists could pursue their individual local leads.

The *Süddeutsche Zeitung* reached out to the International Consortium of Investigative Journalists (ICIJ), based in Washington, DC. The ICIJ helped triage the mass of data, carving it up among countries like a digital clearing house. There were two remarkable things about the ICIJ's work: first, that they managed to farm the information out to so many places, including countries such as Russia (which featured strongly in the leaks), while still keeping it secret. Second, that they managed to coordinate a global group of journalists to observe an embargo. As anyone who's dealt with journalists will attest, even getting them all to arrive at a press conference at the same time can be a tricky endeavour.

The ICIJ had been the linchpin, coordinating a global network of a hundred media outlets (including the BBC and *The Guardian* in the UK) in 25 languages, who in turn were helped by powerful software tools to analyse the giant databases for leads.[37] From that moment on, anyone, anywhere in the world who had damaging information about serious corporate malpractice need only make one call to their local ICIJ outlet, and if the story had global dimensions it could be distributed internationally. It was the data-leak equivalent of Interflora.

Eighteen months later, the next major leak came out.

After the Panama Papers came the Paradise Papers, which broke on 5 November 2017. The new leaked data detailed the inner workings of, among others, another offshore consultancy firm named Appleby. Again, the BBC and *The Guardian* were part of a 96-member consortium of journalists coordinated by the ICIJ to break the news internationally.

The data leaks showed, among many, many other stories, that millions of pounds from the queen's private estate had been invested in a Cayman Islands fund; that racing driver Lewis Hamilton avoided tax payments on his private jet; and that Apple had moved parts of its corporate structure to Jersey after Ireland tightened its tax rules.[38] All the parties concerned strongly denied any wrongdoing and said they had acted lawfully (taking others' advice, in the case of the queen's private estate). Appleby said its work for clients was legitimate and lawful (again: using offshore tax havens isn't necessarily illegal). Unlike Mossack Fonseca, the firm managed to weather the storm, and at the time of writing is still in business.

The data leak had once again been given initially to the same team of journalists at *Süddeutsche Zeitung* before being farmed out via the ICIJ. But this time there was something different. In the Mossack Fonseca case, the journalists had been in touch directly with the alleged leaker, albeit anonymously, and they had given an ostensible motivation for their actions. In the Appleby case, there was less information about the source of the leak. 'For their protection, *Süddeutsche Zeitung* does as a general policy not comment on its sources,' read a response on the BBC News website.[39]

After the story broke, Appleby claimed it had been the victim of a cyberattack in 2016. 'Our firm was not the subject of a leak but of a serious criminal act,' it said in a statement. 'This was an illegal computer hack. Our systems were accessed by an intruder who deployed the tactics of a professional hacker.'[40] The company sued the BBC and *The Guardian* for breach of confidence, and the parties later settled their differences without going to court.[41]

The BBC and other outlets that carried the Paradise Papers stories about Appleby's dealings were open and honest about the fact that they did not know the origin of the leak. They'd worked hard to verify the data, they said, but had no idea as to its source. If true, it means that an alleged computer hacker was able to steal sensitive data from a financial company and get it published by some of the world's most high-profile news outlets, without ever giving journalists the slightest bit of information about their identity or motivations. That's a lot of power.

In some ways, this isn't new: anonymous sources have always been used by journalists. No one would want to see a world where a whistle-blower could leak important information only if their identity was exposed, and the 'brown envelope' full of documents handed over in secret has been the bedrock of some of the world's most important scoops. The extent to which there is public interest in the leak is a key consideration, and in the journalists' eyes the ethical concerns around tax avoidance made both Mossack Fonseca and Appleby fair game.

'Anonymous source', however, can mean different things. Sometimes, the identity of the source is known to the journalist, but not to the wider public, meaning the journalist can attempt to verify the leaker's identity and get a rough idea of their motives. But not always. There are instances, such as the Paradise Papers, where the journalist knows nothing about the source's identity. For some whistle-blowers, the ability to leak in this way has become critical in today's high-surveillance world, where trusting even one individual reporter with their personal information is risky.

Even in cases where a journalist is given the source's identity and motivations, can they believe what they're told? In the Sony case, for example, the hackers lied about both who they were and why they were operating (they suggested to journalists that they were working on behalf of aggrieved Sony employees, but the FBI evidence points to North Korean government hackers).[42] Again, this is not new: the harsh reality is that governments, corporations and others have always been able to use fake identities and fronts to leak news, so as to hide its true source and their motivations.

In short, there is a long tradition of leaks to journalists from anonymous sources, 'unknown' sources and sources lying about their identity. What is new is the ability, thanks to the Internet, for sources to bypass the media entirely and leak straight to the public, knowing that the media will subsequently pick up on the story. We saw this in the case of hacker groups like LulzSec, who would often publish their information straight onto the Web and point journalists and others to it. And what's even newer is the tactic of leaking straight to the public in a highly strategic way, as in the Ashley Madison case, for example, where the data was leaked online in two tranches.

Now, we're seeing a combination of the various tactics: hackers have leaked strategically online, while making direct approaches to journalists and lying about their identity, as in the Sony case. Or they have dumped masses of information anonymously on journalists who are able to publish it strategically, as happened with the Paradise Papers. The risk with these approaches is that they leave journalists open to manipulation. What if, for example, the Paradise Papers leaks actually came from a competitor firm of Appleby, who'd hacked into their rival's computer networks? Does the merit of exposing tax avoidance outweigh the risk of unwittingly doing someone else's dirty work? These questions have always been around, but they come to the fore when data can so easily and untraceably be obtained, and leaked, and with such devastating consequences.

To be able to answer these questions, ideally journalists need to be able to make an assessment as to who's pulling their strings and why. In the case of the leak that I found from the dating website Adult Friend Finder, for example, the hacker gave a motivation: revenge. He claimed a friend of his had worked for them and hadn't been paid, so he was leaking the data to punish the company. I didn't like this motivation, but at least it gave me an idea of whom I was dealing with. I couldn't be absolutely sure he wasn't lying, of course, or wasn't actually a competitor of Adult Friend Finder trying to harm the company. But on balance I felt the merit of revealing the company's failure to protect sensitive data outweighed the risk of fulfilling the hacker's malicious motives.

The problem with the highly strategic leaking tactics outlined above, however, is that journalists have little ability to question the source or their motivation. Either the journalist is following in the source's wake (if the data is dumped online) or the source is feeding the media strategically timed information – in which case, what incentive is there for the journalist to question their motives or identity?

The data-leaking examples above are in many ways unalike. There's clearly a big difference between hackers cynically breaking into a company with the sole aim of damaging it, and a whistle-blower leaking tax avoidance information to a global network of legitimate media outlets. But in between is a large, grey expanse.

Journalists now work in an era in which anyone can dump huge swathes of stolen data anonymously. They can parcel it up and leak it strategically. They can contact journalists worldwide directly and urge them to cover it, or they can cut out the middleman and leak directly to the public. And they can lie about their identity. It's murky territory, and any journalist who gets involved in it needs to ask some hard questions of themselves and, if possible, of their sources.

And to add to the complications, there's another issue: can you even trust that the data is real?

TAINTED LEAKS

On 5 October 2016, David Satter received an urgent-looking message. 'Someone has your password,' read the email, which appeared to come from Google, urging Satter to change his Gmail password by clicking a link.

It was a textbook phishing attempt. This time, the target was a high-profile journalist who'd been critical of the Russian government, notably in his book *Darkness at Dawn*, in which Satter investigated corruption and cronyism in post-Soviet Russia. He was later expelled from the country.

Satter clicked on the link and entered his password. But the website he typed it into didn't belong to Google. Instead he'd revealed his password to computer hackers, who proceeded to raid his email account. Within three weeks documents from his mails had been leaked online by a pro-Russian group of hackers who claimed Satter was part of a shadowy campaign to plant disinformation about Vladimir Putin's government. At first sight it looked like a classic hack-and-dump operation. But on closer inspection, there was something odd about the documents that had been leaked. Some were published in their original form, but one had been given a subtle but significant makeover.

Satter worked with Citizen Lab, a Canadian research organization, to get to the bottom of what happened.[43] As they compared his original document with the leaked version, they discovered a minutely engineered operation to take Satter's original material and subtly tweak it to give it a sinister twist. In his original document, written before the hackers struck, Satter had mentioned a project run by Radio Liberty, a U.S.-government funded pro-democracy operation.[44] Satter had written about Radio Liberty's Russian Investigative Reporting Project, which aimed, he said, 'to provide the Russian population with objective information', partly by publishing articles on the Radio Liberty website.

Yet somewhere between the hack and its eventual publication, Satter's document had been changed. References to Radio Liberty had been taken out. This meant that rather than a specific project for an identifiable outlet, the 'Russian investigative reporting project' looked more like a wide-ranging, shadowy attempt to plant articles across the Russian media.

'We believe that by removing specific references to Radio Liberty, the perpetrators are aiming to give the impression of a broader subversive campaign not limited to a single news organization,' Citizen Lab wrote in its report, which it titled 'Tainted Leaks'.[45]

Satter had compiled a list of fourteen articles that the project had published. But in the doctored version, suddenly there were 24. Of the ones that were added, several were written by Alexei Navalny, a fierce critic of Putin's regime. The researchers believe that this was an attempt to smear Navalny by linking him to what readers of the document would now think was a u.s.-funded information operation in Russia. 'By repeatedly adding [Navalny's] reporting to the document, the tainting creates the appearance of "foreign" funding for his work,' they wrote.[46]

Most remarkable was the attention to detail in the alterations carried out. Satter had mentioned the 'fourteen' articles elsewhere in the document, but his text was changed before publication to read 'twenty-four', commensurate with the extra ones that had been added. Satter said they'd all been published 'in the first nine months of 2016 as of September 30.' But in the doctored version this was changed to 'ten months' and 'October 20', to encompass the date of one of the extra articles that had been inserted. Whoever made the changes paid very close attention to ensure their faked version of Satter's document was as plausible as possible. It was almost as though they expected their work to be highly scrutinized and wanted to make sure there were no discrepancies that would arouse suspicion.

On 22 October, the hacked documents appeared on the website of a group of pro-Russian hackers called CyberBerkut, complete with the doctored report. Citizen Lab surmised: 'they were releasing the document to provide evidence that the

United States was attempting to support a "colour revolution" in Russia. In the CyberBerkut narrative, David Satter was an agent directing the publication of articles critical of the Russian government.'[47]

The leaked documents were then reported by various media outlets across Russia, including at least one run by the state-operated RIA Novosti.[48]

There is a key difference between this tainted leaks case and the others discussed in this chapter. David Satter's doctored material was handled by news outlets that seemed to have little interest in checking whether it was true: for example, Satter says he was never approached for a comment by any of the publications that carried the CyberBerkut leak, possibly because the tweaked document told the story they wanted their readers to hear. But his case is a lesson for all journalists working with data leaks – it's not unfeasible that information may have been manipulated to tell a story, sometimes very subtly. This is especially true if, as in the Sony case, the hackers are trying to draw journalists into covering particular aspects of the leak.

The new possibilities created by Internet anonymity make it all the more important for journalists to check the veracity of the data (as the BBC, *The Guardian* and others tried to do with the leaks from offshore companies). But if the stolen data is leaked online, mainstream media has limited time to react and check its authenticity. And as the old saying goes: a lie gets halfway around the world before truth puts on its boots – an adage made all the more true in a world of social media and instant, ubiquitous access available to all, and with furious competition between media outlets as to who can publish first.

The pressures and dynamics of the news media have been well understood by the hackers. Over the last decade, they have learned not only how to access forbidden data, but how to use it selectively to inflict maximum damage and how media can be co-opted into that process. In 2016, the world witnessed another campaign to hack data, leak it and influence journalists. This time, the target would be far bigger than dating sites, movie companies and offshore consultancies. The hackers were about to take on the fiercest political battle in one of the most powerful countries on the planet.

TEN

HACK THE VOTE

After months of speculation, on 16 June 2015 Donald J. Trump finally announced his intention to run for the office of president of the United States. His descent on the golden escalator to a press conference in the basement of Trump Tower in New York presaged America's headlong tilt into a new and bewildering form of politics.

The photos show that the event was attended by several hundred people, compared to the thousands who attended his later rallies. In those early days, many regarded his candidacy as a sideshow and believed he would never make it into the Oval Office. But his campaign not only became one of the most controversial and compelling in modern history; it proved to be the testing ground for a shocking and insidious new form of online propaganda, one that brought to a peak the strategic leaking and media manipulation tactics that had been honed in the cyberattacks of the preceding years.

Even before Trump announced his candidacy, tech security was proving an explosive issue in U.S. politics: Hillary Clinton had been forced to admit that, as Secretary of State under Barack Obama in 2009, she had stored all her work emails on a personal computer server, reportedly in the basement of the family home in Chappaqua, New York state.[1]

It was a decision that turned into a rolling PR disaster, buffeting the veteran Democrat's slick campaign, particularly when it emerged that a small number of classified messages passed through the non-government system she set up.[2] The more details that came out, the more weight grew behind allegations of a cover-up, dismissed by Clinton but quickly weaponized by her opponents. Trump made hay with the accusation, using it to stoke his argument that Clinton was duplicitous, and part of the 'swamp' of Capitol Hill lifers. The controversy became a thorn in the side of Clinton's camp right up to polling day. The FBI flip-flopped over whether to pursue a prosecution until just two days before the election.[3] For a campaign that was meant to run on rails, such last-minute headlines were a disaster.

But even without Trump's brickbats and the email contro-versy, the Democrats were struggling with internal divisions. A bitter rivalry had emerged between supporters of Washington stalwart Clinton and her iconoclastic, left-leaning rival, Bernie Sanders.

As they prepared for the Convention that would decide between the two candidates, the waters were choppy for the Democratic Party. What they didn't know was that they were sail-ing into a perfect storm. A deadly combination of hacker rivalry and online dissemination was about to hit the Democrats, and their vulnerable computer security made them sitting ducks.

Although it only became public in summer 2016, the hacking of the Democrats was probably well underway even as Trump was declaring his candidacy the year before. From at least summer 2015, hackers were inside the Democrats' networks, according to the security company that eventually uncovered their presence.[4]

As we have seen, cyber investigators often recognize hacking groups by the software they use, which becomes a kind of digital calling card. The tools that breached the Democrats' systems had a very long history. They were first spotted back in 2008. As Russia battled with a rebellion in Chechnya, researchers discovered a new set of viruses targeting pro-Chechen campaigners. The researchers called the hacking group Cozy Duke, because one of its hacking tools was called Cozer, and it used file names with the prefix 'dq'.[5]

By 2013, Cozy Duke was hacking victims in Ukraine, Hungary and Poland (where the U.S. was negotiating the placement of missile bases). The targeting of anti-Russian interests led many to suspect Cozy Duke was a Russian operation. Added to which, the Cozer tool didn't look like a run-of-the-mill virus. It was stealthy, effective and constantly refined by what looked like a single group with impressive skills and considerable resources.

The hacking tool may have been sophisticated, but the delivery mechanism was depressingly familiar: the virus arrived in phishing emails containing dodgy attachments with titles such as 'Ukraine's Search for a Regional Foreign Policy'.[6] When a victim opened the attachment, the virus would be triggered, and the Dukes were given full covert access to their computer.

By summer 2014, the Cozy Duke group was ready to take on its biggest target yet: the U.S. government. But unknown to the hackers, they were being watched. According to Dutch media, the Netherlands' intelligence agencies had hacked into Cozy Duke's operation.[7] They reportedly traced the group back to a university building near Moscow's Red Square.

If Cozy Duke's choice of victims wasn't enough to convince security watchers that it was a Russian operation, the Dutch spies' access seemed to provide the smoking gun. They even managed to hack into the security cameras in Cozy Duke's building, according to the Dutch reports, gathering footage of the hacking group as they clocked in for work. Western intelligence agencies assessed that Cozy Duke was led by the Russian Foreign Intelligence Service, the SVR. President Vladimir Putin's spokesman dismissed the reports as fuelling 'anti-Russian hysteria in the U.S.'[8]

As Dutch intelligence watched, they gained a worrying insight: Cozy Duke had managed to plant its viruses on computers within the White House, the State Department and the offices of the Joint Chiefs of Staff. The group was ready to strike at the very heart of the U.S. government.

As the Dukes geared up to strike in November 2014, the Dutch informed U.S. intelligence agencies of an imminent attack. What ensued was the cyber equivalent of an urban shoot-out. The hackers tried to activate their viruses, issuing commands to grab information. The u.s. defenders would cut off access to the server that was issuing the commands, only to see fresh instructions coming from another infected server. The battle lasted 24 hours and shut down State Department email for days.[9]

Eventually, the u.s. side won, but at a cost. Dutch spies were reportedly shut out of the Cozy Duke network, cutting off their access to its computers and office cctv cameras. But the hacker group was far from giving up after this setback. By summer 2015 they were back in action, this time inside the Democratic Party. And they might well have remained there were it not for a series of slip-ups by a rival hacking group.

As the election clock ticked down, it still wasn't clear whether Clinton or Sanders would be the Democrats' nominee for the White House. But the political rivalry was about to be detonated by a hack that would eviscerate the party and arguably change the course of u.s. history. And the sad thing is, the victims had been given months of warning.

From September 2015, the FBI had spotted Cozy Duke inside the Democrats' networks and began telling the Democratic National Committee (DNC), the party's governing body, of the threat. But they were put through to the equivalent of computer support, according to Donna Brazile, who became the DNC's interim chair in the wake of the attack:

> The FBI agent was transferred to the DNC's helpdesk – you know, the people who answer your calls if you're having trouble logging onto the network or your mouse stopped working right.
>
> The technician thought the call . . . might be a prank call, not an unusual occurrence at the DNC.
>
> Instead of alerting his superior, the IT contractor decided to look for a compromised computer in the system. The

technician's scan of the system didn't turn up anything, so he let it go.[10]

Other techies in the party knew full well that its IT was at risk, but claim that their concerns weren't acted upon. A former senior DNC employee, who did not want to be named, says that the organization's technology team asked for hundreds of thousands of dollars to sort out their security. But the amount approved was only tens of thousands, as the party prioritized front-line campaigning instead. 'Cybersecurity was important to us, but there was always the need to send money to campaigns,' said the source. The DNC did not respond to requests for comment for this book.

More warnings from the FBI followed in December 2015 and January 2016, according to Brazile, but the DNC's technicians said they still couldn't verify the problems that the FBI was seeing. Then in April 2016, the DNC finally spotted an intrusion and called in a tech security company. Suddenly, the Democratic National Committee learned it had been raided by not one, but two sophisticated hacking groups who had stolen large amounts of confidential internal information.

The first group was Cozy Duke, who had lurked inside the DNC since summer 2015, as the FBI had warned.[11] The second group also had a long and ignominious history, and its name would become a byword for the modern world of high-level, aggressive hacking: Fancy Bear. The group got its name because one of the viruses they used was called 'Sofacy'. A security researcher working on the hacking group reportedly said this reminded him of a song called 'Fancy' by Iggy Azalea, and Bear was the suffix his company gave to suspected Russian hacking groups, so the name Fancy Bear was born.[12]

The use of the Sofacy virus dates back at least as far as 2004. By December 2014, it was being used to hack into the German Parliament, infecting many of its 20,000 computers.[13] In April 2015, the same tools were used to attack a French television network, TV5 Monde, taking down a dozen channels for several hours. They were then deployed against British TV station the Islam Channel just a few months later.[14]

Perhaps the most telling incident, however, was the hacking of the World Anti-Doping Agency, WADA. In July 2016, its officials called for a ban on Russian athletes participating in the Rio Olympics later that year. Two months later, WADA announced it had been hacked by the same group that hit the German Parliament, the TV stations and others.[15] Documents stolen from WADA were later published on a website that proclaimed it was run by the 'Fancy Bears hack team', complete with cartoon images of bears. The hackers may not have come up with their name, but they wasted no time in embracing it.

But it was the hacking of the Democratic National Committee that was to cement the Fancy Bear group's reputation. It was perhaps its most audacious (certainly its most well-documented) attack to date, and it called upon all of the strategic leaking and media manipulation tactics displayed in hacks from Ashley Madison to Sony Pictures Entertainment.

Once again, however, their way in was via a simple email. On 19 March 2016, Hillary Clinton's campaign chairman John Podesta received a message with a worrying warning. Someone had tried to use his password to log into his Gmail account. The warning appeared to come from Google and it included a link for Podesta to reset his password for safety reasons.[16]

Podesta was rightly suspicious. He forwarded the message to his chief of staff, who sent it to the IT team, who told Podesta that the email was real, and he needed to change his password. They sent him the genuine link to do the reset, but somehow Podesta didn't use it, and instead clicked the link in the original email and entered his password.[17] That original email had been sent by the Fancy Bear group. They hoovered up Podesta's password and would go on to steal 50,000 of his messages, according to the FBI.[18]

Podesta was an impressive scalp, but the hackers wanted more. Rather than just accessing one sensitive inbox, they wanted entry to the entire organization – not only Clinton's team but the wider Democratic Party machine.

On 6 April, the hackers targeted an employee of the Democratic Congressional Campaign Committee (DCCC), which works to get Democrats into Congressional seats. She fell for a phishing email, leaking her password. Six days later, the hackers used it to log into the DCCC network, and installed their viruses on at least ten computers. The software allowed them to record everything typed on the keyboard and shown on the screen. According to FBI documents, the hackers spent eight hours watching the employee's activity, capturing every password she used to access the DCCC's systems (as well as her personal banking details).[19]

On 18 April, a DCCC employee logged into the Democratic National Committee's systems. The hackers were, of course, recording everything they typed in, so now they were able to log into the very heart of the Democrats. It was, as the leaked emails would later show, a vipers' nest of division and discord. The hackers accessed around thirty computers, according to the FBI, installing the spy software and hoovering up yet more screenshots and keyboard activity.[20] They copied gigabytes of research that the Democrats had carried out on the Republicans, plus thousands of emails. All of it was spirited away by the Fancy Bear group.

Put plainly: for several weeks the hackers were watching everything that happened on dozens of computers handling some of the most politically sensitive data in America. They could see everything displayed on screen, record every word typed and see every password that was entered. For most of this time, the Democrats' leadership had no idea they were under surveillance.

By late April 2016, however, the DNC realized it was under attack. They called in CrowdStrike, a U.S. tech security firm. The company was co-founded in 2011 by a Russian-born coding expert called Dmitri Alperovitch. It had a reputation for naming names when it came to hacking incidents. According to CrowdStrike, once their software was installed it took around ten seconds to work out who was behind the attack. The malicious software pointed to Fancy Bear, and some of the data was being sent to servers previously attributed to Cozy Duke, the group that Dutch intelligence had managed to hack into (now renamed 'Cozy Bear' by CrowdStrike). As the FBI had warned, Cozy Bear had been sitting inside the organization's systems for around a year. Fancy Bear, by contrast, had been in for only a few weeks. But in that time they had harvested an impressive amount of sensitive information, and in the next few months it would be Fancy Bear that would do the Democrats the most harm.

After weeks of analysis, CrowdStrike moved to lock out the hackers. On 10 June, all DNC staff were told to leave their laptops in the office (sparking unfounded fears they were all about to be fired).[21] CrowdStrike changed employees' passwords and deleted the hackers' software. The hackers fought back, but ultimately the Democrats' defences seemed to hold, and it looked like the Bears had been shut out.

The hole in the Democrats' security may have closed, but if they were breathing a sigh of relief, it was premature. The stolen data was now out of their control, and the impact of the hack was far from over. The next phase would prove to be a remarkable moment in hacking history.

On 15 June 2016, CrowdStrike went public with its findings. On its own blog, the company was circumspect about the ultimate source of the hack. They stated Fancy Bear and Cozy Bear worked 'for the benefit of' the Russian Federation government and were 'believed to be closely linked' with its intelligence agencies.[22] However, the *Washington Post*, having also spoken with DNC staff, pulled no punches: 'Russian Government Hackers Penetrated DNC', declared its headline.[23]

Perhaps the decision to go public was a tactical one for the Democrats. Stories were already beginning to swirl about Trump's links to Russia. Blaming the country for a hack on his political opponents might have seemed a useful way to feed the fire. If this was indeed the Democrats' calculation, then they got it catastrophically wrong. When the story went public, it began a truly incredible chain of events that would, arguably, cost the party the election.

Within a day of the *Washington Post* and CrowdStrike articles, a blog suddenly appeared, declaring 'DNC's Servers Hacked by a Lone Hacker'. Far from a Russian government operation, the author claimed, the cyberattack had been carried out by a sole individual who was now ready to leak the information and tell his story.[24]

The blog was published under the pseudonym Guccifer 2.0 – a name that instantly sparked intrigue, since it summoned up the ghost of a previous hack. Guccifer had been the online alter ego of Marcel Lehel Lazar, a Romanian taxi-driver-turned-hacker who had gone on a spree from late 2012 to early 2014, raiding email and social media accounts and publishing the juiciest pickings, including nude self-portraits painted by former president George W. Bush. More pertinently, Lazar was the man who revealed that Hillary Clinton had used a private email address while Secretary of State, unleashing the controversy that dogged her presidential campaign.[25]

Lazar, however, was sentenced in Romania in 2014, extradited to the U.S., sentenced again, then sent back to Romania to serve out the rest of his jail time there.[26] Clearly he couldn't be the real face of this new hacker, Guccifer 2.0, because he was in prison. But whoever had adopted his nickname was making a shrewd insinuation that they were linked to a previous hacking episode targeting U.S. politicians.

Meanwhile on his blog, Guccifer 2.0 openly mocked CrowdStrike (*sic*):

Worldwide known cyber security company CrowdStrike announced that the Democratic National Committee (DNC) servers had been hacked by 'sophisticated' hacker groups.

I'm very pleased the company appreciated my skills so highly))) But in fact, it was easy, very easy.

I guess CrowdStrike customers should think twice about company's competence.

Fuck the Illuminati and their conspiracies!!!!!!!!! Fuck CrowdStrike!!!!!!!![27]

The posts were accompanied by documents stolen from the DNC, and more posts followed with yet more documents. His claims seemed to pour cold water on the theory that Russian hackers (and specifically the Russian government) were behind the attack. Guccifer 2.0 not only claimed to be working alone; he explicitly stated that he was not linked to Russia, and in fact claimed to be Romanian (neatly dovetailing with the previous Guccifer identity).

Some in the media began to question CrowdStrike's research, and the assertion of Russian government involvement. Guccifer 2.0 continued on the offensive, emailing journalists, including reporters at Gawker, and prodding them to publish stories – echoing the media exhortation tactics used by the group that hacked into Sony Pictures Entertainment.[28] Gradually, the coverage started to gain traction; some news outlets started to trawl through the leaked dossiers and spreadsheets and run stories on their findings. And perhaps equally importantly for the hackers, Guccifer 2.0's vociferous crowing had created question marks over who was behind the digital break-in.

More confusion was sown by the arrival of a website called DCleaks, which claimed to be run by 'American hacktivists', and began publishing hacked information from Clinton's inner circle, including emails (along with a much smaller trove of Republican Party emails).[29]

Yet despite Guccifer 2.0 and DCleaks' efforts, in the immediate aftermath they weren't grabbing mainstream media attention. Even some senior staff within the DNC say they didn't notice the hackers' work. And much of the limited media coverage was still focusing on the hack itself and who was behind it, rather than the substance of the data. If the hackers' aim was to harm the Democrats, they needed to shift the lens away from attribution and towards the content of the leaks. The imminent Democratic National Convention (when the party was finally to decide between Clinton and Sanders) was the perfect opportunity, and it was seized on by an organization set up by a man who's arguably been one of the early twenty-first century's greatest influencers: Julian Assange.

Assange created the WikiLeaks website in 2006 to be a secure, anonymized platform for whistle-blowers. Its huge dumps of data and its refusal to censor them have exposed a string of stories highly embarrassing to the U.S. government, including its misdeeds in Iraq and sensitive information contained in its diplomatic cables.

At the time of the DNC hack, Assange was still in the Ecuadorean embassy in London. He'd gained asylum there after allegations of sexual assault emerged against him in Sweden (the case has recently been dropped by Swedish prosecutors). Assange also feared extradition to the U.S. over the leaks his site had published. Yet despite his restricted physical freedom, Assange remained a powerful force in the information battle being waged across politics and journalism. Leaks were still his business, and the gigabytes of DNC information would prove no exception. He also harboured a deep-seated distrust of Hillary Clinton.

When the supposedly Romanian hacker Guccifer 2.0 first leaked the DNC documents on his blog on 15 June 2016, he said he'd given 'thousands of files and mails' to WikiLeaks. 'They will publish them soon,' he wrote.[30] In a later indictment released by the FBI, it's alleged that there was direct contact between Guccifer 2.0 and a group the FBI called 'Organization 1', widely reported to be WikiLeaks.[31] The FBI alleges that Organization 1 messaged Guccifer 2.0, stating: '[s]end any new material [stolen from the DNC] here for us to review and it will have a much higher impact than what you are doing,' and later adding:

if you have anything hillaryrelated we want it in the next two days prefablebecause the DNC [Democratic National Convention] is approaching and she will solidify bernie supporters behind after her.

We think trump has only a 25 per cent chance of winning against hillary...so conflict between bernie and hillary is interesting.[32]

The Democratic National Convention was meant to be a high point in the party's bid for the Presidency – a slick, glitzy schmooze-fest in which the Clinton/Sanders rivalry would finally be laid to rest and the successful nominee would be propelled towards the White House.

WikiLeaks had other ideas.

On 22 July, three days before the Democrats' big convention, WikiLeaks published. But unlike Guccifer 2.0, they didn't just release documents about campaign financing and strategy. They published almost 20,000 emails from the cache of stolen DNC data.[33] If the aim was to increase the impact of the leak, it worked. For a start, WikiLeaks had a far bigger platform for promotion and dissemination than Guccifer 2.0's blog. But more importantly, they had the experience and the technology to create a searchable database of information. The Democrats' dirty washing tumbled out.

As the media ferreted through the mass of communications, they found startling instances in which DNC grandees openly plotted to prevent Bernie Sanders gaining the nomination, despite the committee publicly remaining neutral on the candidates.[34] The exposure of such divisions couldn't have come at a worse time for the Democrats, as one former senior DNC employee explains:

The primary battle was so contentious between Hillary and Bernie, and they were going to try and use the Convention as a get-together where the Hillary side and the Bernie side could come together as one, and create a unified force to go out for the fall campaign. Instead [WikiLeaks] drops these very incendiary emails that would do nothing but cause the Bernie people's heads to explode.

The fallout was immediate and, for the Democratic Party, massively destabilizing. Just two days after WikiLeaks' publication, on the eve of the Convention, the DNC's chairwoman Debbie Wasserman Schultz resigned.[35] Instead of being a showcase to crown their candidate for the White House, the event was eclipsed by controversy as more and more of the Democrats' emails were exposed in the press. Clinton gained the presidential nomination, but the political bloodshed continued: DNC chief executive Amy Dacey resigned, along with chief financial officer Brad Marshall and communications director Luis Miranda.[36] 'We were effectively decapitated as an organization,' said one former DNC staff member.

It's hard to overstate the enervating effect that the leak had on the Democrats. Personal relationships, the bedrock of any high-pressure organization, were subject to creeping corrosion. 'It created such intense stress and pressure that a lot of the really close bonds . . . they kind of dissolved,' recalls Scott Comer, the DNC finance office's chief of staff. 'Not just professional relationships but friendships as well. It was very painful.'

As they looked more closely at their leaked emails, some DNC employees were shocked to find that they included messages sent during May – weeks after the organization knew it had been hacked, but before all staff were informed. In effect, some of them had been sending ill-advised, controversial messages even though others in the DNC knew they were almost certainly under surveillance.

'They knew in April but didn't shut it down until June,' says a former senior DNC employee. 'I think they wanted to leave it active to see what the [hackers] were capable of. If not, why not shut it down immediately?' Like others, he is also suspicious of how quickly the media rooted out the most damaging emails from the 20,000 that were leaked, and suspects they had been prepped by someone with a solid grasp of the U.S. political system:

> From the time of the initial dump, it was only hours before ... very incendiary emails were dropped [by news outlets]. I think our emails were already selected. Someone had already gone through and picked out the bad ones. And that person or persons had to have a good understanding of U.S. politics and U.S. culture.

The leaks also damaged the party's fundraising efforts. Small donor contributions had already been drying up thanks to the Bernie/Hillary squabble, according to an insider. Now big donors were seeing their personal information leaked out in the stolen emails, some of which had come from the DNC's fundraising team. Senior staff spent hours phoning round donors trying to smooth things over – hours they could have spent campaigning rather than apologizing.[37]

As the presidential race entered its final, adversarial phase, Clinton remained standing, nomination in hand, while her party machine lay in ruins around her.

Trump's response in campaign speeches was gleeful: 'WikiLeaks, I love WikiLeaks,' he told a Pennsylvania rally on 10 October.[38]

Meanwhile, the true scale of what had happened was starting to sink in: a hacking group had not only penetrated a key part of American politics, but had brazenly smeared the stolen goods all over the Internet in a way that seemed calculated to influence the course of the election. Even seasoned tech security sources couldn't quite believe what they were seeing, and politicians brought up in a more traditional era were gobsmacked. Donna Brazile, who came in as interim DNC chairperson, claimed:

No one thought they would be bold enough to try something like that in the United States. Nor did anyone suspect that they had the political sophistication to weaponize the information they had gathered from our servers, understanding exactly when they should release which emails they had stolen . . . Our hacking was unlike anything members of our expert task force had ever seen.[39]

Those experts, it seems, hadn't been paying enough attention to hacking incidents such as those outlined in the previous chapter. Highly strategic leaking and media manipulation was fast becoming the norm. Now the same wave was crashing over u.s. politics, too. And as in previous hacks there seemed to be increasing willingness among some media outlets to run with the salacious leaks without questioning who was putting them out, and why.

In fact, tech and its interface with the media was a faultline that ran through the entire election. The attempts to influence its outcome using technology didn't only come via the cybercrime tactics of the Fancy Bear group. Those who wished to sway the campaign also exploited the online platforms that many of us are hooked on, harnessing the power of Facebook and Twitter for a new propaganda campaign.

The 2016 u.s. presidential campaign was partly fought, as are all modern elections, via social media. Two-thirds of Americans use Facebook, for example, and three-quarters of them are on it daily.[40] It was a battle for which Donald J. Trump seemed tailor-made. Already a tv celebrity, by the time he entered the presidential race he'd amassed almost three million followers on Twitter – a shoot-from-the-hip, short-attention-span medium in which he operated effortlessly.[41]

In addition, his campaign was fought in an era of immense distrust of mainstream media worldwide.[42] Again, Trump understood this innately, twisting the knife with his cries of 'fake news', driving his followers away from the shared space of the TV set and the newspapers and into the atomized filter bubble of online media where (sometimes contradictory) messages could be targeted at small groups.

Those who leaked the hacked DNC emails also understood the importance of social media. WikiLeaks' extensive online promotion machine went into action to publicize the data. Twitter accounts were set up for DCleaks and Guccifer 2.0. But it seems they didn't stop there. When U.S. investigators researched the Twitter account for DCleaks, for example, they found something intriguing: the same computer had also been used to set up a Twitter account called @BaltimoreIsWhr, which was used to post messages under the slogan 'Blacks Against Hillary'.[43] It was an apparently U.S.-based Clinton-bashing account, and as investigators would discover, it was just one of a slew of social media accounts, not just on Twitter but on Facebook, targeting divisive messages into the heart of one of the most vicious presidential campaigns of recent history.

On 6 September 2017, ten months after Trump won the election, a post appeared on Facebook's corporate site. Although written in the anodyne, chummy-yet-robotic style of many tech corporation comms, the content was stunning, as hinted at by the title: 'Information Operations on Facebook'.[44]

Facebook's chief security officer Alex Stamos said the company had found 470 fake accounts all affiliated with each other and 'likely operated out of Russia' that had spent $100,000 to run 3,000 adverts across Facebook from the summer of 2015 to May 2017. They had been placed by the Internet Research Agency, a St Petersburg-based firm that, according to media reports and U.S. investigators, functioned as a 'troll farm', getting pro-Russian content on social media sites and combating anti-Putin messages.[45] The adverts didn't necessarily support either party in the election. Rather, according to Stamos, they 'appeared to focus on amplifying divisive social and political messages . . . touching on topics from LGBT matters to race issues to immigration to gun rights'.[46]

It seems the Russian influencers felt that tapping into such controversial undercurrents was enough to achieve their aims.

And Russian troll farms weren't the only ones capitalizing on Facebook's growing influence over American voters. The political parties themselves were harnessing the power of social media, supported by a rash of political consultancy firms. Among them was Cambridge Analytica.

Up until the 2016 U.S. presidential election the company was little-known outside political circles. It had been founded in 2013 by a major Republican donor and run by Steve Bannon, who became Trump's strategist.[47] Among its offerings was a claim to be able to use psychological insights to increase the potency of messages put out on social media (for example, an extroverted, gun-loving risk-taker would be shown a different advert to a shy, liberal bookworm). The problem was that it had gained its psychological data deceptively. Cambridge Analytica had paid several hundred thousand people to take a personality quiz, then used them to gain access to the public bits of their Facebook friends' profiles – 87 million in all – something Facebook was later fined for allowing to happen ($5 billion in the U.S., and £500,000 in the UK).[48] The details of Cambridge Analytica's activities were revealed in an exposé by *Guardian* journalist Harry Davies, which reported that Republican candidate Ted Cruz's campaign worked with the company and used the illicitly obtained data.[49] Things got worse for the firm when its chief executive was caught in an undercover TV sting apparently claiming, among other things, that his company could organize 'honeytrap' operations to influence foreign elections.[50] The company closed less than two months later.[51]

As more of its work was exposed, however, the headlines swirling around Cambridge Analytica became increasingly hyperbolic: if the reporting was to be believed, the company was a shadowy digital Svengali whose tech tricks helped put Trump in the White House.

The problem is, that's far from proven. For a start, although we know that Trump paid Cambridge Analytica, we don't know what the company did for his campaign.[52] Trump's digital direc-tor admitted using a massive amount of (perfectly legal) targeted advertising on Facebook, but denied using Cambridge Analytica's illicitly obtained psychological data, stating of such tactics: 'I just don't think it works.'[53] Even if it turns out that Trump's cam-paign did use the data, it's almost impossible to say how much sway it had. As the UK's data watchdog wrote: 'We may never know whether individuals were unknowingly influenced to vote a certain way in . . . the U.S. election campaign.'[54]

The same is true of the Facebook ads placed by the Russian propagandists at the Internet Research Agency. Facebook esti-mated that around ten million people in the U.S. saw the 3,000 ads, less than half of which were shown prior to polling day.[55] And there's a big difference between 'seeing' an ad on Facebook and paying attention to it, let alone being influenced by it afterwards.

Those who argue for social media's influence point to the tightness of the final result: Trump actually lost the popular vote by 2.8 million, but won by a majority of 74 votes in the electoral college (77 after subsequent defections).[56] So it's possible to argue that swaying a few thousand voters in the right places using Facebook, Twitter and other social media may have been enough to change the result in critical districts.

But that dramatically underplays the influence of the wide-spread media coverage Trump enjoyed. His provocative policies, his no-nonsense speaking style and his outsider status made him catnip for the news media, from both the left and the right. By the middle of 2016, every major news organization was turning up to his rapidly growing rallies, and the more outspoken he became, the harder it was to stay away. Around 83 million Americans watched his September debate with Hillary Clinton on broadcast and cable channels.[57]

Ultimately, what tipped the balance: 3,000 Facebook ads? Or the three-word chants that encapsulated Trump's campaign: 'build that wall', 'drain the swamp', 'lock her up'? One thing is for sure: away from the world of social media voodoo, Trump's opposition was reeling, hit with a damaging combination of cybercrime and weaponized data leaks that had cost the Democrats their entire senior team. The question was: who was really behind the hack?

A misinformation campaign had created confusion as to who had hacked the Democrats and leaked their emails in the months preceding the vote. But as the election came to a conclusion, the truth was starting to emerge.

Guccifer 2.0, the lone Romanian hacker, claimed he'd single-handedly broken into the DNC and had no links with Russia. Yet both the U.S. tech security firm CrowdStrike and the FBI found Fancy Bear's hacking tools on the Democrats' systems. In addition, holes had started to appear in his claims to be Romanian. In an online interview with a journalist, Guccifer 2.0 reportedly struggled to speak the language, raising suspicions that whoever was doing the talking was actually using an online translator to communicate.[58]

Meanwhile, questions were also being asked about the DCleaks website. It claimed to be run by 'American hacktivists' to publicize the leaked emails, yet somehow it had begun releasing the documents on 8 June, six days before the hack went public. Whoever set up the site was in on the operation almost from the outset.[59]

Researchers from UK tech security company Secureworks started looking at the phishing email link sent to Clinton's campaign chairman John Podesta. They managed to reverse-engineer the link to reveal a list of all the other people targeted by the hackers. It was, they said, a who's who of anti-Russian interests, including Ukrainian politicians and even a member of the punk band Pussy Riot. What's more, the links had all been created between 9 a.m. and 5 p.m., Moscow time, between Monday and Friday – with one day off, which happened to coincide with a holiday for technical military staff in the Russian Federation.[60] Tech security researchers and the U.S. intelligence agencies were quickly coalescing around the view that Russian government hackers were behind the DNC job.

Questions started being asked about WikiLeaks' decision to publish the stolen data. The response from its co-founder Julian Assange was typically combative. Characterizing the questions about his sources as a 'distraction attack' and dismissing Russian government involvement, Assange stated: 'No, it's not a state party. Stop trying to distract in that way and pay attention to the content of the publication.'[61]

The Russian president gave a similar response. Denying accusations of Russian state involvement, Vladimir Putin said it was 'hysteria', which he claimed was 'merely caused by the fact that somebody needs to divert the attention of the American people from the essence of what was exposed by the hackers'.[62]

The message from both was clear: pay less attention to the source of the leaks, and more attention to what's in them. As illustrated by the Sony hack, it was an instruction with which some media outlets were only too happy to comply.

For his part, Trump seemed to put out contradictory messages about whether he thought Russia was to blame. At one point he said the idea Russia had leaked the emails to help his campaign was a 'joke'.[63] Then two days later he said: 'Russia, if you're listening, I hope you're able to find the 30,000 emails that are missing,' once again raising the spectre of the controversy around Clinton's private email server.[64]

There was far less ambiguity from intelligence officials, however. By late July 2016, they were reportedly expressing 'high confidence' to the White House (still under Barack Obama's presidency) that Russia was behind the DNC hacks. But it would take until July 2018 for the full allegations to come out, in what would be one of the most comprehensive cybercrime indictments ever seen.

Special Counsel Robert Mueller was tasked with investigating alleged collusion between the Trump campaign and the Russian government. The inquiry claimed several critical scalps, with a string of former Trump loyalists turning on their former leader and agreeing to assist. In the end it found no conclusive evidence of the collusion that Trump's opponents were hoping for. What it did do, however, was file criminal charges on 13 July 2018 against what U.S. intelligence claims is one of Russia's most prolific state hacking groups.[65] The indictment lists twelve Russian nationals whom it says formed the bulk of the team that penetrated the DNC's systems to such devastating effect. Finally, Fancy Bear's members were named – at least, according to the U.S. government.

The indictment maps out in detail every twist and turn of the hack, from the phishing email sent to Clinton's campaign chairman John Podesta, to the setting up of DCleaks, to the alleged communication with WikiLeaks and even the Web searches the hackers carried out. The job descriptions and seniority of each member of the group are described in detail, including the pseudonyms they allegedly used to run various social media accounts and to purchase services used for their hacking campaigns.

How could the Americans know so much about the gang's work? One member of the cybergroup, it seems, let the side down.

Ivan Yermakov was, according to the FBI, a Russian military officer assigned to Unit 26165, a team within Russia's Main Intelligence Directorate, the GRU.[66] He was also, on occasion, 'Kate S. Milton', 'James McMorgans' and 'Karen W. Millen' – just some of his social media pseudonyms, said investigators. While the FBI documents are clear about the alleged roles and responsibilities of the twelve alleged hackers, when it comes to Yermakov they have so much information it almost seems as though U.S. spies were watching over his shoulder as he typed.

The indictment alleges he searched the Web for details about the DNC and Clinton, analysed the organization's Internet connections to see what computers they ran, and researched what commands to type into Microsoft software to pilfer emails. And when CrowdStrike moved in to sort the problems out, the Americans claim Yermakov started searching online for information about the company, including any details CrowdStrike might know about Fancy Bear's precious hacking tools.

Yermakov wasn't the only person the FBI claimed to have under observation. The day the Guccifer 2.0 blog was published claiming sole responsibility for the hack, the FBI say that Fancy Bear operatives searched online for a very specific set of phrases, including 'illuminati', 'worldwide known' and 'think twice about'. If the phrases look familiar, that's because they later appeared word-for-word on the blog post written by Guccifer 2.0. The 'solo Romanian hacker' claimed to be unconnected to the Russian government, but the FBI's indictment seems to show his words were drafted by the very Russian military unit that hacked into the DNC. If true, it shows impressively fast work by the Russians. Within a day of the DNC going public with news of the hack, the intruders had a fake persona ready to go – and not just any persona, but one with plausible connections to a previous hacking campaign under the Guccifer name.

The FBI also alleged that, when Guccifer 2.0 had contacted journalists with information, he'd given them the password to a hidden part of the DCleaks website. It became increasingly hard to separate Guccifer 2.0 from DCleaks from Fancy Bear.

Of course, this is all according to the FBI. Theirs is a lengthy indictment full of data, some of which is independently verifiable, but much of which is not. The Russian government has consistently denied having anything to do with the hacking of the DNC, and claims such allegations are part of a conspiracy directed at the Federation. (Requests for an interview for this book made via its foreign office and its embassy in London went unanswered.)

What the indictment doesn't include, however, is any reference to Cozy Bear, the other allegedly Russian hacking group that CrowdStrike claims to have found lurking inside the DNC. It seems their stealthy behaviour has kept them under the radar – at least for now.

The two hacking teams seem to have been treading on each other's toes. CrowdStrike claims they saw evidence of both groups going after the same information. If both were part of the Russian government, as security researchers believe, why weren't they cooperating? The answer may lie in the labyrinthine networks of Russia's intelligence services. A report by the European Council on Foreign Relations (perhaps not the most impartial source, but thorough in its mapping-out of Russian state intelligence agencies) shows the overlap of roles between the GRU, suspected of being behind Fancy Bear, and the SVR (Russia's Foreign Intelligence Service), suspected of being behind Cozy Bear.[67]

This overlap, combined with Putin's leadership style, deliberately fosters tension, competitiveness and distrust, according to the report. It also describes the GRU as 'aggressive and risk-taking'. If the GRU was indeed the agency behind Fancy Bear, it would explain why their raid on the Democratic National Committee was rumbled (comparatively) quickly – in just a few weeks, compared to Cozy Bear's stealthy year-or-more undercover.

And if the report is correct in its picture of the fierce rivalry between the agencies, one can only guess at the conversations that must have taken place when Fancy Bear got caught inside the DNC, potentially ruining the intelligence access of both the groups. It wasn't the last time the GRU would be caught red-handed in its hacking activities, according to Western intelligence agencies.

On 13 April 2018, Dutch law enforcement detained four Russian men in The Hague. They'd hired a car and parked it at the Marriott hotel, according to the Dutch intelligence service. But it seems they weren't interested in the four-star amenities.

The Marriott is next to the office of the Organization for the Prohibition of Chemical Weapons (OPCW), which was playing a key role in an investigation into the attempted murder in March 2018 of former Russian double agent Sergei Skripal and his daughter Yulia, who were poisoned in Salisbury, in the southwest of England.

The Dutch intelligence agency claimed that the four men picked up in The Hague were part of a Russian government 'close access' hacking team, who had parked nearby the OPCW in order to intercept the Internet signals emitted from the building.[68] They released photos of the boot of the car, which appeared to be full of interception equipment.

Dutch intelligence also claimed they had seized a laptop from the men which, when analysed, showed signs of having been used in Malaysia, Switzerland and Brazil. The connection? According to the Netherlands, in Malaysia the laptop was used to target the investigation into Malaysia Airlines flight MH17, which was shot down in July 2014 over territory held by Russian-backed rebels in Ukraine.[69] In Switzerland it was used in Lausanne, where it was linked to the hacking of a laptop belonging to the World Anti-Doping Authority, which had exposed doping by Russian athletes. Brazil is also home to a key anti-doping agency site. The implication was that the Russian close access team had been on a 'world tour', targeting organizations threatening Russian interests.

The Russian government strongly denied any connection to the hacking allegations. It called the incident in The Hague 'Western spy mania', saying it was the victim of 'yet another stage-managed propaganda campaign'. Its statement said: 'It's unclear who is supposed to believe these statements accusing Russian citizens of attempting to mount cyber-attacks . . . Any Russian citizen carrying a mobile device is seen as a spy.'[70]

The four Russians detained in the Netherlands were using diplomatic passports. On the one hand, that meant they could not be charged with offences by the Dutch, who simply expelled them instead. But on the other, when the Dutch released photos of the passports, it gave journalists a new lead. Reporters at investigative website Bellingcat looked up the passport holders' names on a Russian database and claimed to find one of them registered at the address of the GRU, the Russian military intelligence agency that the FBI claims is behind Fancy Bear. The journalists also said that a search of a car ownership database revealed that one of the four men arrested had registered his Lada at another GRU office. This, in turn, enabled journalists to identify 305 other people with cars registered there (as well as their passport and mobile phone numbers): all presumably GRU employees.[71]

If the Dutch government and Bellingcat claims are true, it seems the GRU's 'aggressive and risk-taking' approach was their undoing. With their faces known (not to mention the identities of hundreds of their colleagues), Russia's alleged hacking team may find it much harder to mount such close access operations again.

It seemed like a closing chapter in the Fancy Bear story. But it was far from the end of tech security's influence on U.S. politics. As his election victory faded into history and his bellicose White House reign began, President Trump became embroiled in an escalating trade war with China. As the conflict heated up, technology once again proved to be a pivotal issue: this time, one which straddled the Atlantic divide and put serious strain on America's 'special relationship' with the UK.

In early 2013 I had lunch with a long-serving MP who was a member of the Parliamentary Intelligence and Security Committee. Towards the dessert course the politician lowered their voice and told me the committee was 'concerned about this company, Huawei'. Being an evidence-based journalist I asked for, well . . . evidence. None was forthcoming. Perhaps any that existed was just too secret to share: the committee often hears from intelligence sources behind closed doors.

But it seemed the committee was indeed worried about the Chinese technology giant. In June 2013 it released a report entitled *Foreign Involvement in the Critical National Infrastructure.*[72] The foreign involvement was Huawei. And the critical national infrastructure turned out to be the backbone of the UK's communications system, run by BT. The British company had signed a contract with Huawei in 2005 to provide equipment for an overhaul of the telecoms network. As the Intelligence and Security Committee was 'shocked' to discover, government ministers weren't even told about the deal, let alone asked their opinion. The committee's report still didn't provide specific evidence of any alleged Chinese government interference in Huawei, but did make it crystal clear how worried its members were.

It was one of the first of a series of blows for Huawei, as the company became embroiled in a damaging mix of geopolitics, tech security and trade war, despite firmly denying any accusations that it enabled spying by Beijing.

To understand why Huawei is big news, you have to understand 5G – short for Fifth Generation mobile phone technology. Over the years, the speed, coverage and capacity of the mobile networks has expanded rapidly. 5G is the next leap forward, but it means more than just faster downloads of cat videos. There is an edifice of cutting-edge equipment waiting in the wings for the new network's arrival. Part of the leap in 5G is that it can send signals faster, meaning less 'latency' (the delay in transmitting and receiving a signal). Think about driverless cars: a delay of even a few microseconds in transmitting or receiving an instruction to stop could mean the difference between life and death.

Remote-controlled surgery, smart traffic controls, drone flights: many, many future innovations can only really take off (quite literally, in some cases) once 5G has arrived. As a result, the rush is on to get it installed. For that, you need someone to supply the equipment (transmitters and receivers, for example) and right now, there are only three players in that game: Huawei, Nokia and Ericsson.[73] The Chinese company is estimated by some to be a good two years ahead of the competition – a vital lead in the high-tech marketplace.

The problem is that several countries around the world have decided they simply cannot trust equipment made in China, especially if it's installed wide and deep into their communications networks, carrying everything from Facebook updates to politicians' emails. They fear the Chinese government may have installed so-called 'backdoors' into the kit, allowing it to intercept communications.

Australia has blocked the company from providing equipment for its 5G roll-out (a decision being challenged by Huawei). New

Zealand has followed suit.[74] In the U.S. it is banned from government networks, and in May 2019 American companies were briefly banned from trading with the company.

Usefully, here in the UK we have the answer. Or at least, we should have. In the wake of concerns over the BT contract, the UK government tasked GCHQ, the government's communications intelligence agency, to set up a team to test Huawei kit in collaboration with the company. The results, predictably enough, have never been made public. But senior people within UK government cyber circles have almost certainly seen the conclusions, and their subsequent comments have been very revealing.

In April 2019, Ian Levy, technical director of the UK's National Cyber Security Centre, told the BBC: 'The security engineering in Huawei is unlike anything else. It's engineering like it's back in the year 2000. It's very, very shoddy and leads to cybersecurity issues that we need to manage long term.' Crucially, though, he went on to say: 'We don't think the things we're reporting on are evidence of Chinese state malfeasance. It's poor engineering.'[75]

In other words, the UK isn't so much worried about China having built covert access into Huawei kit: if it's that badly built, they fear *anyone* could potentially hack into it. (Huawei did not respond to requests for comment for this book.)

At the time of writing, the solution the UK was edging towards was installing Huawei, but not on 'critical' parts of the network. This solution didn't seem to satisfy the U.S., however, which threatened to rein in its data-sharing and security partnerships with the UK if it went ahead with installing the Chinese company's products in Britain's 5G network.

The U.S. is extremely suspicious that Huawei will allow the Chinese government a backdoor into the communications on which many of us rely. Which is ironic, since it's only a few years since we learned about a system which allows the U.S. government a backdoor into the communications on which many of us rely.

In December 2012, journalist Glenn Greenwald received a peculiar message. A whistle-blower wanted to make contact with some confidential information, but would only do so if Greenwald used a highly secure method of communication. Not being especially tech-savvy, the journalist struggled to make it work.[76] Increasingly frustrated, the source (who by this time had adopted the pseudonym Citizenfour) sent an encrypted message instead to a contemporary of Greenwald's, a fellow journalist called Laura Poitras. It would change her life, and those of many others:

> I am a senior government employee in the intelligence community. I hope you understand that contacting you is extremely high risk and you are willing to agree to the following precautions before I share more. This will not be a waste of your time.[77]

Citizenfour was, of course, Edward Snowden, a former contractor for the u.s. National Security Agency (NSA), America's answer to GCHQ.

Snowden was employed by a consultancy called Booz Allen Hamilton to work at the NSA. He was an infrastructure analyst, someone who 'looks for new ways to break into Internet and telephone traffic around the world'.[78] He'd watched with alarm as his work had revealed to him more and more of the u.s. government's surveillance apparatus.

In the mid-2000s, the American intelligence agencies had woken up to the fact that around 80 per cent of the world's tidal wave of digital communications traffic flowed through the u.s., and they'd seen an unprecedented opportunity to generate and exploit intelligence leads.[79] Snowden was concerned at the capacity for innocent people to be caught up in this dragnet. Eventually, he decided to steal top-secret information about the u.s. government's interception programmes and leak it. He smuggled tens of thousands of documents out of a high-security facility in Hawaii.

Holed up in a hotel in Hong Kong, Snowden had handed much of the material to Greenwald and other journalists from *The Guardian*. He then tried to flee, reportedly to Cuba, but only got as far as Russia, where he remained as the U.S. had cancelled his passport mid-flight.[80]

What the leaked documents revealed was astonishing to anyone ignorant of the modern state's surveillance capability (which was almost everyone). Among many other revelations they detailed how the U.S. government, via secret court orders, was able to access information from the world's biggest technology brands. Under a programme called PRISM, the documents showed the NSA had legally sanctioned access enabling 'collection directly from the servers' of Facebook, Google, YouTube, Skype, AOL, Apple, Microsoft and Yahoo.[81] Some of the companies denied any knowledge of the programme and others claimed they had not consented to such access, leading many to assume it was done in secret via a sealed court order.

Historically, the NSA was banned from collecting data on American citizens en masse without specific legal permission. But it got round this by changing the definition of 'collecting', according to journalist Fred Kaplan's detailed history of the NSA, *Dark Territory*. 'Under the new terminology, the NSA was just *storing* the data, the *collecting* wouldn't happen until an analyst went to retrieve it from the files,' Kaplan writes.[82] But even that was problematic because under U.S. law, as Kaplan explains: 'data could only be stored if it was deemed "relevant" to an investigation of foreign intelligence or terrorism.'

Once again, the NSA changed the definition: 'under this new definition, *everything* was potentially relevant, there was no way of knowing what *was* relevant until it *became* relevant; therefore, you had to have everything on hand to make a definitive assessment.'[83]

Language is a powerful tool, and when you change it, you redistribute power. Thus was the legal path paved to the mass data-gathering programmes of the NSA.

But the agency wasn't just a passive collector. Over the preceding decades the NSA (once jokingly referred to as 'No Such Agency', due to its highly secret nature) had merged defensive cybersecurity work with offensive teams: government-employed hackers tasked and protected under U.S. law with breaking into companies and governments overseas. 'Getting the ungettable' was reportedly their motto.

It wasn't only in the U.S. that state-sponsored hackers were at work. The documents published during 2013 by *The Guardian*, among others, also revealed the extent of collaboration between the NSA in the U.S. and GCHQ in the UK. It was a position of primacy Britain achieved partly through an accident of geography: as one of its nearest neighbours in Europe, the UK had a physically close relationship with the U.S. Some of the first transatlantic cables to America had been laid from a tiny beach in Cornwall on the far southwest coast. As telegrams had given way to telephones and finally high-speed data streams, the route had remained the same. Even now, at low tide you can still see huge cables running up to the beach. These days they are packed full of fibre-optic lines carrying data around the world in staccato pulses of light. No surprise, then, that in addition to its main base in the west of England, GCHQ also has a large outpost at Bude in Cornwall.[84]

The Snowden leaks showed how the UK's listening station obsessively fought to increase its ability to intercept the wealth of information flooding through these fibre-optic cables; an activity which it called, charmingly, 'access to light'. Equally poetic (though perhaps not for those on the receiving end of them) were the code names given to the various interception tools, among them Mutant Broth, Rickety Pig and Fretting Yeti.

Like the NSA, GCHQ wasn't just a passive collector. It also ran offensive hacking operations. It's easy to get overwhelmed by the mass of Snowden documents and the bewildering maze of state surveillance they expose. But honing in on just one of the GCHQ operations covered in the documents indicates how far the agency could go while still claiming to be acting within its boundaries. According to an article in *The Intercept* in February 2015 based on the Snowden documents, the UK's signals intelligence agency accessed the personal email and Facebook accounts of employees of a Dutch technology company to enable Britain's spies to intercept phonecalls and texts around the world.[85]

GCHQ, wrote *The Intercept*, was targeting SIM cards – the little rectangles of plastic inside mobile phones that connect the handset to the phone network. The information sent to and from the SIM card is encrypted, so it can't be spied upon. According to *The Intercept*, GCHQ wanted access to the encryption codes for these SIM cards so that it could tap into mobile communications in countries from Iran and Afghanistan to India and Iceland. To do so, in 2010 GCHQ is alleged to have targeted a company called Gemalto, headquartered in the Netherlands, which was one of the biggest global suppliers of encryption software for SIMs. According to documents released by *The Intercept*, GCHQ first profiled which Gemalto employees might be useful for their operation, finding out where they worked and what their job roles were. Then they used the American NSA's tools to access the employees' personal email and Facebook accounts to find out further information about them. GCHQ reportedly eventually managed to break into Gemalto digitally and gain the precious encryption keys, enabling them to unscramble mobile phone communications from millions of devices. Gemalto launched an investigation, and discovered hacks carried out on its systems in 2010 and 2011, which it said looked like the alleged GCHQ operation *The Intercept* had reported on. But the company said the hack didn't penetrate its confidential internal networks.[86]

At the time, GCHQ responded to *The Intercept*'s report by stating its work was done within a 'strict legal and policy framework' and that it ensures its activities are 'authorized, necessary and proportionate'.[87] If this looks like a stock response, that's because it was. Throughout much of the era of the Snowden revelations (and the above example of Gemalto is just one of many allegations that emerged from the documents), the agency's response to media enquiries barely changed. It's possible this was because of the sensitivity of much of its work: responding to the minutiae of each new revelation might have risked revealing, jigsaw-style, where its strengths and weaknesses lay.

But if *The Intercept*'s story is true, and the GCHQ response is correct, then the consequences are striking: it means it was considered authorized, necessary and proportionate for UK government cyberteams to target completely innocent people, hack their personal email and Facebook accounts to get inside their company – which was in a non-hostile territory and acting completely legally – and attempt to steal its intellectual property with the wider aim of eventually accessing people's private communications.

Is that cybercrime?

Absolutely not, according to GCHQ's response. It was all authorized, legal and proportionate. And of course, we don't know how many criminal activities were derailed as a result of GCHQ's access to all those mobile phonecalls and texts. Perhaps they felt the ends justified the means. And yet in order to achieve those ends, innocent individuals allegedly had their private information tapped into, pored over and utilized without their knowledge or consent, and a private company in a Western European country had its systems hacked by a country it probably considered an ally.

In GCHQ's defence, it operates under considerable legal restrictions, and its staff have to jump through many hoops before being able to carry out any offensive operations. But isn't the same argument available to other countries' hackers? What if it emerged that, for example, the Fancy Bear hacking group had received legal permission to carry out their aggressive raids on foreign political organizations? Would that make their actions acceptable? What if the Lazarus group – the allegedly North Korean state hacking team that unleashed WannaCry and broke into Sony Pictures and Bangladesh Bank – had the personal blessing of their leader?

We may not like these countries' governments, but ultimately they are sovereign states, and if the test of a hack's legitimacy is whether the government that carried it out can say it's 'authorized, legal and proportionate', then that leaves considerable room for other countries to exploit the same argument. We can wax lyrical about how much better our legal frameworks are compared to theirs but because decisions about nation-state hacking are almost always made behind closed doors, in our country as well as others, we have limited opportunity to vet the decision-making processes that countries use to justify their actions.

In a way, much of this isn't new: nations have always spied on other nations and given themselves legal and political cover to do so. But in the past, this espionage was stealthier: it was about strategic, informational advantage and rarely broke out into the 'real world'. As we've seen throughout the course of this book, that's no longer the case. Government hackers no longer hide in the shadows. Their work increasingly relies on the highly public media manipulation tactics employed by the Fancy Bear and Lazarus group attacks. They're noisy, disruptive and in some cases deeply damaging to the critical services on which we all rely. And they're often using tools indistinguishable from those of the cybercrime gangs.

There is of course a big difference between the credit card fraud and bank account hacking that started this book, and the legally sanctioned hacking of the NSA, GCHQ and others that finishes it. But in between there is a growing area of thick, grey mud, and the number of players within it is expanding all the time. That's a direct result of a crossover between the three types of hacking groups: organized cybercrime gangs, hacktivists and nation-state hackers.

The crooks may have started out with a pure profit motive, but as the preceding chapters have shown, that's not how it's remained. Their tools have become ever more damaging, creating mass, indiscriminate attacks.

Hacktivists have seen their digital protest tactics turned to cybercrime, and their media manipulation techniques have been refined and honed by powerful forces.

And most worryingly of all, the crooks' and hacktivists' techniques are increasingly being adopted by nation-state teams, where they can be applied with all of the time, money and strategic direction that a government can exert. We've seen the damage this has caused to our hospitals, power stations and political processes.

This book started with hackers making millions out of raiding bank accounts, holding people to ransom, stealing their data and defrauding them. It went through hackers launching reputational damage campaigns and manipulating the media. And it ends with high-level, nation-state campaigns that are, apparently, legal, necessary and proportionate. Along the way, the tools and tactics used by the different groups have become increasingly indistinguishable.

As these groups converge, and as politics, journalism and critical services are increasingly affected, where does cybercrime end and state power begin?

Perhaps, once, the dividing line between them all was clear. That's not how it looks now.

EPILOGUE

As I was writing this book, yet another remake of *Godzilla* was hitting the movie screens. It's an age-old tale of a nuclear-charged, prehistoric creature who waddles out of the sea to wreak havoc before disappearing back beneath the waves.

It seemed an apt analogy for how a lot of people feel about cybercrime. Hacking attacks can sometimes seem like the work of monsters from the digital deep. They rear up, swallowing personal data, grabbing credit card numbers, crashing computer networks and sowing disinformation, before vanishing back into the dark, leaving the populace terrified and unsure where they will strike next. This has created fertile ground for the growing cybersecurity industry, which claims to offer protection against these techno-beasts' attacks.

The media (myself included) hasn't always covered itself in glory in its coverage of hacking. Alarmist headlines and terrifying predictions are too often followed by an absence of subsequent information, advice or investigation. Over the years it struck me that it might be better to understand why these monsters emerged in the first place, and how they evolved. This might give us an idea of where they'll strike next. As we've seen throughout this book, after decades of modern cybercrime it is possible to discern some patterns. Notably, we've seen the confluence of different hacker groups and a convergence of their tools, tactics and techniques.

And it's not going to stop. Our society is only going to become more reliant on technology, partly driven by the wonderful and profitable things we can do with all the data such technology creates. The increasing trend for connecting parts of the energy grid to the Internet is just one example: it's a boon for power companies looking to manage their equipment and optimize their business – it's also handy for hackers who want to try to switch the lights off.

Organized cybercrime gangs, too, show few signs of fading away – they've made too much money to give up now. Security researchers have watched as the early bank-hacking gangs moved on to launch ransomware attacks. They are probably even now cooking up their next money-making projects.

Hackers' use of the media will continue as well: with organizations like the International Consortium of Investigative Journalists and WikiLeaks there are now ready conduits for getting big, impactful data leaks in front of a world audience, pre-sifted and pre-packaged. And with news outlets struggling for revenue and eyeballs against behemoths such as Facebook, there will always be journalists willing to run a salacious story with little regard to who the source is or what their motivations might be.

Governments aren't giving up hacking either. Among the general public, the Snowden revelations may have been a disturbing insight into the scale of state surveillance. But for some regimes they seem to have been a wake-up call to the potential for snooping on and controlling populations at home and abroad in our increasingly digitized world. For nation states, the cybercriminals' tools also represent exceptional value for money compared to conventional weapons. You may look with terror at the story of Daniel Kaye, the thirty-year-old who tried to take down Liberia's entire Internet connection armed only with a mobile phone. But for $10,000 a month (reportedly the amount he was paid by those funding the attack) I bet there are military recruiters who'd hire him in a flash.

It's easy to feel as though the whole situation has got out of hand: too many monsters, not enough heroes. And yet, there are steps we can all take to tackle the threat. The good news is that it doesn't necessarily require lots of expensive new kit. After all, as we learned from the Love Bug story, from the earliest days hackers have often relied on exploiting the humans behind the computers. If we want to tackle cybercrime, it's humans, not necessarily computers, that we need to harden up.

The first and most important step will hopefully be obvious enough to anyone who's read this book: be very careful about emails.

It's depressing to note that, time and again, phishing emails are the criminals' way in. Whether it's sending a fake password reset message to the chairman of Hillary Clinton's presidential campaign, or convincing hundreds of thousands of people to open a 'love letter' attachment, email spam is the number one infection vector for hackers. We need to move away from the quaint idea that our inboxes can somehow be protected by our Internet companies, email providers or IT support departments. No amount of filtering will stop every malicious attachment, and it takes only one click to get infected. The quid pro quo for our brave new world of 24/7 access is that each of us is now our own security guard.

Perhaps we can take a leaf out of the corporate playbook. Cybersecurity experts talk about companies' 'deterrence' and 'resilience' to attacks. What does that look like for the ordinary person in the street? Keeping software up to date, using strong passwords and making regular backups (and keeping them disconnected somewhere safe). None of it's rocket science, but all of these steps will raise you up from being the low-hanging fruit on which so many cybercriminals prey. They'll also help get you back on your feet if the worst happens.

For organizations, the uncomfortable truth is that conventional risk assessment is no longer going to work. In days gone by, it might have been possible to assess how likely a target you were for hackers, and what data they might try to go for based on its value. But with the increasing convergence of hacking tactics, such assessments become harder to make. The indiscriminate, mass hacking tools of cybercrime have, as we've seen, occasionally been used by nation states with no profit motive. Hacktivists occasionally break in for fun and steal everything they can lay their hands on. This makes it increasingly hard to calculate your risk of being hacked (the NHS, for example, clearly placed itself low on the cyberthreat scale prior to the WannaCry attack).

Instead, organizations may benefit from having both an 'if' team and a 'when' team. The former works on the basis that hacks are preventable and tries to secure the organization, working out what its sensitive data and systems are, where they sit and how well protected they are. For example, it would be this team's responsibility to educate staff about the dangers of phishing emails, weak passwords and so on. (Too much of this work, in my opinion, uses the stick rather than the carrot – I suspect most employees would respond better to receiving a bottle of champagne for having the strongest password, than having to do an online training course because they failed a phishing email test exercise).

The 'when' team, by contrast, would work on the basis that the hack has already happened – what's the worst type of data a hacker could have accessed, and what's the worst thing they could do with it? How will you go about informing customers? Regulators? Staff? (Especially if corporate email is one of the services that's been hit.) From a worst-case scenario, how would you get back to normal operation, and how long would it take?

The former team would rely more on techies, the latter team on PR and legal. But it's vital the two teams mix – one of the big problems in the October 2015 TalkTalk hack, for example, was the company's PR decision to send the chief executive into newsrooms without sufficient information from the IT folks. In fact, had the company been quicker at assessing the scale of the attack, it might not have become a news story at all.

Even if it doesn't result in a massive cybersecurity investment, simply going through such an 'if and when' process and recording the outcomes might pay dividends in a hacking incident. For example, under the new European data regulations, when assessing an incident the UK's data watchdog partly takes into account the extent to which organizations have considered where their important data is and what rules are in place to protect it.

The media also needs to take its role more seriously, not only in making its coverage of hacks more helpful to everyday audiences, but in being more diligent about how it uses hacked information leaked by unknown sources with opaque motivations. In an age of mass data leaks and shadowplay, it's painfully easy for the media to become the puppet of the hackers. Salacious data-leak stories may look like an easy win at first, but they can have sour consequences in the long term – particularly if, as apparently happened in the Democratic Party and Sony hacks, it later emerges that journalists effectively became a tool of cynical manipulation by nation states.

At a government level, things are inevitably a lot more complex. Wonderful as it would be to 'ban state hacking' overnight, as we have seen, it's not easy to work out the parameters. In reality, there are always going to be occasions on which arms of government must make unauthorized intrusions into people's digital lives. We hope our own governments use this power wisely and legitimately. But since we'll almost certainly never know how their decisions were reached, this leaves open the door to other countries to use the same justification for their own hacks.

There are legitimate fears about the tools governments are developing to enable such hacks, and how safely they're kept. The malicious software that drove the WannaCry attack that disproportionately affected the NHS, for example, was allegedly developed by the U.S. government before it somehow leaked out onto the Internet. It incorporated so-called 'zero days' in Windows operating systems that arguably should have been flagged up to Microsoft for fixing and helping keep the public safe, rather than squirrelled away for government hackers' use.

The u.s. government now reportedly runs a type of internal clearing house for such powerful hacking tools, in an attempt to control which of its agencies are exploiting them and when they can be made public.[1] This sounds an eminently sensible idea that other governments could adopt.

There is also more that could be done to tackle the growing and unrestrained market of companies brokering such zero days. It's fast becoming clear that some of these companies' claims to sell only to 'legitimate' government buyers are pretty thin. Instead, critical holes in apps and programs that we all use are being sold to the highest bidder, who sometimes uses them in unscrupulous ways, even if they are a government organization.

Just as the trade in weapons is controlled, this business might also be regulated. Some would argue that the zero-day brokers are international players with opaque corporate setups, and therefore hard to police. But they must put their profits in a bank somewhere. And besides, the difficulty of regulating the global trade in traditional weapons hasn't stopped us trying.

None of this, of course, will stop cybercrime in its tracks. Our modern, data-rich world is too full of increasingly complex, inter-reliant technologies and unpatched holes to prevent the hackers getting through. In the original 1954 *Godzilla* movie, an electrified fence was erected to keep the monster out. It didn't work then, and there's no Big Wall solution that's going to save us now. But perhaps if we pay attention to the lessons of the past few decades, our future can be made just that little bit safer.

REFERENCES

1 MEET THE HACKERS

1 'Love Bug May Have Been Accident', www.news.bbc.co.uk, 11 May 2000.
2 Barry M. Leiner, Vinton G. Cerf, David D. Clark, Robert E. Kahn, Leonard Kleinrock, Daniel C. Lynch, Jon Postel, Larry G. Roberts and Stephen Wolff, 'Brief History of the Internet', *Internet Society* (1997), pp. 2–4, online at www.internetsociety.org.
3 'History of the Web', www.webfoundation.org, accessed 21 June 2019.
4 Jason Scott, 'The BBS Documentary', www.bbsdocumentary.com, accessed 21 June 2019.
5 'What Is the Well?', www.well.com, accessed 24 June 2019.
6 John Perry Barlow, 'Crime and Puzzlement', www.eff.org, 8 June 1990.
7 Ibid.
8 'A History of Protecting Freedom Where Law and Technology Collide', www.eff.org, accessed 26 June 2019.
9 John Perry Barlow, 'A Declaration of the Independence of Cyberspace', www.eff.org, 8 February 1996.
10 This practice was not confined to American academic settings, as evidenced by books such as *The Night Climbers of Cambridge*, first published in the 1930s under the pseudonym Whipplesnaith (Cambridge, 2007), and *LA Climbs: Alternative Uses for Architecture* by Alex Hartley (London and New York, 2003).
11 Dennis Fisher, '"We Got to Be Cool About This": An Oral History of the L0pht', www.duo.com, 6 March 2018.
12 'Weak Computer Security in Government: Is the Public at Risk? Hearing Before the Committee on Governmental Affairs, United States Senate', U.S. Government Printing Office, 19 May 1998.
13 International Criminal Tribunal for the Former Yugoslavia, www.icty.org, 14 March 2002.
14 Barlow, 'Crime and Puzzlement'.
15 Ibid.
16 Eric Chien, 'VBS.Loveletter.Var', www.symantec.com, accessed 26 June 2019.
17 James Meek, 'Love Bug Virus Creates Worldwide Chaos', *The Guardian* (5 May 2000).
18 'Love Bug May Have Been Accident'.

2 FALL OF THE BERLIN FIREWALL

1 Unemployment rate, OECD Data, www.data.oecd.org, accessed 22 July 2018.

2 Figures kindly provided by Anna Smolentseva, Senior Researcher, Institute of Education, National Research University Higher School of Economics, Moscow, Russia, 31 July 2018.

3 Dan Bloom, 'Putin's Great Russian Brain-drain', *Daily Mail* (2 December 2014).

4 'Russian Scam Artist Sentenced in "Forbes List" ID Theft', NBC New York, www.nbcnewyork.com, 16 July 2009.

5 Igor Klopov, 'DECADE/TRUESTORY/', undated, shared directly with the author via online message.

6 See 'Case 1:07-cr-00707-ARR Document 102-1', https://ddosecrets.com, accessed 26 June 2019.

7 U.S. Department of Commerce News, via www.census.gov, 2 March 2000.

8 'Fraud, the Facts 2009', UK Cards Association (London, 2009).

9 Samuel Burke, 'In the Mind of a Hacker', CNN Business (29 October 2014).

10 Benjamin Peters, *How Not to Network a Nation: The Uneasy History of the Soviet Internet* (Boston, MA, 2017).

11 Ed Cabrera, Robert McArdle and the U.S. Secret Service Criminal Investigation Division (CID), 'The Evolution of Cybercrime and Cyberdefense', *Trend Micro* (29 October 2018).

12 'Albert Gonzalez', Berkman Klein Center for Internet and Society at Harvard University, https://cyber.harvard.edu, 8 August 2012.

13 Misha Glenny, *DarkMarket: How Hackers Became the New Mafia* (London, 2012), p. 93.

14 U.S. Department of Justice, 'Leader of Hacking Ring Sentenced for Massive Identity Thefts from Payment Processor and U.S. Retail Networks', www.justice.gov, 26 March 2010.

15 Kevin Poulsen, 'Feds Charge 11 in Breaches at TJ Maxx, OfficeMax, DSW, Others', *Wired* (5 August 2008).

16 'International Credit Card Trafficker Sentenced to 88 Months in Prison', www.justice.gov, 5 April 2013.

17 Jim Bruene, 'Online Banking: 2003 Results', www.finovate.com, 3 January 2004.

18 See www.thefinancialbrand.com, accessed 23 December 2018.

19 Glenny, *DarkMarket*, p. 77.

20 'What Is Zeus Malware?', https://enterprise.comodo.com, 31 July 2018.

21 Michael Schwirtz and Joseph Goldstein, 'Russian Espionage Piggybacks on a Cybercriminal's Hacking', *New York Times* (12 March 2017).

22 Don Jackson and Kevin Stevens, 'Zeus Banking Trojan Report', www.secureworks.com, 10 March 2010.

23 Aleksandr Panin, 'Solution of Cancer', 'Solution of Aging', www.ssrn.com, 26 February 2018.

24 U.S. Department of Justice, 'Two Major International Hackers Who Developed the "SpyEye" Malware get over 24 Years Combined in Federal Prison', www.justice.gov, 20 April 2016.

25 Pushpa Mishra, 'Creators of SpyEye Trojan Aleksandr Panin, Hamza Bendelladj Sentenced', Hack Read, 22 April 2016.

26 Garrett M. Graff, 'Inside the Hunt for Russia's Most Notorious Hacker', *Wired* (21 March 2017).

27 Ibid.

28 Ibid.

29 U.S. Department of Justice, 'Motion for Temporary Restraining Order', www.justice.gov, 30 May 2014.

30 Ibid.

31 Benny Evangelista, 'Napster Runs Out of Lives: Judge Rules Against Sale', *San Francisco Chronicle* (4 September 2002). The Napster name is now used by a different music service that states its operation is '100% legal'. Megan Guess, 'Napster Returns!', *Ars Technica* (15 June 2016).

32 Violet Blue, 'CryptoLocker's Crimewave: A Trail of Millions in Laundered Bitcoin', *ZDNet* (22 December 2013).

33 Fahmida Y. Rashid, 'Zeus Criminals Launch DDOS Attacks to Hide Fraudulent Wire Transfers', eWeek (1 December 2011).

34 Jim Edwards, 'This Is What It Looks Like When a Click-fraud Botnet Secretly Controls Your Web Browser', *Business Insider* (27 November 2013).

35 U.S. Department of Justice, United States of America v Evgeniy Mikhailovich Bogachev et al., 'Motion for Entry of Default', www.justice.gov, 11 July 2014.

36 See www.fox-it.com, 21 March 2017.

37 Graff, 'Inside the Hunt for Russia's Most Notorious Hacker'.

38 Will Stewart, '"Fantomas", the FBI's Most Wanted', *Daily Mail* (27 February 2015).

39 See www.fox-it.com, 21 March 2017.

40 'Actions in Response to Russian Malicious Cyber Activity and Harassment', www.obamawhitehouse.archives.gov, 29 December 2016.

3 *OCEAN'S 11* DOT COM

1 See www.pust.co., accessed 1 July 2019.

2 'DPR Korea: UN Says $111 million Needed to Provide Life-saving Aid, Tackle Malnutrition', www.news.un.org, 12 April 2018.

3 Sophie Schmidt, 'It Might Not Get Weirder Than This', https://sites.google.com/site/sophieinnorthkorea, accessed 26 June 2019.

4 See www.northkoreatech.org, accessed 1 July 2019.

5 Ahn Yong-hyun, 'What Is North Korea's Electronic Warfare Capability?', www.chosun.com, 23 March 2011.

6 Joseph S. Bermudez Jr, 'A New Emphasis on Operations Against South Korea?', www.38north.org, 11 June 2010.

7 'North Korea Boosted "Cyber Forces" to 6,000 Troops, South Says', *Reuters* (6 January 2015).

8 'New Cyber Reserve Unit Created', Ministry of Defence, Joint Forces Command, and the Rt Hon. Philip Hammond MP, www.gov.uk, 29 September 2013.

9 'Security Council Strengthens Sanctions on Democratic People's Republic of Korea, in Response to 12 February Nuclear Test', www.un.org, 7 March 2013.

10 'Report of the Panel of Experts Established Pursuant to Resolution 1874 (2009)', United Nations Security Council, 5 March 2019, p. 48.

11 Ibid., p. 328.

12 United States of America v PARK JIN HYOK, Criminal Complaint, 8 June 2018, p. 133.

13 Ibid., p. 136.

14 'Letter dated 27 June 2014 from the Permanent Representative of the
   Democratic People's Republic of Korea to the United Nations addressed to
   the Secretary-General', United Nations General Assembly Security Council,
   27 June 2014.

15 United States of America v PARK JIN HYOK, Criminal Complaint, 8 June 2018,
   p. 34.

16 Ibid., p. 25.

17 James Cook, 'Staff at Sony Pictures Are Being Forced to Use Pens and Paper
   After a Massive Hack', *Business Insider* (28 November 2014).

18 United States of America v PARK JIN HYOK, Criminal Complaint, 8 June 2018,
   p. 26.

19 Arik Hesseldahl, 'Sony Pictures Investigates North Korea Link in Hack
   Attack', recode.net, 28 November 2014.

20 'Consolidated Financial Results Forecast for the Third Quarter Ended
   December 31, 2014, and Revision of Consolidated Forecast for the Fiscal
   Year Ending March 31, 2015', Sony News and Information (4 February 2015),
   p. 6.

21 Steve Holland and Matt Spetalnick, 'Obama Vows U.S. Response to North
   Korea over Sony Cyber Attack', *Reuters* (19 December 2014).

22 David E. Sanger, David Barboza and Nicole Perlroth, 'Chinese Army Unit Is
   Seen as Tied to Hacking Against U.S.', *New York Times* (18 February 2013).

23 Ibid.

24 'Sony Hires Mandiant to Help Clean Up After Cyber Attack', *Reuters*
   (30 November 2014).

25 'Update on Sony Investigation', www.fbi.gov, 19 December 2014.

26 United States of America v PARK JIN HYOK, Criminal Complaint, 8 June 2018,
   p. 58.

27 World Bank data, www.data.worldbank.org, accessed 26 June 2019.

28 United States of America v PARK JIN HYOK, Criminal Complaint, 8 June 2018,
   p. 62.

29 Republic of the Philippines Senate, Committee on Accountability of Public
   Officers and Investigations (Blue Ribbon), 17 March 2016, pp. 17–22.

30 See www.shalikafoundation.org, accessed 1 July 2019.

31 Bangladesh Bank v Rizal Commercial Banking Corporation et al., Complaint,
   United States District Court, Southern District of New York, 31 January 2019,
   p. 9.

32 See www.swift.com, accessed 1 July 2019.

33 United States of America v PARK JIN HYOK, Criminal Complaint, 8 June 2018,
   p. 71.

34 Clare Baldwin and Joseph Menn, 'Hacker Documents Show NSA Tools
   for Breaching Global Money Transfer System', *Reuters* (16 April 2017).

35 Sergei Shevchenko, 'Two Bytes to $951m', baesystemsai.blogspot.com,
   25 April 2016.

36 Ibid.

37 Bangladesh Bank v Rizal Commercial Banking Corporation et al., Complaint,
   31 January 2019, p. 27.

38 Ibid., p.28.

39 See www.jica.go.jp, accessed 1 July 2019.

40 Republic of the Philippines Senate, Committee on Accountability of Public Officers and Investigations (Blue Ribbon), 17 March 2016, p. 16.

41 Bangladesh Bank v Rizal Commercial Banking Corporation et al., Complaint, 31 January 2019, p. 35.

42 Romualdo Agarrado testimony to Republic of the Philippines Senate, Committee on Accountability of Public Officers and Investigations (Blue Ribbon), 17 March 2016, broadcast by ABS-CBN News, accessed via www.youtube.com, 2 July 2019.

43 Bangladesh Bank v Rizal Commercial Banking Corporation et al., Complaint, 31 January 2019, p. 39.

44 Republic of the Philippines Senate, Committee on Accountability of Public Officers and Investigations (Blue Ribbon), 6 June 2016, p. 28.

45 Bangladesh Bank v Rizal Commercial Banking Corporation et al., Complaint, 31 January 2019, p. 55.

46 Republic of the Philippines Senate, Committee on Accountability of Public Officers and Investigations (Blue Ribbon), 6 June 2016.

47 Alan Katz and Wenxin Fan, 'A Baccarat Binge Helped Launder the World's Biggest Cyberheist', Bloomberg (3 August 2017).

48 Republic of the Philippines Senate, Committee on Accountability of Public Officers and Investigations (Blue Ribbon), 6 June 2016, p. 67.

49 Mark Merueñas, 'RCBC Sues Bank of Bangladesh for Defamation', *MSN Money* (12 March 2019).

50 Manolo Serapio Jr and Enrico Dela Cruz, 'Philippine Central Bank Fines Rizal Bank over Bangladesh Cyber Heist Failings', *Reuters* (5 August 2016).

51 Republic of the Philippines Senate, Committee on Accountability of Public Officers and Investigations (Blue Ribbon), 6 June 2016, p. 81.

52 'Roanu Damages Tk 250 Crore Crops, Properties', *Daily Asian Age* (24 May 2016).

53 United States of America v PARK JIN HYOK, Criminal Complaint, 8 June 2018, p. 2.

54 Banco del Austro v Wells Fargo Bank, Notice of Commencement of Action, 28 January 2016.

55 'Taiwan's Far Eastern International Fined T$8 million over SWIFT Hacking Incident', *Reuters* (12 December 2017).

56 'Report of the Panel of Experts Established Pursuant to Resolution 1874 (2009)', United Nations Security Council, 5 March 2019, p. 51.

57 Ibid., p. 51.

58 'Cosmos Bank Fraud: Cops Say Four of 7 Suspects Also Hacked Chennai Bank', *Times of India* (19 September 2018).

59 'Report of the Panel of Experts Established Pursuant to Resolution 1874 (2009)', United Nations Security Council, 5 March 2019, p. 197.

60 See www.mfa.gov.kp, accessed 1 March 2019.

61 'North Korea Says Sony, WannaCry Hack Charges Are a Smear Campaign', *ABC News* (14 September 2018).

4 DIGITAL EXTORTION

1 'NHS Cyber Attack: "My Heart Surgery Was Cancelled"', *BBC News*, 12 May 2017.

2 'Telefonica, Other Spanish Firms Hit in "Ransomware" Attack', *Reuters* (12 May 2017).

3 'Information about the PC CYBORG (AIDS) Trojan Horse', *Computer Incident Advisory Capability Information Bulletin*, www.ciac.org, 19 December 1989, accessed 28 June 2019 via www.archive.org.

4 Merck, 'Merck Announces Fourth-quarter and Full-year 2017 Financial Results', www.investors.merck.com, 2 February 2018.

5 'Cyber Threat Alliance Cracks the Code on Cryptowall Crimeware Associated with $325 Million in Payments', www.cyberthreatalliance.org, 28 October 2015.

6 Brad Smith, 'The Need for Urgent Collective Action to Keep People Safe online: Lessons from Last Week's Cyberattack', blogs.microsoft.com, 14 May 2017.

7 Iain Thomson, 'Leaked NSA Point-and-pwn Hack Tools Menace Win2k to Windows 8', www.theregister.co.uk, 14 April 2017.

8 Michael Mimoso, 'ShadowBrokers Expose NSA Access to SWIFT Service Bureaus', threatpost.com, 14 April 2017.

9 Its name is a twist on the file name of a predecessor virus called WCRYPT.EXE, short for Windows Cryptor.

10 William Smart, 'Lessons Learned Review of the Wannacry Ransomware Cyber Attack', Department of Health and Social Care, NHS Improvement, NHS England, February 2018, p. 5.

11 Ibid., p. 40.

12 Ruth Alexander, 'Which Is the World's Biggest Employer?', *BBC News*, 20 March 2012.

13 'DoH Extends BT N3 Deal', www.guardian.com, 20 December 2010.

14 Julian King, speaking at the Europol–Interpol Cybercrime Conference 2017 in The Hague, www.ec.europa.eu, 27 September 2017.

15 MalwareTech, 'Finding the Kill Switch to Stop the Spread of Ransomware', www.ncsc.gov.uk, 13 May 2017.

16 Ibid.

17 'Legal Case Update', www.malwaretech.com, accessed 20 April 2019.

18 United States of America v PARK JIN HYOK, Criminal Complaint, 8 June 2018, p. 123.

19 Ibid., p. 125.

20 Ibid., p. 112.

21 Ibid.

22 Encyclopaedia Britannica, 'Pound', www.britannica.com, accessed 28 June 2019.

23 House of Commons Library, 'Inflation: The Value of the Pound, 1750–2011', 29 May 2012, p. 2.

24 C. Wilson Peck, 'The Royal Farthing Tokens of James I', *British Numismatic Journal*, vol. XXVII, III/8 (1952–4), pp. 313–33.

25 Clive Emsley, Tim Hitchcock and Robert Shoemaker, 'Crime and Justice: Crimes Tried at the Old Bailey', *Old Bailey Proceedings Online*, www.oldbaileyonline.org, 28 June 2019.

26 Geoff White and Bernard P. Achampong, *The Dark Web*, www.audible.com, Episode 3, 'Bitcoin's Days Are Numbered', 2016.

27 See www.article.gmane.org, accessed via www.archive.org, 20 April 2019.

28 'Confirmed Transactions Per Day', www.blockchain.com, accessed 28 June 2019.

29 'Frequently Asked Questions', www.bitcoin.org, accessed 28 June 2019.

30 Leah McGrath Goodman, 'The Face Behind Bitcoin', *Newsweek* (3 June 2014).

31 Data from www.xe.com, accessed 28 June 2019.

32 Although some claim it was a mistaken misspelling of the word 'hold'.

33 Geoff White, Nicola Dowling and Gail Champion, 'File on Four: The Missing Bitcoin Billions', *BBC Radio 4*, 11 March 2018.

34 *What Bitcoin Did* podcast, 'Mark Karpeles on the Collapse of Mt. Gox', www.hatbitcoindid.com, 19 February 2019.

35 Ibid.

36 White et al., 'The Missing Bitcoin Billions'.

37 *What Bitcoin Did* podcast, 'Mark Karpeles on the Collapse of Mt. Gox'.

38 Yuki Furukawa, 'Former Mt. Gox CEO Mark Karpeles Gets Suspended Jail Term', Bloomberg, 15 March 2019.

39 '"U.S. Wanted Him for His Intellect" – Wife of Russian Arrested for Alleged Bitcoin Fraud to RT', *RT*, 8 September 2017.

40 United States of America v BTC-E A/K/A Canton Business Corporation and Alexander Vinnik, 17 January 2017.

41 Ibid., p. 2.

42 Elie Bursztein, Kylie McRoberts and Luca Invernizzi, 'Tracking Desktop Ransomware Payments', *Research at Google*, www.g.co/research/protect, accessed 19 April 2019.

43 White et al., 'The Missing Bitcoin Billions'.

44 As this book was completed, France's extradition request was granted.

45 Taiga Uranaka and Thomas Wilson, 'Japan Raps Coincheck, Orders Broader Checks after $530 Million Cryptocurrency Theft', *Reuters* (29 January 2018).

46 'How to Steal $500 Million in Cryptocurrency', Bloomberg (31 January 2018).

47 'NEM Protocol Tracks Funds Stolen from Coincheck Exchange', www.blog.nem.io, 1 February 2018.

48 Jonathan Foster, 'Coincheck Hackers Have Laundered All of Their NEM', www.deepdotweb.com, 9 April 2018.

49 'Cryptocurrency Group Gives Up Search for Coincheck Loot', *Nikkei Asian Review* (21 March 2018).

50 'South Korean Intelligence Says N. Korean Hackers Possibly Behind Coincheck Heist – sources', *Reuters* (5 February 2018).

51 'North Korea "Hacked Crypto-currency Exchange in South"', *BBC News*, 16 December 2017.

52 'Hi-tech Crime Trends 2018', *Group-IB*, October 2018.

53 '2018 Q3 Cryptocurrency Anti-money Laundering Report', CipherTrace, 2018.

54 Sergio Pastrana and Guillermo Suarez-Tangil, 'A First Look at the Crypto-mining Malware Ecosystem: A Decade of Unrestricted Wealth', www.arXiv.org, 3 January 2019.

5 YOUR DATA FOR SALE

1 Adam Shepherd, '"It's the legacy that gets you", Warns Ex-TalkTalk Boss', *IT Pro* (5 June 2018).

2 'TalkTalk Hacker Daniel Kelley Sentenced to Four Years', *BBC News* (10 June 2019).

3 Arrestees, especially children, are not meant to be identified. The *Daily Mail*'s picture was manipulated to hide his identity, but it barely did, and the boy's family later sued the *Mail* and several other newspapers over their coverage. See Alan Erwin, 'TalkTalk Hack: Co. Antrim Schoolboy Suing *Daily Telegraph*, *Daily Mail* and *The Sun* for Alleged Breach of Privacy', *Belfast Telegraph* (6 November 2015). However, as charges were brought and the cases chugged through the legal system, the mask of anonymity inevitably slipped. Alan Erwin, 'Teenager Involved in TalkTalk Hacking Can Be Named, Court Rules', *Belfast Telegraph* (14 March 2018). At the time of writing, Sterritt is still suing three British newspapers over their coverage of his arrest while he was still fifteen.

4 'TalkTalk Hacker Claimed He Would Be a "Millionaire"', *BBC News* (2 April 2019).

5 'TalkTalk Hack Attack: Friends Jailed for Cyber-crimes', *BBC News* (19 November 2018).

6 'TalkTalk Cyber Attack – How the ICO's Investigation Unfolded', Information Commissioner's Office, www.ico.org.uk, accessed 27 June 2019.

7 See www.ofcom.org.uk, accessed 21 May 2019.

8 David W. Maurer, *The Big Con: The Story of the Confidence Man and the Confidence Trick* (London, 2000).

9 'Over £1bn Lost by Businesses to Online Crime in a Year', Get Safe Online, www.getsafeonline.org, 13 June 2016.

10 Geoff White, 'How Scammers Conned TalkTalk Customers out of Thousands of Pounds', *Channel 4 News*, 7 December 2015.

11 'TalkTalk Outsources to Wipro', *Light Reading*, www.lightreading.com, 3 August 2011.

12 Information Commissioner's Office, 'Personal Data Belonging to Up to 21,000 TalkTalk Customers Could Have Been Used for Scams and Fraud', www.ico.org.uk, 10 August 2017.

13 Rahul Sachitanand, 'India's $150 Billion Outsourcing Industry Stares at an Uncertain Future', *Economic Times*, www.economictimes.indiatimes.com, 15 January 2017.

14 Joseph Blankenship, 'Defend Your Data as Insiders Monetize Their Access: How the Dark Web Provides a Marketplace For Your Firm's Stolen Data', Forrester Research, www.forrester.com, 30 July 2018.

6 BEYOND THE DARK WEB

1 Seth G. Jones, 'Going on the Offensive: A U.S. Strategy to Combat Russian Information Warfare', Center for Strategic and International Studies, www.csis.org, 1 October 2018.

2 'Onion Routing, Brief Selected History', www.onion-router.net, accessed 27 June 2019.

3 See www.nrl.navy.mil, accessed 27 June 2019.

4 See https://metrics.torproject.org, accessed 1 March 2019.

5 See www.securedrop.org, accessed 27 June 2019.

6 See www.forum.bitcoin.org, accessed 20 February 2019 via archive.org.

7 'Schumer Pushes to Shut Down Online Drug Marketplace', *NBC New York* (5 June 2011).

8 See www.doctorcaudevilla.com, accessed 27 June 2019.

9 United States of America v Ross William Ulbricht, documents unsealed 31 March 2015.

10 United States of America v Ross William Ulbricht, statement of FBI Special Agent Christopher Tarbell, 27 September 2013, p. 25.

11 Ibid., p. 15.

12 Joshua Bearman, 'The Rise and Fall of Silk Road', *Wired*, www.wired.com (May 2015).

13 See www.freeross.org, accessed 28 June 2019.

14 'Former Silk Road Task Force Agent Pleads Guilty to Extortion, Money Laundering and Obstruction', www.justice.gov, 1 July 2015.

15 'Former Secret Service Agent Sentenced to 71 Months in Scheme Related to Silk Road Investigation', www.fbi.gov, 7 December 2015.

16 Dr Gareth Owenson and Dr Nick Savage, 'The Tor Dark Net', GCIG Paper No. 20, Global Commission on Internet Governance, www.cigionline.org, 30 September 2015.

17 See www.iwf.org.uk, accessed 28 June 2019.

18 See https://metrics.torproject.org, accessed 1 March 2019.

19 Dr Adam R. Winstock, Dr Monica Barrett, Dr Jason Ferris and Dr Larissa Maier, 'Global Drug Survey 2016', www.globaldrugsurvey.com, accessed 1 March 2019.

20 'Portsmouth Dark Net Drug Dealer Jailed for 16 Years', *BBC News*, 20 December 2017.

21 See www.dea.gov, accessed 28 June 2019.

22 'Deaths Related to Drug Poisoning in England and Wales: 2017 Registrations', Office for National Statistics, www.ons.gov.uk, 6 August 2018. Despite the decline of 4 per cent in deaths involving heroin and morphine, there were still 1,164 fatalities from those drugs in 2017.

23 'Fentanyl Sales in the Deep and Dark Web', www.flashpoint-intel.com, 28 July 2017.

24 'Dark Web Drug Supermarket Duo from Huddersfield Jailed', *BBC News*, 25 September 2017.

25 Mark Townsend, 'Dark Web Dealers Voluntarily Ban Deadly Fentanyl', *The Guardian* (1 December 2018).

26 A. J. Dellinger, 'AlphaBay Marketplace Shutdown: Former Public Relations Specialist Indicted by Feds', *International Business Times* (16 November 2017).

27 Andrea Bellamare, 'The Secret Life of Alexandre Cazes, Alleged Dark Web Mastermind', *CBS News*, 23 July 2017.

28 'Massive Blow to Criminal Dark Web Activities after Globally Coordinated Operation', Europol press release, www.europol.europa.eu, 20 July 2017.

29 Geoff White, David Lewis and Gail Champion, 'File on Four: Swipe Right for Crime', *BBC Radio 4*, 24 February 2019.

30 See www.philzimmermann.com, accessed 28 June 2019.

31 Glenn Greenwald and Ewen MacAskill, 'NSA Prism Program Taps in to User Data of Apple, Google and Others', *The Guardian* (7 June 2013).

7 THE INTERNET HATE MACHINE

1 '/b/', *Encyclopedia Dramatica*, www.encyclopediadramatica.rs, accessed 28 June 2019.

2 Whitney Phillips, *This Is Why We Can't Have Nice Things: Mapping the Relationship between Online Trolling and Mainstream Culture* (Boston, MA, 2016).

3 Jamie Bartlett, 'A Life Ruin: Inside the Digital Underworld', *Medium*, www.medium.com, 30 November 2015.

4 Parmy Olson, *We Are Anonymous: Inside the Hacker World of LulzSec, Anonymous and the Global Cyber Insurgency* (New York, 2012), p. 28.

5 'Fox 11 Investigates: "Anonymous"', *Fox 11*, www.myfoxla.com, 28 July 2007, accessed via www.archive.org.

6 Nick Denton, 'Church of Scientology Claims Copyright Infringement', Gawker, www.gawker.com, 16 January 2008.

7 Ibid.

8 Olson, *We Are Anonymous*, pp. 65–7.

9 'Masked Protest over Scientology', *BBC News*, 11 February 2008.

10 Ibid.

11 'Press Release: Secret U.S. Embassy Cables', WikiLeaks, www.wikileaks.org, 28 November 2010.

12 Maha Azzam, 'Opinion: How WikiLeaks Helped Fuel Tunisian Revolution', *CNN*, www.edition.cnn.com, 18 January 2011.

13 'PayPal Suspends WikiLeaks Donations Account', *Reuters*, 4 December 2010.

14 Olson, *We Are Anonymous*, p. 74.

15 Carole Cadwalladr, 'Anonymous: Behind the Masks of the Cyber Insurgents', *The Guardian* (8 September 2012).

16 'Update on PayPal Site Status', www.thepaypalblog.com, 9 December 2010, accessed via www.archive.org, 29 June 2019.

17 'Anonymous Hackers "Cost PayPal £3.5m"', *BBC News*, 22 November 2012.

18 Robert McMillan, 'Group Used 30,000-node Botnet in MasterCard, PayPal Attacks', *Computerworld* (9 December 2010).

19 Olson, *We Are Anonymous*, p. 116.

20 Ibid., p. 127.

21 Nebraska Man Agrees to Plead Guilty in Attack of Scientology Websites Orchestrated by "Anonymous"', *FBI Los Angeles Division*, www.archives.fbi.gov, 25 January 2010.

22 Joseph Menn, 'Cyberactivists Warned of Arrest', *Financial Times* (5 February 2011).

23 See www.secunit.org, accessed via www.webcache.googleusercontent.com, 11 March 2019.

24 Parmy Olson, 'Is This the Girl that Hacked HBGary?', *Forbes* (16 March 2011).

25 United States of America v Jake Davis et al., criminal indictment, 6 March 2011, p. 5.

26 'In Conversation with Former Anonymous and LulzSec Hackers', Royal Court Theatre, 29 September 2014, transcript taken from 'The Big Idea: In Conversation with LULZSEC', www.youtube.com, accessed 29 June 2019.

27 United States of America v Jake Davis et al., criminal indictment, 6 March 2011, p. 5. Ultimately, the group was never prosecuted in the U.S.

28 Peter Bright, 'Anonymous Speaks: The Inside Story of the HBGary Hack',
    Ars Technica (16 February 2011).
29 Olson, *We Are Anonymous*, p. 19.
30 Andrew McInnes, 'Hail Xenu: Anonymous Defends Due Process against FBI',
    Letters from a Broken Country Blog, timeoutcorner.wordpress.com,
    8 February 2011.
31 See www.hackadaycom.files.wordpress.com, accessed 11 March 2019.
32 Joost Schellevis, 'Anonymous hackt beveiligingsbedrijf HBGary'
    ('Anonymous hacks security company HBGary'), www.tweakers.net,
    7 February 2011.
33 Olson, *We Are Anonymous*, p. 158.
34 'HBGary Federal CEO Aaron Barr Steps Down', www.threatpost.com,
    28 February 2011, accessed via www.archive.org, 11 March 2019. The affiliated
    company, HBGary, was later taken over by another firm.
35 United States of America v Jake Davis et al., criminal indictment, 6 March
    2011, p. 5.
36 Charles Arthur, 'LulzSec: What They Did, Who They Were and How They
    Were Caught', *The Guardian* (16 May 2013).
37 Ibid.
38 'Sony Pictures Says LulzSec Hacked 37,500 User Accounts, Not 1 Million',
    LA Times (9 June 2011).
39 The Queen v Ryan Cleary, Jake Davis, Ryan Ackroyd, Mustafa Al-Bassam,
    indictment document, 11 May 2012.
40 Richard Godwin, 'Hacked Off: Jake Davis Talks about His Life on the Dark
    Web', *Evening Standard* (17 September 2014).
41 Charles Arthur and Ryan Gallagher, 'LulzSec IRC Leak: The Full Record', *The
    Guardian* (24 June 2011). The motives for and executions of the hacks varied:
    in the case of the NHS, for example, LulzSec praised the organization's work
    and urged it to improve its security.
42 See www.backtracesecurity.com, accessed via www.archive.org,
    11 March 2019.
43 United States of America v Hector Xavier Monsegur, aka 'Sabu',
    23 May 2014, p. 6.
44 Olson, *We Are Anonymous*, pp. 317–23.
45 See www.shetland.org, accessed 11 March 2019.
46 Peter Bright, '"The Cutting Edge of Cybercrime" – Lulzsec Hackers Get up
    to 32 Months in Jail', *Ars Technica* (16 May 2013).
47 'Criminal Justice System Statistics Quarterly: December 2017', Ministry of
    Justice, accessed 29 June 2019. It is worth noting that the Computer Misuse
    Act doesn't cover all hacking offenders, some of whom are convicted under
    other crimes that are easier to prosecute and attract longer sentences, such
    as fraud.
48 Christina Dunbar-Hester, *Hacking Diversity: The Politics of Inclusion in Open
    Technology Cultures* (Princeton, NJ, 2019), p. 15.
49 'LulzSec Computer Hackers Jailed for a Total of 7 Years', Crown Prosecution
    Service, www.cps.gov.uk, 16 May 2013, accessed www.archive.org, 29 June
    2019.
50 'LulzSec Hacker Given Community Order for Possessing Child Abuse
    Images', *Press Association* (12 June 2013).

51 'Profile: Gary McKinnon', *BBC News*, 14 December 2012.

52 Mark Brosnan, Katy-Louise Payne, Ailsa Russell, Richard Mills, Katie Maras and Dheeraj Rai, 'Is There a Relationship between Cyber-dependent Crime, Autistic-like Traits and Autism?', *Journal of Autism and Developmental Disorders* (2019).

53 United States of America v Hector Xavier Monsegur, aka 'Sabu', 23 May 2014, p. 6.

54 Stan Schroeder, 'Facebook Acquires Team Behind Blockchain Startup Chainspace', Mashable (5 February 2019).

55 'Teen Becomes World's First $1 Million Bug Bounty Hacker on HackerOne', www.hackerone.com, accessed 29 June 2019.

56 See www.mojang.com, accessed 13 March 2019.

57 Manos Antonakakis, Tim April, Michael Bailey, Matthew Bernhard, Elie Bursztein, Jaime Cochran, Zakir Durumeric, J. Alex Halderman, Luca Invernizz, Michalis Kallitsis, Deepak Kumar, Chaz Lever, Zane Ma, Joshua Mason, Damian Menscher, Chad Seaman, Nick Sullivan, Kurt Thomas and Yi Zhou, 'Understanding the Mirai Botnet', 26th USENIX Security Symposium, 16–18 August 2017.

58 Ibid., p. 1103.

59 Ibid., p. 1094.

60 Ibid., p. 1093.

61 Ibid., p. 1104.

62 United States of America v Josiah White, Paras Jha and Dalton Norman, 11 September 2018, p. 2.

63 Ibid., p. 15.

64 Ibid., pp. 23–4.

65 Manos Antonakakis et al., 'Understanding the Mirai Botnet', p. 1105.

66 Brian Krebs, 'Who Is Anna-Senpai, the Mirai Worm Author?', Krebs on Security, wwwkrebsonsecurity.com, 18 January 2017.

67 United States of America v Josiah White, Paras Jha and Dalton Norman, 11 September 2018, p. 7.

68 Ibid., p. 28.

69 Manos Antonakakis et al., 'Understanding the Mirai Botnet', p. 1101.

70 Dominic Casciani, 'Briton Who Knocked Liberia Offline with Cyber Attack Jailed', *BBC News*, 11 January 2019.

71 Manos Antonakakis et al., 'Understanding the Mirai Botnet', p. 1102.

72 'International Hacker-for-hire Jailed for Cyber Attacks on Liberian Telecommunications Provider', National Crime Agency, www.nationalcrimeagency.gov.uk, accessed 29 June 2019.

73 Brian Krebs, 'Did the Mirai Botnet Really Take Liberia Offline?', Krebs on Security, www.krebsonsecurity.com, 4 November 2016.

74 'International Hacker-for-hire Jailed for Cyber Attacks on Liberian Telecommunications Provider', National Crime Agency.

75 Ibid.

76 Mattijs Jonker, Alistair King, Johannes Krupp, Christian Rossow, Anna Sperotto and Alberto Dainotti, 'Millions of Targets under Attack: A Macroscopic Characterization of the DoS Ecosystem', *Proceedings of IMC '17*, 1–3 November 2017.

8 LIGHTS OUT

1 Eugene Kaspersky, 'The Man Who Found Stuxnet – Sergey Ulasen in the Spotlight', Nota Bene, Notes, Comment and Buzz from Eugene Kaspersky – official blog, www.eugene.kaspersky.com, 2 November 2011.

2 The U.S. government, for example, has had a 'presumption of denial' for software exports to Iran since 1992 ('Iran Sanctions', RS20871, Congressional Research Service, updated 4 February 2019).

3 See www.zerodium.com, accessed 29 June 2019.

4 'Tor Browser Bounty', www.zerodium.com, 13 September 2017.

5 At www.twitter.com/Zerodium, accessed 25 May 2019.

6 Liam O'Murchu, 'Stuxnet Using Three Additional Zero-day Vulnerabilities', Symantec Official Blog, www.symantec.com, 14 September 2010.

7 Kaspersky, 'The Man Who Found Stuxnet'.

8 'Rootkit.TmpHider', *VirusBlokAda*, www.anti-virus.by, 17 June 2010.

9 Ibid.

10 User frank_boldewin, www.wildersecurity.com, 14 July 2010.

11 Nicolas Falliere, Liam O Murchu and Eric Chien, 'W32.Stuxnet DossierVersion 1.4', Symantec Security Response (February 2011), p. 2.

12 Ralph Langner, 'To Kill a Centrifuge: A Technical Analysis of What Stuxnet's Creators Tried to Achieve', Langner Group (November 2013).

13 'Country Analysis Briefs – Iran', U.S. Energy Information Administration (9 April 2018), p. 1.

14 'Country Analysis Briefs – Iran', U.S. Energy Information Administration (16 April 2010), p. 5.

15 'Implementation of the NPT Safeguards Agreement in the Islamic Republic of Iran – Report by the Director General', International Atomic Energy Agency (6 June 2003), p. 2.

16 'Implementation of the NPT Safeguards Agreement in the Islamic Republic of Iran – Report by the Director General', International Atomic Energy Agency (15 November 2004), p. 9. Inspectors acknowledged the highly enriched traces may have been due to contamination from imported equipment.

17 Dafna Linzer, 'Iran Was Offered Nuclear Parts', *Washington Post* (27 February 2005).

18 Falliere et al., 'W32.Stuxnet DossierVersion 1.4', p. 5.

19 Kim Zetter, *Countdown to Zero Day* (New York, 2014), p. 222.

20 'Stuxnet Patient Zero: First Victims of the Infamous Worm Revealed', Kaspersky Lab, www.kaspersky.com, 11 November 2014, p.2.

21 William J. Broad, 'A Tantalizing Look at Iran's Nuclear Program', *New York Times* (29 April 2008).

22 Langner, 'To Kill a Centrifuge', p. 12.

23 Zetter, *Countdown to Zero Day*, p. 3.

24 Langner, 'To Kill a Centrifuge', p. 10.

25 Kim Zetter and Huib Modderkolk, 'Revealed: How a Secret Dutch Mole Aided the U.S.–Israeli Stuxnet Cyberattack on Iran', *Yahoo! News*, news.yahoo.com, 2 September 2019.

26 'Stuxnet 0.5: How It Evolved', *Symantec Security Response* (26 February 2013).

27 Zetter, *Countdown to Zero Day*, p. 333.

28 Ibid., p. 238.

29 Ibid., pp. 359–62.
30 Langner, 'To Kill a Centrifuge', p. 15.
31 Norton Santos, 'BlackEnergy APT Malware', RSA NetWitness Platform, www.community.rsa.com, 23 March 2016.
32 John Hultquist, 'Sandworm Team and the Ukrainian Power Authority Attacks', *FireEye Threat Research*, www.fireeye.com, 7 January 2016.
33 'General Assembly Adopts Resolution Urging Russian Federation to Withdraw Its Armed Forces from Crimea, Expressing Grave Concern about Rising Military Presence', United Nations General Assembly Plenary Seventy-third Session, 56th Meeting (PM), 17 December 2018.
34 'Cybercrime BlackEnergy2 / 3: The History of Attacks on Critical IT Infrastructure of Ukraine', CyS Centrum, www.cys-centrum.com, 6 January 2016.
35 Jake Styczynski, Nate Beach-Westmoreland and Scott Stables, 'When the Lights Went Out: A Comprehensive Review of the 2015 Attacks on Ukrainian Critical Infrastructure', *Booz Allen Hamilton* (September 2016), p. 14.
36 Israel Barak and Ross Rustici, 'ICS Threat Broadens: Nation-State Hackers Are No Longer the Only Game in Town', *Cybereason*, www.cybereason.com, 7 August 2018.
37 'Analysis of the Cyber Attack on the Ukrainian Power Grid', *Electricity Information Sharing and Analysis Centre*, www.eisac.com, 18 March 2016, p. 4.
38 Kim Zetter, 'Inside the Cunning, Unprecedented Hack of Ukraine's Power Grid', *Wired* (3 March 2016).
39 Styczynski et al., 'When the Lights Went Out', pp. 20–21.
40 Ibid., p. 21.
41 Ibid., p. 22.
42 Andy Greenberg, 'How an Entire Nation Became Russia's Test Lab for Cyberwar', *Wired* (20 June 2017).
43 Ibid.
44 'Міністерство енергетики та вугільної промисловості Україн' ('Ministry of Energy and Coal Industry of Ukraine'), www.pe.kmu.gov.ua, 12 February 2016.
45 Norton Santos, 'BlackEnergy APT Malware'.
46 Greenberg, 'How an Entire Nation Became Russia's Test Lab for Cyberwar'.
47 Pavel Polityuk, 'Ukraine Sees Russian Hand in Cyber Attacks on Power Grid', *Reuters* (12 February 2016).
48 'Reckless Campaign of Cyber Attacks by Russian Military Intelligence Service Exposed', National Cyber Security Centre, www.ncsc.gov.uk, 3 October 2018.
49 Alert (TA18-074A) 'Russian Government Cyber Activity Targeting Energy and Other Critical Infrastructure Sectors', U.S. Department of Homeland Security, 15 March 2018.
50 'Resurgent Iron Liberty Targeting Energy Sector', Secureworks Counter Threat Unit Research Team, www.securworks.com, 24 July 2019.

9 WEAPONIZING DATA

1 Parmy Olson, *We Are Anonymous: Inside the Hacker World of LulzSec, Anonymous and the Global Cyber Insurgency* (New York, 2012), p. 250.

2 Chris Taylor, 'Murdoch's Sun Newspaper Hacked by LulzSec', www.mashable.com, 18 July 2011.

3 David Mikkelson, 'Jenkem – Bulletin Warns of a Purported New Drug Called "Jenkem," Made by Fermenting Raw Sewage', www.snopes.com, 30 October 2007.

4 Whitney Phillips, *This Is Why We Can't Have Nice Things: Mapping the Relationship between Online Trolling and Mainstream Culture* (Boston, MA, 2016), p.6.

5 'Online Cheating Site AshleyMadison Hacked', www.krebsonsecurity.com, 19 July 2015.

6 See www.avidlifemedia.com, accessed via www.archive.org, 28 June 2019.

7 'Online Cheating Site AshleyMadison Hacked', www.krebsonsecurity.com, 19 July 2015.

8 'We Are the Impact Team: We Are Releasing the Ashley Madison Data', www.reddit.com, 16 August 2015.

9 'Radio Hosts Tell Woman Live on Air Her Husband Had Ashley Madison Account', Australian Associated Press via www.guardian.com, 20 August 2015.

10 See www.adultfriendfinder.com, accessed 28 June 2019.

11 Geoff White, 'Adult Dating Site Hack Exposes Millions of Users', *Channel 4 News* (21 May 2015).

12 Laurie Segall, 'Pastor Outed on Ashley Madison Commits Suicide', CNN, 8 September 2015.

13 Steve Spriester, 'Widow of SAPD Captain Trying to Clear Husband's Name Following His Death', www.ksat.com, 16 November 2016.

14 Geoff White, 'Ashley Madison Fallout: Blackmail Risk', *Channel 4 News* (21 August 2015).

15 Alastair Sharp and Allison Martell, 'Infidelity Website Ashley Madison Facing FTC Probe, CEO Apologizes', *Reuters* (5 July 2016).

16 Annalee Newitz, 'Ashley Madison Code Shows More Women, and More Bots', *Gizmodo*, 31 August 2015.

17 United States of America v PARK JIN HYOK, Criminal Complaint, 8 June 2018.

18 Mark Seal, 'An Exclusive Look at Sony's Hacking Saga', *Vanity Fair* (4 February 2015).

19 Kevin Roose, 'Sony Pictures Hack Exposes Hollywood Celebrities' Secret Aliases', *Splinter* (8 December 2014).

20 Seal, 'An Exclusive Look at Sony's Hacking Saga'.

21 Kevin Roose, 'Hacked Documents Reveal a Hollywood Studio's Stunning Gender and Race Gap', *Splinter* (1 December 2014).

22 Dominic Rushe, 'Amy Pascal Steps Down from Sony Pictures in Wake of Damaging Email Hack', *The Guardian* (5 February 2015).

23 Aaron Sorkin, 'The Sony Hack and the Yellow Press', *New York Times* (14 December 2014).

24 See www.wikileaks.org, accessed 28 June 2019.

25 Sam Biddle, 'More Embarrassing Emails: The Sony Hack B-sides', Gawker (17 April 2015).

26 Anousha Sakoui, 'Sony Says News Outlets Should Stop Using Hacked Documents', Bloomberg (14 December 2014).

27 Hope King, 'Ashley Madison Tries to Stop the Spread of its Leaked Data', CNN Business (21 August 2015).

28 Jen Yamato, 'Sony Hack: "Christmas Gift" Reveals Michael Lynton Emails Stolen Days Before Attack', Deadline (16 December 2014).

29 'Consolidated Financial Results Forecast for the Third Quarter Ended December 31, 2014, and Revision of Consolidated Forecast for the Fiscal Year Ending March 31, 2015', Sony News and Information (4 February 2015), p. 6.

30 Luke Harding, 'Revealed: The $2bn Offshore Trail that Leads to Vladimir Putin', *The Guardian* (3 April 2016).

31 'Panama Papers: A Special Investigation', www.guardian.com, accessed 28 June 2019.

32 John Henley, 'Iceland PM Steps Aside After Protests over Panama Papers Revelations', *The Guardian* (5 April 2016).

33 Vishakha Sonawane, 'Panama Papers: Spain's Industry Minister José Manuel Soria Resigns Over Links to Offshore Account', *International Business Times* (15 April 2016).

34 Juliette Garside, Holly Watt and David Pegg, 'The Panama Papers: How the World's Rich and Famous Hide their Money Offshore', *The Guardian* (3 April 2016).

35 'Panama Papers Law Firm Mossack Fonseca to Shut Down after Tax Scandal', *Reuters* (14 March 2018).

36 Frederik Obermaier, Bastian Obermayer, Vanessa Wormer and Wolfgang Jaschensky, 'About the Panama Papers', www.panamapapers.sueddeutsche. de, accessed 28 June 2019.

37 'About the Investigation', www.icij.org, accessed 28 June 2019.

38 'Paradise Papers', *BBC News*, accessed 28 June 2019.

39 'Paradise Papers: Everything You Need to Know About the Leak', *BBC News*, 10 November 2017.

40 'Appleby Reaction to Media Coverage', www.applebyglobal.com, 5 November 2017, accessed via www.archive.org, 28 June 2019.

41 Charlotte Tobitt, 'Guardian and BBC Settle Paradise Papers Dispute with Offshore Law Firm Appleby', *Press Gazette* (22 May 2018).

42 United States of America v PARK JIN HYOK, Criminal Complaint, 8 June 2018, p. 123.

43 Adam Hulcoop, John Scott-Railton, Peter Tanchak, Matt Brooks and Ron Deibert, 'Tainted Leaks Disinformation and Phishing with a Russian Nexus', www.citizenlab.ca, 25 May 2017.

44 See pressroom.rferl.org, accessed 28 June 2019.

45 Hulcoop et al., 'Tainted Leaks Disinformation and Phishing with a Russian Nexus'.

46 Ibid.

47 Ibid.

48 'Политолог о «цветной революции» в РФ: пора бы США подключить фантазию' ('Political Scientist on the "Color Revolution" in the Russian Federation: It's Time for the United States to Promote a Fantasy'), www.radiosputnik.ria.ru, 24 October 2016.

10 HACK THE VOTE

1 Michael S. Schmidt, 'Hillary Clinton Used Personal Email Account at State Dept., Possibly Breaking Rules', *New York Times* (2 March 2015).

2 Anthony Zurcher, 'Hillary Clinton Emails: What's It All About?', *BBC News*, 6 November 2016.

3 Ibid.

4 Dmitri Alperovitch, 'Bears in the Midst: Intrusion into the Democratic National Committee', CrowdStrike, www.crowdstrike.com, 15 June 2016.

5 Artturi Lehtiö, 'THE DUKES – 7 Years of Russian Cyberespionage', F-Secure Labs Threat Intelligence, www.f-secure.com, 17 September 2015. At one point the group was briefly referred to as Office Monkeys, a reference to an email attachment into which they had embedded their virus – a video of a group of monkeys trashing an office.

6 Ibid., p. 9.

7 Huib Modderkolk, 'Dutch Agencies Provide Crucial Intel about Russia's Interference in U.S.-Elections', *de Volksrant*, 25 January 2018.

8 Ibid.

9 Evan Perez and Shimon Prokupecz, 'Sources: State Dept. Hack the "Worst Ever"', *CNN*, 10 March 2015.

10 Donna Brazile, *Hacks: The Inside Story of the Break-ins and Breakdowns That Put Donald Trump in the White House* (New York, 2017), pp. 118–19.

11 Alperovitch, 'Bears in the Midst'.

12 Vicky Ward, 'The Russian Expat Leading the Fight to Protect America', *Esquire* (24 October 2016). The success of the Fancy Bear moniker is controversial within the cybersecurity community, with some experts arguing that it detracts from the seriousness of the group's activities.

13 'German Parliament Cyber-attack Still "Live"', *BBC News*, 11 June 2015.

14 'GRU Took "Complete Control" of UK-based TV Station in 2015', *Financial Times* (5 October 2018).

15 'WADA Confirms Attack by Russian Cyber Espionage Group', World Anti-Doping Agency, www.wada-ama.org, 13 September 2016.

16 United States of America v Viktor Borisovich Netyksho et al., Criminal Indictment, 13 July 2018, p. 6.

17 Eric Lipton, David E. Sanger and Scott Shane, 'The Perfect Weapon: How Russian Cyberpower Invaded the U.S.', *New York Times* (13 December 2016).

18 United States of America v Viktor Borisovich Netyksho et al., Criminal Indictment, 13 July 2018, p. 19.

19 Ibid., p. 9.

20 Ibid., p. 10.

21 Ward, 'The Russian Expat Leading the Fight to Protect America'.

22 Alperovitch, 'Bears in the Midst'.

23 Ellen Nakashima, 'Russian Government Hackers Penetrated DNC', *Washington Post* (14 June 2016).

24 Guccifer2, 'Guccifer 2.0 DNC's Servers Hacked by a Lone Hacker', www.guccifer2.wordpress.com, 15 June 2016.

25 John Cook, 'Hacked Emails Show Hillary Clinton Was Receiving Advice at a Private Email Account from Banned, Obama-hating Former Staffer', Gawker, 20 March 2013, accessed via www.archive.org, 30 June 2019.

26 'Romanian Hacker "Guccifer" Sentenced to 52 Months in Prison for Computer Hacking Crimes', U.S. Department of Justice, www.justice.gov.uk, 1 September 2016.

27 Guccifer2, 'Guccifer 2.0 DNC's Servers Hacked by a Lone Hacker'.

28 Sam Biddle, 'Contrary to DNC Claim, Hacked Data Contains a Ton of Personal Donor Information', Gawker, 17 June 2016.

29 See www.dcleaks.com, accessed via www.archive.org, 30 June 2019.

30 Guccifer2, 'Guccifer 2.0 DNC's Servers Hacked by a Lone Hacker'.

31 'Mueller Says Searches Yielded Evidence of Stone–WikiLeaks Communications', *Reuters*, 16 February 2019. WikiLeaks did not respond to repeated email requests for comment for this book.

32 United States of America v Viktor Borisovich Netyksho et al., Criminal Indictment, 13 July 2018, pp. 17–18. Square brackets as per original document, added by U.S. Department of Justice.

33 See www.wikileaks.org, accessed 30 June 2019.

34 Alana Abramson and Shushannah Walshe, 'The 4 Most Damaging Emails from the DNC WikiLeaks Dump', *ABC News*, 25 July 2016.

35 Jonathan Martin and Alan Rappeport, 'Debbie Wasserman Schultz to Resign DNC Post', *New York Times* (24 July 2016).

36 David Sherfinski and Dave Boyer, 'DNC Shakes Up Leadership as Brazile Takes Charge in Wake of WikiLeaks Email Scandal', *Washington Times* (2 August 2016).

37 Brazile, *Hacks*, pp. 70–71.

38 Jason Lemon, 'Julian Assange and Donald Trump: All the Times President Has Praised WikiLeaks Founder as U.S. Files Extradition Request', *Newsweek* (11 April 2019).

39 Brazile, *Hacks*, p. 135.

40 Aaron Smith and Monica Anderson, 'Social Media Use in 2018', Pew Research Center, www.assets.pewresearch.org, 1 March 2018.

41 '@realDonaldTrump', *Twitter*, www.twitter.com, accessed via www.archive.org, 30 June 2019.

42 '2015 Edelman Trust Barometer', www.edelman.com, 19 January 2016.

43 United States of America v Viktor Borisovich Netyksho et al., Criminal Indictment, 13 July 2018, p. 14.

44 Alex Stamos, 'An Update on Information Operations on Facebook', www.newsroom.fb.com, 6 September 2017.

45 United States of America v. Internet Research Agency LLC et al., 16 February 2018.

46 Stamos, 'An Update on Information Operations on Facebook'.

47 Harry Davies, 'Ted Cruz Campaign Using Firm That Harvested Data on Millions of Unwitting Facebook Users', *The Guardian* (11 December 2015).

48 'Investigation into the Use of Data Analytics in Political Campaigns', Information Commissioner's Office, p. 38.

49 Davies, 'Ted Cruz Campaign Using Firm That Harvested Data on Millions of Unwitting Facebook Users'.

50 'Revealed: Trump's Election Consultants Filmed Saying They Use Bribes and Sex Workers to Entrap Politicians', *Channel 4 News*, 19 March 2018.

51 'Cambridge Analytica and Scl Elections Commence Insolvency Proceedings and Release Results of Independent Investigation into Recent Allegations',

www.ca-commercial.com, 2 May 2018, accessed via www.archive.org,
3 July 2019.

52 Kate Kaye, 'Trump Spending with Cambridge Analytica Looks Like Peanuts
Compared to Cruz', *AdAge* (24 August 2016).

53 Lesley Stahl, 'Facebook "Embeds", Russia and the Trump Campaign's Secret
Weapon', *CBS*, 8 October 2017.

54 'Investigation into the Use of Data Analytics in Political Campaigns',
The Information Commissioner's Office, p. 4.

55 Elliot Shrage, 'Hard Questions: Russian Ads Delivered to Congress',
www.facebook.com, 2 October 2017. (On 30 October 2017, Facebook
reportedly told Congress that material had potentially been seen by
126 million Americans – see David Ingram, 'Facebook Says 126 Million
Americans May Have Seen Russia-linked Political Posts', *Reuters* (30 October
2017). However, this was referring to 'posts' by 'Russians', as distinct from
'ads' by the 'Internet Research Agency'.)

56 'U.S. Election 2016', *BBC News*, accessed 30 June 2019.

57 Sam Thielman, 'Presidential Debate Breaks U.S. Ratings Record in Clinton–
Trump Face-off', *The Guardian* (27 September 2016).

58 Lorenzo Franceschi-Bicchierai, 'Why Does DNC Hacker "Guccifer 2.0" Talk
Like This?', *Vice News*, 23 June 2016.

59 'Does a BEAR Leak in the Woods?', Threatconnect Research Team,
www.threatconnect.com, 12 August 2016.

60 Raphael Satter, 'Russia Hackers Pursued Putin Foes, Not Just U.S. Democrats',
Associated Press (2 November 2017).

61 'WikiLeaks Founder Assange on Hacked Podesta, DNC Emails: "Our source
is not the Russian government"', *Fox News*, 16 December 2016.

62 Patrick Healy, David E. Sanger and Maggie Haberman, 'Donald Trump Finds
Improbable Ally in WikiLeaks', *New York Times* (12 October 2016).

63 'Trump Slams "Desperate" Claims that Russia Hacked DNC Emails for Him',
Associated Press (25 July 2016).

64 Ivan Levingston, 'Trump: I Hope Russia Finds "the 30,000 emails that are
missing"', *CNBC*, 27 July 2016.

65 United States of America v Viktor Borisovich Netyksho et al., Criminal
Indictment, 13 July 2018, p. 14.

66 Ibid., p. 4.

67 Mark Galeotti, 'Putin's Hydra: Inside Russia's Intelligence Services',
European Council on Foreign Relations, www.ecfr.eu, May 2016.

68 'Netherlands Defence Intelligence and Security Service Disrupts Russian
Cyber Operation Targeting OPCW', *Netherlands Ministry of Defence*,
www.english.defensie.nl, 4 October 2018.

69 'MH17 Ukraine Plane Crash: What We Know', *BBC News*, www.bbc.co.uk,
19 June 2019.

70 'Russia Cyber-plots: U.S, UK and Netherlands Allege Hacking', *BBC News*,
www.bbc.co.uk, 4 October 2018.

71 '305 Car Registrations May Point to Massive GRU Security Breach',
Bellingcat, www.bellingcat.com, 4 October 2018.

72 'Foreign Involvement in the Critical National Infrastructure: The
Implications for National Security', Intelligence and Security Committee,
TSO, June 2013.

73 'We Compete Favourably with Huawei in 5G – Nokia CEO', Bloomberg
   (11 June 2019).

74 John McDuling, 'New Zealand Joins Australia in Banning Huawei', *Sydney
   Morning Herald* (28 November 2018).

75 'Can We Trust Huawei?', *BBC Panorama*, 8 April 2019.

76 Roy Greenslade, 'How Edward Snowden Led Journalist and Film-maker
   to Reveal NSA Secrets', *The Guardian* (19 August 2013).

77 Andy Greenberg, 'These Are the Emails Snowden Sent to First Introduce
   His Epic NSA Leaks', *Wired* (13 October 2014).

78 Scott Shane and David E. Sanger, 'Job Title Key to Inner Access Held
   by Leaker', *New York Times* (1 July 2013).

79 Fred Kaplan, *Dark Territory: The Secret History of Cyber War*
   (New York, 2016), p. 191.

80 'Fidel Castro Labels Libellous Report Cuba Blocked Snowden Travel',
   Reuters (28 August 2013).

81 Glenn Greenwald and Ewen MacAskill, 'NSA Prism Program Taps in
   to User Data of Apple, Google and Others', *The Guardian* (7 June 2013).

82 Kaplan, *Dark Territory*, p. 196, emphasis as per original.

83 Ibid., p. 197, emphasis as per original.

84 GCHQ Bude, www.gchq.gov.uk, accessed via www.archive.org, 4 July 2019.

85 Jeremy Scahill and Josh Begley, 'How Spies Stole the Keys to the Encryption
   Castle', The Intercept, www.theintercept.com, 19 February 2015.

86 'Gemalto Presents the Findings of its Investigations into the Alleged Hacking
   of SIM Card Encryption Keys by Britain's Government Communications
   Headquarters (GCHQ) and the U.S. National Security Agency (NSA)', Gemalto,
   www.gemalto.com, 25 February 2015.

87 'Scahill and Begley, 'How Spies Stole the Keys to the Encryption Castle'.

EPILOGUE

1 Kim Zetter, *Countdown to Zero Day* (New York, 2014), pp. 224–5.

FURTHER READING

Aiken, Mary, *The Cyber Effect: A Pioneering Cyberpsychologist Explains How Human Behaviour Changes Online* (London, 2017)

Psychologist Dr Mary Aiken's study of online behaviour, probing how we are responding to the new territory of digital space.

Bartlett, Jamie, *The Dark Net* (London, 2015)

Bartlett's book goes beyond the narrow, specific confines of the 'dark web' and looks at fringe movements around the Web, from political extremism to the porn industry.

Glenny, Misha, *DarkMarket: How Hackers Became the New Mafia* (London, 2012)

A compelling book on the convergence of the Russian card fraud and hacking scenes in the decade or so after the turn of the millennium, and their links to global organized crime.

Mitnick, Kevin, *Ghost in the Wires: My Adventures as the World's Most Wanted Hacker* (New York, 2012)

Written by a man who spent a long time on the FBI's cyber most-wanted list, Mitnick's account of his years in the early computer hacking scene is astonishing, and shows how dangerous are those individuals who combine technical acumen with an innate ability to exploit human nature.

Olson, Parmy, *We Are Anonymous* (New York, 2013)

As a *Forbes* journalist, Olson gained unrivalled access to the chatrooms and personalities behind the Anonymous movement, and her book reads like a near-contemporaneous account of the community's emergence, with all its twists and turns.

Petzold, Charles, *Code: The Hidden Language of Computer Hardware and Software* (Redmond, WA, 2000)

A brilliant explanation, from first principles, of how computers actually work. Occasionally quite technical, but having read it you will truly understand (almost) everything that happens between you touching the keyboard and the words appearing on screen.

Popper, Nathaniel, *Digital Gold: The Untold Story of Bitcoin* (London, 2016)

A comprehensive account of the emergence of Bitcoin (including a quite bizarre cast of characters), starting in the very earliest days of the crypto-currency world and going almost right up to the recent heyday.

Phillips, Whitney, *This Is Why We Can't Have Nice Things: Mapping the Relationship between Online Trolling and Mainstream Culture* (Boston, MA, 2016)

An academically rigorous, fascinating account of Internet troll culture, in all its many dimensions. Phillips traces the origins and evolution of this diverse group of people, including their often-fractious, mutually manipulative relationship with the media.

Stoll, Clifford, *The Cuckoo's Egg: Tracking a Spy through the Maze of Computer Espionage* (New York, 2007)

A page-turner tale of how Stoll obsessively investigated a 75-cent accounting discrepancy and revealed an international espionage operation targeting the highest levels of the u.s. government and military. A little old now, but still (rightly) considered a masterwork of tech security writing.

Zetter, Kim, *Countdown to Zero Day: Stuxnet and the Launch of the World's First Digital Weapon* (New York, 2015)

A comprehensive and concise book by *Wired* journalist Zetter on the Stuxnet virus that hit Iran's Natanz nuclear enrichment facility. Very detailed, with excellent sources and a good overview of the geopolitical environment in which the attack took place.

ACKNOWLEDGEMENTS

The email that led to the creation of this work was as prescient as it was polite. Apologizing for contacting me out of the blue, David Watkins, Commissioning Editor at Reaktion Books, went on to suggest I write a book about cybercrime, which he called a 'fascinating, varied and frightening topic'. As the previous chapters have hopefully shown, his assessment was spot on.

David had emailed me after reading a long article I'd published on my website about the hacking of TalkTalk. After years of investigation, I'd ended up sitting on a heap of information about the incident. I thought it was a fascinating tale. Sadly, it seemed most commissioning editors disagreed – no one I approached would publish or broadcast the whole thing, so in exasperation I did it myself. The lesson is clear: don't assume people in positions of power and responsibility have better judgement than you do. Believe in yourself and good things will happen.

In addition to the wisdom imparted by the authors listed in the short further reading list, and the others who are referenced throughout this book, I am indebted to the many other people who have helped me write it.

The list below is incomplete for several reasons: first, my memory for names is highly fallible; second, some sources for this book wished to remain anonymous, for obvious reasons; third, my team of proofreaders included my friends and family, and it's safer that their names are not connected with me and my work; lastly, I have been guided by innumerable rambling, off-record chats with excellent people, conducted in the heat of conferences, the backs of taxis and the depths of noisy bars, which have informed and shaped my thinking.

If you believe you helped with this book and you're not on the list below, please accept my apologies, and claim your free drink when next we meet.

Mustafa Al-Bassam; Chris Barker and colleagues at the Royal Mint; Jessica Barker; David Bell at Vocal PR and all at Digital Shadows; Mark Brosnan; Paul Chichester and colleagues at the National Cyber Security Centre; Eric Chien at Symantec; Robert Coelho; Mick Coggin; Tamsin Collison, and all the TalkTalk victims and Indian sources; Scott Comer; Jake Davis; Deth Veggie; Russell Diona; Bas Doorn; Jennifer Emick; Dave Fermin Sevilla at PAGCOR; Stewart Garrick; members of the GRAMMERsoft group; Curtis Green; Onel de Guzman; Mike Hulett; Don Jackson; Brett Johnson; Mitch Kapor; Mark Karpelès; Jonathan Kemp; Igor Klopov;

Kevin Mandia, John Hultquist, Nalani Fraser and colleagues at FireEye; Charlie McMurdie; Hector Xavier Monsegur; Dave Palmer and Andrew Tsonchev at Darktrace; Aleksandr Panin; Shalika Perera; Oliver Price; Rodolfo Noel S. Quimbo; Mel Georgie B. Racela; Mike Rendall; Christien Rioux; Vencent Salido; Michael Sandee; Will Scott; Andrew Smith; Don Smith, Rafe Pilling and colleagues at Secureworks; Anna Smolentseva; Takayuki Sugiura; Paul Syverson; Lynn Ulbricht; Mark Van Staalduinen; Patrick Ward; David Watkins and colleagues at Reaktion Books; Ollie Whitehouse and John Cartwright at NCC Group; Glenn Wilkinson; Martyn Williams.

INDEX